How to Deal with
OCD

How to Deal with
OCD

Elizabeth Forrester

JOHN MURRAY LEARNING

First published in Great Britain in 2015 by Hodder and Stoughton. An Hachette UK company.

First published in US in 2015 by Quercus

British Library Cataloguing in Publication Data: a catalogue record for this title is available from the British Library.

Library of Congress Catalog Card Number: on file.

Paperback ISBN 978 1 47360131 4

eBook ISBN 978 1 47360133 8

1

This book is for information or educational purposes only and is not intended to act as a substitute for medical advice or treatment. Any person with a condition requiring medical attention should consult a qualified medical practitioner or suitable therapist.

The publisher has used its best endeavours to ensure that any website addresses referred to in this book are correct and active at the time of going to press. However, the publisher and the author have no responsibility for the websites and can make no guarantee that a site will remain live or that the content will remain relevant, decent or appropriate.

The publisher has made every effort to mark as such all words which it believes to be trademarks. The publisher should also like to make it clear that the presence of a word in the book, whether marked or unmarked, in no way affects its legal status as a trademark.

Every reasonable effort has been made by the publisher to trace the copyright holders of material in this book. Any errors or omissions should be notified in writing to the publisher, who will endeavour to rectify the situation for any reprints and future editions.

Typeset by Cenveo Publisher Services.

Printed and bound in Great Britain by CPI Group (UK) Ltd., Croydon, CR0 4YY.

John Murray Learning policy is to use papers that are natural, renewable and recyclable products and made from wood grown in sustainable forests. The logging and manufacturing processes are expected to conform to the environmental regulations of the country of origin.

Carmelite House
50 Victoria Embankment
London EC4Y 0DZ
www.hodder.co.uk

Also available
in ebook

Contents

Acknowledgements

I have had the great good fortune to have had some wonderful opportunities over the years to learn and grow as a clinician. Although I have worked with some exceptionally talented colleagues, my biggest inspiration has come from the people who have trusted me to help them get better.

Grateful thanks to those of you who read and commented on early drafts, offered enthusiasm and encouragement, and helped to turn it all into its finished form.

Without the love and support of my husband and son, writing this book could not have been the positive experience it was. Not least for their input on practical and technological matters (thanks, Henry).

And finally, I am indebted to my parents for allowing me to become the person I am today.

Foreword

OCD is an unnecessary problem, so it needs to be dealt with. Start here!

Fifty years ago, Obsessive-Compulsive Disorder (OCD) was regarded as untreatable and most likely to lead to a progressive decline, at best requiring adjustments by those around the sufferer to allow a diminished life and at worst resulting in long-term hospitalization. The dominant theoretical view was Freudian psychoanalysis, which defined OCD as the consequence of 'weak ego boundaries'; in this view, obsessional thoughts were in fact the unpleasant contents of the subconscious 'id' breaking through into the conscious 'ego'. Compulsions were supposed to shore up this weak 'boundary' as a mechanism preventing the sufferer from going mad. The conclusion from this view was that compulsions should be supported or even encouraged by those around the patient; failure to do so would result in psychosis. Not surprisingly, this tended to be a pretty scary way of thinking about a problem that was pretty scary even without this nasty little twist.

This is clearly nonsense; how come nobody spotted that? Actually, it's easy to understand. Confrontation of obsessional fears without the person ritualizing did lead to an alarming and rapid increase in anxiety, which may well have looked and felt like it would progress to a point where the person might even go mad! In my experience, in the early stages of OCD those affected and people around them can think that they are indeed losing their mind.

However, what then happened is that some psychological researchers took a radically different view, which was that OCD represented a complex pattern of interlinked and, most importantly, *learned* reactions and linked behaviours, and that all of us were capable of such reactions as an exaggeration of normal thinking, feeling and behaving. The importance of this view was, of course, the implication that if OCD could be learned, then maybe it could also be unlearned. This optimism proved justified, and researchers and clinicians showed that a combination of changing expectations and helping sufferers confront their obsessional fears without ritualizing was a highly effective treatment for OCD. It was also clear that those who did 'Exposure and Response Prevention' (ERP), which is what this approach to treatment became known as, did not develop a psychosis. In fact, they got better! This unambiguous result dealt a scientific death-blow to psychoanalysis, although there are those who still doggedly persist with it. Most importantly, however, OCD went from being a problem which was seen as incurable to one that was treatable. What's more, it later became clear that it was treatable in an astonishingly short time. The progress made in those early days has since been built upon further, which leads to the conclusion that, because the problem is entirely treatable, it is an unnecessary illness. It can be treated and ultimately, in the near future, it will be preventable.

How we got from 'hopeless problem' to 'unnecessary illness' gives important clues as to how best to treat OCD today, and what further needs to happen in order to eradicate OCD. Elizabeth Forrester's book provides the fundamentals in terms of an understanding which can then be built on to help the person suffering from OCD to make the changes necessary to overcome their obsessional fears and behaviours and, crucially, to reclaim their life.

So, how did this positive change happen? Professor Jack Rachman and his colleagues in the 1970s undertook the really important research which gave us the way forward. They showed, firstly, that for people with OCD, carrying out their ritual typically brought immediate relief from anxiety and discomfort ... but also that their distress quickly returned, alongside a strengthened urge to further ritualize, in what amounts to a progressive downward spiral leading, in the worst case, to complete obsessional paralysis. What these researchers then showed was that if the sufferer could choose to *not* ritualize and instead stay with the discomfort, then the anxiety and discomfort reduced anyway (often to the great surprise of the person with OCD), just that it took a bit longer. Even more importantly, they also were able to show that provoking the fear *while choosing not to ritualize* meant that the anxiety and discomfort progressively decreased until it disappeared entirely! This is the foundation of ERP, and Elizabeth helpfully describes the way this works in a clear way in Chapters 9 and 10 of this book. That research gives people with OCD (and their therapists) confidence that if they are able to stop all ritualizing, their OCD will inevitably be eliminated, and there are no exceptions. Notice the language here; it's really important. The key feature is *choosing not to ritualize*. You could confront people with their fears against their will, but all you would be doing is torturing them with no benefit. So perhaps it's just about stopping doing those compulsions?

Ah, I hear you say, if only it were that easy! And, of course, you would be right; for someone with OCD, it's the hardest thing of all. Being told 'stop it!' is worse than useless; it is demoralizing and implies criticism, just another way of telling someone to 'get over it' or 'pull yourself together'. In my experience of trying to help people suffering from OCD, they would like nothing better than to be able to get over it. The problem is that they don't know how and haven't got the resources to do so. Which is, of course, the purpose of this book; to help those who suffer from OCD and their loved ones find the understanding and guidance they need to rid themselves of the problem and get on with their life. Underpinning OCD is a set of beliefs and fears, not only about harm but about the responsibility for harm. It is the inflated sense of responsibility, usually as a response to an unwanted and unacceptable intrusion, which motivates the person to carry out their compulsions. What needs to happen is for the belief to be weakened enough that the person can deliberately, and without planning to reverse their action, find out what happens if they don't engage with rituals, compulsions or other types of neutralizing behaviour. That's the 'cognitive' bit of cognitive behavioural therapy.

Often, of course, there is more to it than this. If people can be helped to deal with their OCD early on, it may be that confronting their fears will do the trick. However, we know that for many it takes several years to even begin the process by identifying that OCD is the problem. On average, people develop OCD in its full form at age 20. It then takes an average of six to ten years for people to seek help. In that period between OCD developing and seeking help, a great deal can happen … and not happen. Education is cut short, friends are lost or not found, jobs stall, don't progress or are lost. In the meantime, OCD worms its way into every area of the sufferer's life, it affects the way they view themselves, and erodes and destroys their hopes, dreams and ambitions. So when they do seek help, the OCD has become subtly entrenched not just in the area it started, but often in many other areas. Understandably, people develop other problems; many people with long-standing OCD become so demoralized that they are clinically depressed.

So, as you will read in this book, fears of being responsible for harm (or preventing harm) is a key trigger for obsessional fears and motivator of compulsive behaviour; understandably, people with OCD feel terrifyingly responsible and then seek to ensure that the harm they do fear does not happen and/or that they are not responsible if it does. These fears and efforts to deal with them can distort important aspects of life, such as relationships, work, making your own home, having children, even thinking itself. The terror of being contaminated, of sexually molesting children, of blaspheming, of causing a fire, can lead people to increasingly frantic and pervasive efforts to seek safety. With the benefit of an outside view (that is, the point of view of someone other than the sufferer or their loved ones), it is possible so see that for the person with OCD the solution becomes the problem. The person with contamination fears is not infected, but they spend hours each day washing. The person troubled by horrible thoughts devotes all their efforts to pushing these out of their mind or 'fixing them' through prayer, mental argument and efforts at avoidance, and they get good at doing these things. The problem is, of course, that in doing so they nail their fears in place, so that even confronting the original fear can leave some of these complicated efforts at control untouched or even strengthens them, which in turn results in persistence of their obsessional fears. These efforts become ingrained and habitual, and at times automatic, so even when the person is able to successfully confront their fears, many aspects of the OCD remain untouched. As you will read in this book, the ultimate solution is to engage with what is important and in doing so eradicate the OCD.

One conclusion may be that after many years of pervasive OCD, the problems can become entrenched and intractable so that sometimes self-help is not enough and skilled therapy is required. Is that really so? Yes … and no. Yes, it is usually very helpful to go through an empirically grounded self-help book like this even when your problem seems to you and those around you, including therapists, to be relatively complicated and severe. That is because OCD is OCD, and it follows particular 'rules', and CBT as helpfully laid out in this book is the way forward. But when the problems are complicated, they can need someone with the ability to understand both you and your problems to put them in perspective, and that's what an appropriately trained therapist will do. If they are worth their salt, they will also have supervision from a colleague, which means that you can benefit from another perspective too!

And the 'no'? All good CBT is self-help, and that includes CBT with a therapist. That's because a therapist does not change you; rather, they help you understand what's happening from a different perspective, help you see the changes that are needed, help you to choose to change and then support you and guide you as you make the changes required. That means that *all good CBT is self-help*! You can be supported in that by a therapist, support groups, your loved ones or a book like this. But in the end, it's not what your therapist or the book says, it's how you then use your new understanding to deal with it. So, if you have OCD or are someone who is trying to help someone with OCD, this book is a great place to start.

Professor Paul Salkovskis
Professor of Clinical Psychology and Applied Science, University of Bath
Director, South West Centre for the Specialist Treatment of Anxiety and Related Problems (AWP NHS Trust and University of Bath)

Introduction

Miss Rayne gathered her infant school class around her, all of us
sitting cross-legged and eager on the floor as she began to read. 'Don't
step on the cracks', the story warned, 'or there'll be a bear around the
corner.' We listened wide-eyed, and when the bell rang at the end
of school and we made our way home, we remained mindful of this
new rule to which we had been introduced. Now, growing up in a
small mining town in the Midlands we all knew the likelihood of
encountering a bear on our way home whether we avoided cracks in
the pavement or not was extremely slim, but it seemed a small price to
pay. Just in case ...

I dare say you did similar things as a youngster. It was just a bit of
fun. Even though I no longer go out of my way to avoid the cracks in
the pavement, the thought of it still comes into my head from time
to time. Although it's many years since I played this game, in certain
situations it just pops into my head, seemingly from nowhere. That's
the thing with thoughts. They furnish our internal life and help us
navigate our daily routines. They're reminders of things we need
to do, of the potential consequences of things we don't do, as well
as memories from the past, daydreams of the future, along with all
manner of ideas and images from the creative to the absurd.

There are all kinds of things we do 'just in case'. We take an umbrella
with us on a sunny day, put some spare underwear in our hand luggage
when flying off on holiday, we go back to check that we locked the
door. These kinds of things are just examples of the everyday worries
and doubts that we all experience. However, sometimes these worries
and doubts become more troubling. Instead of the occasional urge to
check the gas is off, or a doubt about whether you washed your hands
thoroughly after preparing some raw chicken, you notice that these
ideas come into your mind rather frequently. And just to be sure, you
go back to check or give your hands another wash – perhaps with some
antibacterial hand wash. Although on some level we might accept the

doubts as just doubts, something that occurs from time to time but can be easily ignored, when we feel driven to do something in response to that doubt it suggests that there is another link in the chain. That link is that the idea of some kind of threat or danger has occurred to us. In addition, it seems there is something we can do to either reduce or remove this possible danger. Fingers crossed, just in case …

If obsessive–compulsive disorder (OCD) was a drug, it would be taken off the market immediately. It's highly addictive, has horrendous side effects, and doesn't work.

Why have you picked up this book?

Of course, even if you can identify with these examples it doesn't necessarily mean you have a problem but then again I guess that the reason you picked this book up is that you think you may have a problem, or know someone who might. Perhaps you've already come across the term 'obsessive–compulsive disorder' and are now wondering if indeed this might explain what the trouble is. It could be that you have suffered from OCD in the past but the problem has returned. Some of you may have battled with it for a long time but not overcome it. Whatever your reason for reading this book, the message is that you *don't* have to let OCD rule your life any more.

About this book

How to Deal with OCD features the **STEP P**ast method for overcoming OCD. **STEP P**ast is a five-step approach, drawing on cognitive behavioural therapy techniques, to give practical and emotional support to anyone affected by OCD.

S – **Support** helps you come to terms with the problem, and maps out the road to recovery.

T – **Tackle** the negative thoughts and behaviour patterns that hold you back.

E – Escape the behaviours and situations that make your life a struggle.

P – Practice provides coping strategies to help you adjust your responses and replace harmful thoughts, when they occur.

P – Progress to a healthier, happier new life – without fear of setbacks or relapse.

The aim of this book is to help you to gain a better understanding of obsessive–compulsive disorder: what it is, the many different ways in which it can show itself, what keeps the problem going and what you need to do to be able to overcome the problem.

In addition to information about OCD from research studies, I want to share my many years of clinical experience with you to help you make sense of how you, your friend or family member have become caught up in the OCD trap and empower you to take the right steps to help you to live your life free from OCD. In addition, you will read about other people's struggles with OCD and how they have tackled it using this approach. It's tempting to turn the page rather than read about difficulties other than your particular concerns, but I would encourage you to read about all the different types of OCD discussed in the book. By learning how OCD works for other people, you can gain a better understanding of your own particular problems and how to tackle them.

Cognitive behaviour therapy (CBT) has been shown to be particularly helpful for problems like OCD. While the focus is on using techniques from CBT, we will also draw on some of the latest ideas from what is often called 'Third Wave' CBT.

Throughout the book you will find practical exercises which will help you through the process. My intention – as with my face-to-face therapy clients – is to equip you with the skills and knowledge to become your own therapist. The practical exercises come in various forms:

- asking you to reflect on your own experiences
- questions for you to consider

- planning tasks to discover how OCD really works
- trying new ways of approaching your difficulties.

I believe in taking a 'whole person' approach to therapy. In order to tackle a specific problem we should also take a step back and consider the 'bigger picture'. We often overlook some of the basic building blocks of a healthy, happy lifestyle. Yet making some small changes here and there puts us in better shape to take on the challenge of overcoming OCD. For this reason, you will find sections on helpful habits at various points throughout the book.

By taking it step by step, you will:

- build your confidence
- know what you need to do tackle the problem
- learn how to get on with your life despite what OCD might be telling you.

Note

The case studies in this book are an amalgamation of many real-life examples and do not depict any specific individuals. Any resemblance to an individual person is purely coincidental.

PART 1

Support

*Understand where you are now
and where you want to be*

CHAPTER 1

What is OCD?

Overview

Obsessive–compulsive, obsessional, OCD. There's a bit of confusion about what it really is. In this chapter we will:

- learn what OCD is
- recognize the difference between obsessions and compulsions
- understand why interference and distress is key to diagnosis.

In recent times, the term OCD has almost become an everyday expression. Someone who likes to keep their home clean and tidy may excuse themselves as being 'a little bit OCD'. The ardent fan that has been to see *Les Miserables* more than 50 times may be described as 'obsessed'.

It is even seen as a positive attribute, something to strive for – to be obsessed with work is valued by many as a sign of someone conscientious and successful. Even the media messages drummed into us every day insist that we can't be too thin, too rich, or have too flashy a car. But in these examples, the person gets pleasure or satisfaction out of doing these particular things. To claim to be obsessed with something means we like or love something very much.

Yet anyone who suffers from OCD would hardly say they get pleasure from the ideas that come into their minds or the things they have to do. It's far more likely that they feel worried and upset, constantly bothered by the things they have to do in an attempt to feel less worried.

It's interesting to note how advertisers prey on our anxieties too: we can't be too clean or too careful. Even if OCD isn't a problem for us, they often succeed in making us worry … and so we buy their products to ensure our homes are clean, our hands are germ-free, or our families protected in the event of accidents or illness. We have managed to reduce that worry. An idea, a scary consequence, and a means of preventing it from happening. Even if we don't wholeheartedly believe it. Fingers crossed, just in case …

What is OCD?

Already we're beginning to see something of a pattern building up. It helps explain how we can all get the kinds of worries that we might find in obsessive–compulsive disorder. Nevertheless, it isn't only that these kinds of thoughts or worries occur to us. Or that we foresee some kinds of disastrous consequences which make us feel anxious enough to try to prevent them happening. Or even that we take some kind of action in an attempt to prevent this scary outcome. The clincher is how much these things interfere in our lives – how distressing we find them and how much they interfere with our daily routines.

So to meet criteria for the diagnosis of OCD there are three key features:

- obsessions
- compulsions
- interference or distress.

Even if you already feel certain that OCD is the problem, let's look at these in more detail. After all, knowledge is power and the better we can understand a problem the better equipped we are to deal with it.

What are obsessions?

One of the key features of obsessive–compulsive disorder is being bothered by **obsessions**: persistent thoughts or ideas that seem to just pop into our heads again and again, even though we're not trying to have them. They're sometimes called **intrusive thoughts** because they *intrude*. In other words, they interrupt us when we're busy thinking or doing something else.

3

Obsessional thoughts can occur to us in different ways:

- as words, like a statement about something or speech in our head
- as a feeling of doubt
- as an image – a picture in our mind
- as an urge to do something.

To keep it simple, let's just call them all 'thoughts' for the moment. Intrusive thoughts can feel quite different from other thoughts because they seem so difficult to ignore and get in the way of what we're doing. They can also seem different to us since the content of the thoughts – what the thought is about – feels unacceptable to us in certain ways.

Obsessional thoughts often seem to go against the way we see ourselves. It may feel wrong to have them. Perhaps they seem quite shocking and disgusting because they aren't the kinds of things we would usually choose to think about, or they represent things we would never dream of doing. Although they might be triggered by a particular situation we find ourselves in, they can equally just pop into our heads at any time for no particular reason. Here are some examples.

Thoughts
- I could give my family food poisoning.
- It's not safe to leave the kettle plugged in.
- Magpies bring bad luck.

Doubts
- What if I've committed a crime and can't remember?
- What if the binman cuts himself on that broken glass I put in the dustbin?
- Did I switch the iron off?

Images
- Attacking my partner with a knife.
- My baby in hospital because she'd eaten a raisin off the floor.
- Microscope view of germs covering the toilet.

Urges
- To touch a stranger inappropriately.
- To drive into oncoming traffic.
- To steal something.

These are only a few examples. It would be impossible to list every possible obsessional thought that someone might have. In the following chapters, there will be many more examples of different kinds of obsessional thoughts. You may have already found that some of the examples are similar to the kinds of thoughts you have had, although it's likely that there are some differences too. The exact content of obsessional thoughts are as individual as you are, but they still fit into the same categories of thoughts, doubts, images and urges and can be understood in the same way.

What are compulsions?

Compulsions or compulsive behaviours are things that you feel you *have* to do and cannot resist doing. Quite often, compulsions are actions you feel you have to repeat doing, like washing your hands again and again, or having to check something several times to make sure you've done it right in order to relieve the anxiety experienced following an intrusive thought.

Compulsive behaviours are linked to obsessive thoughts in a meaningful way. If we regard obsessive thoughts as fears or worries, compulsions are actions we might take to prevent the fear or worry coming true. So if, for example, you experience a thought such as 'I wonder if I closed the window?' it is likely that you would feel compelled to check to see if you had closed it. These visible, observable behaviours are sometimes referred to as **overt** or physical compulsions.

While we often consider a *behaviour* to be something that we can see – like checking the window or washing hands – compulsive behaviours also refer to other things we feel we have to do in response to an intrusive thought that are not visible to others. The kinds of behaviours that other people can't see because they are things we do in our head are sometimes referred to as **covert** or mental compulsions. It's easy to overlook them since they seem such an ordinary part of our internal life. Here are some examples.

Overt compulsions:

- following a strict routine in the shower
- keeping knives and sharp objects out of sight
- touching, tapping or having to repeat an action.

Covert compulsions:

- trying not to have a particular thought
- trying to decide whether or not something is clean enough
- thinking a 'good' thought after a 'bad' one.

Compulsions or compulsive behaviours are sometimes referred to as **neutralizing**. 'Neutralize' means to cancel out or (especially in this setting) to make something safe.

As with the list of obsessions, these are only a few examples because we will discuss different types of compulsions in more detail later.

The role of interference and distress

Although the presence of obsessive thoughts or behaviours we feel compelled to carry out are important features of OCD, a further key consideration is that the thoughts and/or behaviours cause significant interference in everyday activities or cause a lot of distress. It's likely that if you have OCD both of these things are true. In themselves, you might find the thoughts very upsetting but additionally the things you feel compelled to do might also be distressing, such as having to wash your hands so vigorously that they become really sore and chapped.

A further consequence that adds to levels of both distress and interference can be when compulsive behaviours take a long time. While you're in the middle of carrying out compulsions, it's possible that you become more and more upset and anxious because you find it difficult to stop what you're doing, becoming more and more worked-up the longer it goes on. And, of course, if ordinary everyday activities take such a long time to carry out, e.g. locking the door before going to work, or spending hours checking the internet for crimes that have happened in your area, it can eat into the day, meaning you don't have enough time for other things, or everything takes so long that you can't even manage to get to bed at a reasonable time.

Another critical way in which obsessions or compulsions can interfere with daily life is when they prevent you from doing particular activities or tasks, or there are certain fixed ways in which you have to do them. For example, being unable to go on holiday because you can only use the toilet at home, or having to repeatedly check documents at work so that you get into trouble for sending them out late. In order to prevent yourself from having upsetting thoughts or worries, it's quite usual that you might avoid doing particular things, going to particular places or being with particular people. **Avoidance** can become such a part of how we go about our daily lives that we can kid ourselves that OCD isn't that much of a problem because it's just what we do. However, other people don't usually take the same kinds of precautions or do things in the way we might like them to be done and that, of course, can be upsetting or distressing because it triggers particular worries or concerns. Here are some examples.

You have to do things in particular ways:

- washing your body in a particular order in the shower
- always wearing gloves when you go out, even on a warm day, to prevent your hands getting contaminated
- touching, tapping or counting when you check appliances are switched off.

It is time-consuming:

- having to repeat routines and rituals until you feel satisfied that you've done them correctly
- everyday tasks have so many 'rules' you have to follow that they take much longer than they should.

It affects the way you live:

- you're often late for appointments because it takes so long to leave the house
- you insist your family take the precautions you do
- there are lots of things you don't do to prevent triggering worries.

It might have unwanted or unintended consequences:

- additional costs from buying a lot of cleaning products, or replacing things you have damaged by cleaning too much or because they seem unsafe or unclean
- your home getting cluttered because you can't put out rubbish for fear of contamination or losing something
- losing your job because you're constantly late or can't finish work.

It leads to avoidance:

- people who might have something catching , like a tummy bug
- going past a church or other religious building in case you have blasphemous thoughts
- putting off starting a family.

It causes distress:

- getting upset because you still feel dirty after scrubbing your hands for 30 minutes
- feeling stressed after you've missed the bus because of checking the door several times
- believing you're a bad or evil person because you have unwanted sexual, violent or blasphemous thoughts.

So we can see that there are several aspects to interference and distress.

- You have to do things in particular ways.
- It is time-consuming.
- It affects the way you live.
- It might have unwanted or unintended consequences.
- It leads to avoidance.
- It causes distress.

At this point, you may be thinking 'But I don't have any obsessive thoughts' or 'I don't do anything when I get these thoughts, I'm just really bothered by lots of intrusive thoughts'. We'll have a closer look at both of these claims later in the book but for the moment it should be noted that the key to diagnosis of OCD is not that both obsessions *and* compulsions must be present. As long as two out of the three key features of OCD are experienced, that is sufficient. In other words, if you're troubled by obsessions and/or compulsions which cause significant distress or interference to everyday activities, it is likely that you have obsessive–compulsive disorder.

Chapter summary

In this chapter you have learned:

- OCD is an anxiety disorder
- the difference between obsessions and compulsions
- interference and distress are key to diagnosis.

Obsessive–compulsive disorder is an anxiety problem. If we are bothered by unwanted thoughts that keep coming back to us even when we try hard not to have them, or there are certain things we have to do again and again until it feels right, it might be OCD. Interference and distress are the key to diagnosis. In this way, we can see that someone who claims to be 'obsessed' with shoes or a musical does not have OCD. **Obsession** is to do with *thoughts*; obsessional thoughts also refers to doubts, urges or images. **Compulsion** signifies what we *do* – how we act or behave in response to obsessions. This is often referred to as **neutralizing**. Compulsions can be physical, observable actions like checking the door or washing our hands. They can also be mental actions like attempting to solve a problem, or thinking a nice thought after an upsetting one.

Now that you have a better understanding of obsessions and
compulsions, are you ready to discover more about OCD? Chapter 2
uses a series of real-life experiences to illustrate different ways in which
the problem might affect us.

Have I got OCD?

Overview

Chapter 1 explained the difference between obsessions and compulsions, and how interference and distress are defining features of OCD. This chapter:

- describes the different forms OCD can take
- uses real-life experiences to show different kinds of OCD
- helps you identify how OCD affects your life.

OCD can affect you in different ways to different degrees. There might be one or two things that bother you a lot (like washing or checking). Maybe things that bothered you in the past are no longer a problem but some other worries have crept in. That's one of the features of OCD: the focus of our concerns often changes over time. It reflects the things that are important to us at different points in our lives. Although OCD worries can be about anything and everything, most OCD concerns seem to fall into one of four general categories.

The four dreads of OCD

Although it is unlikely that this book will describe exactly the kinds of worries that you have, it is very likely that your concerns will fall into at least one of four general categories:

- dirty
- dangerous
- doubting
- deviant.

Let's explore a range of examples. Although each personal story has been placed under a key heading, as you read think about how their concerns might also fit with the other OCD dreads. And even if you don't share their particular problem, in what way is their experience similar to yours? How is it different?

Dirty

'I used to think, "If only my problem was washing my hands too much". I'd be able to stop it … no problem … I can't understand why you'd get worried by thinking things were dirty. But after I read how these people were so worried about dirt and germs and all that kind of stuff I realized that my problems aren't all that different. I check everything for the same reasons that they wash things … it's like we just don't trust ourselves to do it right. Reading about other kinds of OCD really helped me understand what was happening to me.'

Most of us wash our hands after going to the toilet, before preparing food, after doing jobs that make our hands visibly dirty such as gardening or changing the oil in the car. We change our clothes regularly, do the washing, clean the house, put fresh sheets on the bed. It's part of our routine – something we do to keep ourselves, our family and our homes clean and pleasant.

From time to time we might get a bit more concerned about dirt, germs and disease … a brand-new beige carpet, sterilizing bottles for a baby, hearing about MRSA or swine flu on the news. Many people feel grubby and unclean after travelling on public transport and want to wash their hands as soon as they get home.

These things aren't usually a problem if they only bother us occasionally, don't worry us much and don't interfere with our lives. And even if you prefer to wash your hands before eating, as long as you don't absolutely *have* to do it before having food, it's not an obsessional problem. However, if you are preoccupied with dirt and germs every day, find these thoughts very upsetting and these worries impact on your daily life in terms of trying to deal with these worries, then you may well have contamination OCD.

Contamination OCD

Concerns with dirt, germs or contamination can affect us in various ways. Common contamination worries include:

- dirt, germs or disease
- bodily fluids, e.g. urine, faeces, saliva, semen
- household products, e.g. bleach, insecticide spray, garden fertilizer
- environmental contaminants, e.g. asbestos, radiation, toxic waste
- animals or insects.

Generally, the concern is that *you* will become contaminated, or you may worry that you may pass on contamination to others because you've not been careful enough.

Case study: Maxine

Maxine spent a lot of her time in cleaning frenzies where she would spend all day and stay up all night cleaning her home from top to bottom. It wasn't so much that she was troubled by worries about germs or being contaminated by things that might make her ill in some way, but she had become very sensitive to smells and odours. Such was her worry about her belongings smelling, she had taken to throwing away many of her possessions, including furniture, she could only wear items of clothing once before discarding them, and she had stopped cooking.

She began to limit the kinds of foods she would eat too, avoiding anything that might have a lingering odour. In addition, Maxine developed a number of routines to minimize the risk of smells, e.g. wrapping sandwiches in a paper napkin to hold them while eating so that her hands wouldn't be tainted, wiping her face after each mouthful, lighting scented candles around her home, taking steps to prevent

---

contaminating treasured possessions, excessive hand washing, bathing and toilet routines.

Maxine scrutinized other people, paying attention to the way in which they would eat, or how they cleaned their homes, although she concluded that the reason others did not take the preventative measures she did was because they did not smell like she did. As her rituals and routines became more elaborate and time-consuming, Maxine became increasingly depressed. Sleep deprivation and erratic, poor eating habits contributed to this downward spiral.

Although she would attempt to wash or clean everything to keep it odour-free, this led to further problems as she either ruined items that don't take kindly to washing (like shoes, books and photographs) or she failed to eliminate smells completely. She slept on the bare floor (the bed had to go because she feared it harboured smells) with only a small blanket to cover her (to reduce the burden of things to wash).

Many of the things she was doing to avoid smell and contamination tended to backfire: her inability to dry clothes thoroughly caused them to become stale and mildewed, and by attempting to keep 'clean' and 'dirty' things separate in the home, certain parts of her home became 'no-go' areas. The additional stress of increasing financial pressure from spending a small fortune on cleaning products and replacing essential items further added to her unhappiness.

Case study: Janet

Janet became increasingly concerned about the effect her contamination worries were having on her son, now aged seven. Because of her fears about dog faeces, she would try to do everything in her power to prevent him from coming into contact with anything that could possibly be contaminated with it. This was becoming more difficult now that he was getting older. It was often a cause of arguments between her and her husband because of the restrictions she placed on their activities. In particular, her husband was keen to take his son to play football in the park but Janet would become extremely upset and angry when they returned, making them both strip off in the garage in case they brought any dog mess into the house. She then insisted that they both had a bath to ensure they were really clean. Because of her reaction, her husband has stopped going to the park.

Janet's concerns about dog faeces began during pregnancy after she read about toxocariasis in a magazine. She'd always been fairly careful about hygiene, and reasoned that any good mother would be careful because children are so vulnerable. She prides herself on her clean home, and is horrified at how dirty some of her friends are. Since this particular concern began, Janet prefers not to have her friends come to her home because she 'can't be sure they don't have something on them'. Although she feels uncomfortable going to their homes, she just about manages by taking antibacterial hand gel and drinks and snacks for her son (she's told her friends that he has food allergies). It's harder now that he is older as other mums don't tend to accompany their children on playdates, and he is also asking to bring friends home. She is worried that he is losing friends because of this.

Due to these preoccupations, Janet is constantly on alert for anything that may pose a risk and this is rubbing off on her son. She walks in the middle of the footpath as she claims there is more dog mess at the edges. And as well as giving dogs a wide berth, she holds her breath until well past them (and gets her son to do the same) in case they breathe in germs. Although she does all she can to avoid encounters with dogs, she gets extremely worried if she has to pass one and would have to use hand gel and then go home to wash even though she crosses the road to avoid the possibility of direct contact. She insists that, like her, her son always wears a coat and gloves when they go out as this limits the amount of washing and cleaning she would need to do (outdoor garments are removed and kept in the garage, which is the only way anyone is allowed in the house).

At home, Janet always uses products that are labelled 'antibacterial' and buys several bottles of disinfectant each week. Although she launders the family's clothing daily, she has stopped hanging it to dry in the garden because she worries that foxes might have soiled there.

Over the past few months, her avoidance behaviours have become more extreme. Janet does all she can to prevent triggering thoughts about dogs: she has thrown out all cuddly toys that look like dogs and picture books with dog pictures, she pre-records TV programmes so that she can fast-forward through adverts that may show dogs, has changed where she does her grocery shopping because the checkout in her local supermarket is right next to the pet food aisle, and even shuns a well-known brand of toilet paper because it often features pictures of puppies on the wrapper. When in the queue, she would check the clothing of other customers for dog hairs and would swap queues if she noticed anything potentially 'dangerous'.

Rules, rituals and avoidance

If contamination OCD is a problem for you, it is likely that some or all of the following are things you do either to prevent or to reduce worries or anxiety:

- frequent hand washing
- washing, showering or bathing routines
- toilet routines
- cleaning and laundry routines
- avoiding 'dirty' things or situations
- taking precautions to avoid contamination
- checking
- seeking reassurance.

Frequent handwashing

Do you wash your hands more often than most people, always washing them very thoroughly and paying close attention to make sure every bit of your hand has been thoroughly washed, washing each finger one by one, or washing past your wrists (or even your elbows) every time, always using soap (and plenty of it)?

Washing, showering and bathing routines

When you have a bath or shower, does it take you a long time or are you driven to bathe or shower more than once a day even if the weather isn't scorching hot or you haven't done something to get noticeably dirty or sweaty? Do you use a lot of bath products? Do you have a particular routine or ritual before you can take a bath or shower? Maybe you have to clean the bath or basin before you use it? Or use a lot of towels each time and have to use a clean towel each time? Do you have rules about when you or others have to wash, bathe or shower, e.g. before and after sex (and getting your partner to do so too)?

Toilet routines

Do you have rules about when you can go, e.g. first thing in the morning before getting washed or dressed? Can you only use certain toilets, e.g. your own, or at your parents' house? Perhaps you use a lot of toilet paper? Avoid sitting down on the seat? Do you have to wash or bathe afterwards? Maybe you avoid drinking to cut down on the need to go?

Cleaning and laundry routines

Are there particular ways in which you have to clean? Do you clean more often than other people you know? Do you get worried or anxious in case things aren't clean enough? Do you use a lot of antibacterial products or only use disposable cloths for cleaning? Are there certain things you feel unable to wash together, e.g. underwear with towels? Do you wash clothing every time you wear it, even if it still looks clean? Do other people consider your cleaning routines to be extreme, e.g. unscrewing sockets to clean behind them or moving wardrobes every week? Have you worn things out because you have cleaned them too much (or tried to wash things that shouldn't be washed)?

Avoiding 'dirty' things or situations

Are there places or situations you avoid because they don't seem clean enough, e.g. travelling by bus, or not sitting down on public transport? Do you get someone else to put out the rubbish? Do you avoid walking or sitting on the grass?

Other precautions to avoid contamination

Are there other precautions you take to prevent or reduce contact with a contaminant? Things like carrying antibacterial hand gel or wipes, keeping separate 'indoor' and 'outdoor' clothes, designating certain areas in your home as clean/dirty? Do you wash things you bring into your home or store things in a special way, e.g. wrapping groceries before storing them in the cupboard? Do you insist on drinking from a disposable cup? Or always carry your own cutlery with you? Or check 'best before' dates on food items?

Checking and reassurance

Do you often check that things are clean enough? Or notice things like dark marks and then worry it might be something dirty? Look closely at other people's reactions to things that seem dirty to you? Or ask how they go about cleaning/using the toilet or similar kinds of things?

If you have answered 'Yes' to one or more of these questions, you may have **contamination** or **washing** OCD.

Mental contamination

Sometimes it's not about becoming physically contaminated but feeling sullied or tainted by somebody or something. This is sometimes called 'sympathetic magic' – the idea that something takes on the characteristics or qualities of something it might resemble or look like, or has some kind of connection with. For example, if you were offered a drink of orange squash that had been poured into a brand-new child's potty you might find it hard to drink even though you had just seen it being taken out of its packaging and protective plastic wrapper and so knew it had never been used before.

In a similar way, many people would not want to put on an item of clothing that used to belong to someone like Hitler or the murderer Myra Hindley. Even if it was freshly washed, it might seem as if it could somehow pass on their 'badness' to anyone who touched it. The result isn't that you've become physically contaminated – you haven't actually come into contact with dirt or germs – but you feel mentally contaminated by it.

Case study: Shiralee

Shiralee felt she had been the victim of sexual harassment when she worked as a barista in her local coffee shop. The manager, Steve, had been friendly at first. But then she thought he seemed a bit too 'friendly' when he brushed past her whenever she was leaning over, making personal remarks about certain parts of her body and standing very close whenever she found herself alone with him. Although it had been a few years since she'd left her job (and she believed Steve had moved on too), Shiralee couldn't bear to be reminded of anything to do with that period in her life. Just the thought of it made her feel disgusted and dirty, and even seeing another branch of the well-known chain of coffee shops or hearing the name 'Steve' would trigger unwanted memories.

If mental contamination is a problem for you, it's possible that you might have some washing or cleaning routines. It's more likely that you do some or all of the following:

- attempt to block thoughts from coming into your mind
- have 'superstitious' behaviours, e.g. touching wood
- try to 'undo' unwanted or upsetting thoughts with a 'good' thought
- avoid certain places, people or things that are connected with bad thoughts
- find it hard to say certain words or names because they make you feel uneasy
- spend a lot of time worrying or ruminating about past events.

If this sounds familiar to you, this kind of OCD might be **mental contamination**.

Dangerous

Even if you have a passion for extreme sports such as bungee jumping or Parkour, there are plenty of things you still do, like most people, to prevent or reduce the risk of harm or danger. We're careful when we use knives or sharp tools, we drive carefully to avoid accidents, and generally try not to be careless enough to leave taps running or the gas on.

Occasionally, we might feel the need to go back and check. Perhaps a thought pops into our head about something that could happen. After seeing a car crash on the motorway, you might imagine being in an accident yourself. It might even make you drive more slowly – for a while, anyway.

However, if you find you're very preoccupied with thoughts or images about bad things that could happen every day and they upset you so much that they interfere with your daily life, you may well have harm and danger OCD.

Harm and danger OCD

Concerns with harm and danger can affect us in a wide variety of ways. There's often a lot of overlap with other kinds of OCD, such as contamination worries and doubting. Common danger and harm concerns include:

- fears about causing a fire, flood or burglary
- causing a road traffic accident
- committing a crime
- cutting yourself on a sharp knife
- losing control and injuring someone
- causing harm because you haven't been careful enough
- offending others either deliberately or accidentally.

It might be that you worry that something bad might happen because you've not been careful enough, even though you didn't wish to cause harm. Or it may be that you're afraid that you might lose control and act on these thoughts, urges or impulses.

Case study: Checking

Trying to leave for work in the morning was a testing time for Tadeusz. Even though he'd found ways to cut out the need for some checks – like having cereal and juice for breakfast instead of toast and a hot drink, and avoiding opening any windows – it would still take ages. But that was so much better than when he had to have his breakfast at least three hours before leaving for work to allow enough time for the kettle and toaster to cool down.

He had a routine that he went through, starting in his bedroom and working his way through his flat room by room: his bedroom, the bathroom, the kitchen, the lounge and finally the hall. 'Window, window, window', he would chant quietly as he rattled the catches on all of the three opening portions of his bedroom window to make sure they were firmly closed and locked. Then 'Socket, socket' as he inspected the electrical sockets in his room, switching off at the wall and pulling out any plugs. He was relieved that his mobile phone had an excellent alarm because he'd got really fed up with having to set his radio alarm clock each night before going to bed.

In the bathroom, he'd make sure no plugs had been left in the sink or bath. He had cut through the chains that attached them so that he could line them up on the windowsill rather than risk them falling into the plughole while he was out. Taps would be turned off so tightly that he struggled to turn them on again.

The kitchen was always the toughest challenge. There were so many sockets and so many things that needed unplugging or switching off or simply checking, although he'd stopped using quite a few things. Instead of using the gas cooker, Tadeusz just heated things in the microwave. It didn't taste as good – and there were so many things he really missed, like fried onions. But using the gas meant he'd have to spend hours each morning checking it was turned off, holding his hand over the top of the burners to feel for any gas escaping and then sniffing to see if he could smell gas. Everything had to be unplugged and switched off at the wall. He'd tried to do that with the fridge too, but as it was a fridge-freezer, food began to defrost and then there'd be a big build-up of ice from plugging it in again once he was home.

On a good day, a 'once-over' would do. Even so, it would take the best part of an hour … and that was before having to tackle locking the front door and everything that involved. On a bad day, doubts would have Tadeusz going back into each room three or four times even if he'd already left the house. And the whole process would have to begin again …

Case study: Causing harm

Carol had been troubled by obsessional thoughts on and off during her life. Now in her late 40s with grown-up children who still lived at home with her and her husband, she had become quite depressed as a result of some family difficulties and it was at this time that she began to get intrusive thoughts about losing control and causing harm. She found thoughts about killing her daughter particularly disturbing. These thoughts occurred frequently throughout the day and terrified her.

Carol was very aware of bodily sensations when she became anxious which she believed were an indication that she really was about to lose control. She would do everything she possibly could to prevent sparking off these thoughts: she hid knives and other sharp objects – even the dog's lead as she feared she might strangle someone with it – and stopped watching her favourite soaps on television in case violent scenes were portrayed. In fact, Carol found that all kinds of things on television and in the newspaper could trigger worries. However, although she generally tended to avoid any media reports about violent incidents, she felt strangely drawn to check newspapers for descriptions of the kind of person who committed horrendous crimes against which she could compare herself.

As the number of thoughts increased, Carol found it harder to go out as she began to worry that she may lose control and kill *anyone*. She also made excuses not to see other relatives, like her parents or her brothers' families, as their presence would make her fearful. In addition, she would always try to block out upsetting thoughts and try not to have them as well as attempting to feel completely in control, always on the look-out for any signs that she was not.

She couldn't understand *why* she was thinking this way. After all, she loved her children so much and her family was so important to her. Because she held the view that thinking bad things is as bad as doing them, she concluded that she must be a really evil, bad person for having these thoughts.

Sometimes we just get vague feelings about harm and danger – something we just can't put our finger on. Nevertheless, we might feel a bit uneasy. My grandmother banned lilac from the house. She couldn't say how it could cause bad things, but her superstitious belief was that it would bring about a death. OCD can also attach itself to these hazy feelings that something bad might happen.

Case study: Numbers and counting

Stefan had always had a thing about numbers. He liked some numbers more than others, thought that certain numbers were lucky for him – like the number three. His birthday was on the third day of the third month, he was one of three children and he lived at number 3. He enjoyed his job as a taxi driver, and felt comfortable with the fact that the registration of his taxicab was a number that was divisible by three.

More of a problem was that some numbers troubled him a lot. Not just the obvious ones like 13, but also some with more personal meanings for him. After the phone call from his brother at 4 a.m. to say that his mother had just died, the number four began to fill him with dread and he began to avoid it whenever possible. At break times, he couldn't bring himself to take the last seat when three of his mates were already sitting at a table for four, and would buy only two-finger chocolate wafer bars instead of the larger four-finger bars. He began to count almost everything, and being pretty good at maths, worked out complicated sums to check whether or not his lucky or unlucky numbers applied.

As time went on, Stefan's number concerns became more and more of a problem. He became increasingly preoccupied with looking out for what he thought were problem numbers, counting how many vehicles were in front of him at the traffic lights and reading their registration numbers. After a particularly tiring night shift, he pulled up behind another cab with a series of three 6s on its licence plate and was struck by a sudden memory: the number of the beast. He wasn't sure where the memory had come from, but knew it had something to do with the Bible. And although he no longer went to church regularly, this felt important and very threatening.

Rules, rituals and avoidance

If harm and danger OCD is a problem for you, it is likely that some or all of the following are things you do either to prevent or to reduce worries or anxiety:

- checking taps, switches and appliances
- checking locks, doors and windows
- having set routines or procedures before leaving the house
- mentally reviewing your actions
- checking that you haven't caused an accident
- avoiding situations that trigger thoughts about harm or danger
- seeking reassurance
- having lucky or unlucky numbers, colours with a special significance, etc.

Checking taps, switches and appliances

Do you repeatedly check taps, switches and appliances before leaving your home? Do you usually unplug electrical appliances before going out or going to bed? Even things that have a clock or timer on them? Do you insist on unplugging an appliance rather than simply switching it off at the wall?

Checking locks, doors and windows

Do you check that all doors and windows are closed or locked before going out? Even if you know they haven't been opened recently? Are there a number of steps you have to take to satisfy you that they are closed, e.g. rattle the handle a certain number of times, or count while you check? Are you satisfied if someone else locks up (or maybe even prefer it so you don't have to)?

Set routines or procedures before leaving the house
Do you have a set routine or procedure before you leave the house? Do you often go back to check something several times?

Mentally reviewing your actions
Do you spend a lot of time going over events in your head to check that you didn't cause harm? Or trying to be sure you haven't caused an accident?

Avoiding situations that trigger thoughts about harm or danger
Do you avoid doing certain things, going to certain places, or being with certain people because of thoughts about harm or danger? Do you avoid using appliances because you think they could be unsafe? Or have to take a lot of precautions when you use them? Do you keep sharp objects out of sight? What about other things that could be used as a weapon? Does seeing such things make you worry that you might lose control and harm someone? Do you find it hard to do certain things (like driving) in case you have an accident? Do you avoid taking on certain responsibilities (such as being in charge of the code for the safe at work)?

Seeking reassurance
Do you ask other people for reassurance? Do you check the news or even phone the police to ask about any accidents that you fear you may have caused? Do you spend a lot of time looking for information on the internet to put your mind at rest?

Lucky or unlucky numbers, colours with a special meaning, etc.
Are there certain numbers that you think of as lucky? Or unlucky? How about colours with a special significance? Or other superstitious behaviours that make you feel safe and that you can't resist doing?

If you have answered 'Yes' to one or more questions, you may have
danger or **harm** OCD.

Doubting

Did I miss Alex's birthday? Is there enough petrol in the tank to get
me home? Does this report need more detail? Are we good parents?
Was that the doorbell? Who doesn't get doubts on a daily basis? In our
hectic and often stressful lives, we're trying to do so many things at
once that it's hardly surprising if we can't always remember what we've
done or what we mean to do. While we mostly deal with such doubts
swiftly or just shrug them off, persistent doubts are a typical feature of
OCD. In fact, OCD is often nicknamed the 'doubting disease'.

Case study: Doubting

Things haven't been going too well at work for David recently. As a
clerk with a large insurance company, one of his main responsibilities
is to update policy files with new correspondence and information and
discard redundant information. He is behind with his work and has a
backlog of filing. He feels that he struggles to concentrate on reading
the documents, which means he is uncertain about where they should
be filed. David generally finds reading hard-going, as if what he's trying
to read just won't sink in. As a result, he feels compelled to constantly
reread everything. Often he gets extremely uptight and stressed, and at
these times his concentration becomes even worse. He distracts himself
by surfing the internet but worries that he will get into trouble if his
manager catches him.

However, David's workplace problems are only the tip of the iceberg.
At home, he has accumulated so much clutter that it spills over into
every room. Most of the clutter is an accumulation of correspondence,
magazines and other paper items. He agrees that it is too much, but
worries about getting rid of it for a number of reasons. First, he is afraid
that he may accidentally throw away something of importance, like a
bank statement, that he might later need. In addition, he worries that he
may become the victim of identity fraud and could lose all his savings

if anything giving his personal details fell into the wrong hands, he feels
this is quite likely as he believes the area he lives in is quite dangerous.
Because the clutter is fairly disorganized, David feels that he has to go
through each item to check whether or not it is something he needs
to keep. This even applies to till receipts, as he is afraid that fraudsters
would be able to identify his bank details from them if he had paid
by card. When contemplating throwing things away, he becomes
increasingly tense and anxious and would want to feel completely
certain, all the time assuring himself that he isn't making a mistake. All
too often, he just gives up as it all seems too much like hard work.

Case study: Repeating

Although Arun had a number of OCD concerns, what bothered him
most was that there were certain things he had to do over and over
again. He could understand why he would repeatedly check he hadn't
dropped his keys or his phone, and even why he felt it would help
to wash his hands a few more times. It was the embarrassment of
the other things he had to repeat. Checking his keys and taking a bit
longer washing his hands didn't look that unusual. But hesitating in
the doorway as he entered a room, swaying to and fro before he could
go in, or stopping dead in the middle of a crowded pavement to step
backwards and forwards a couple of times led to people saying 'What
the hell do you think you're doing?', or less savoury versions, as they
almost tripped over him. Sometimes it was only one or two repetitions,
but on a bad day Arun could get stuck for ages before he felt ready to
carry on. He was sure that work colleagues had noticed because at times
it was hard to miss, particularly when it involved touching and tapping
things in meetings. Of course, what they couldn't see was the way he
wrestled with his mind: constantly debating whether or not he should
just carry on; did he need to do it again; could he be certain he didn't
need to step backwards; were his doubts really just doubts?

Relationship OCD

Since OCD has a tendency to target those areas of our lives that are
important to us, perhaps it's not surprising that relationships can be

another common focus of concern. Obsessional concerns can take various forms, such as:

- doubts about whether your partner is cheating on you
- constantly wondering if you really love your partner (or child)
- asking for reassurance about whether they still love you or find you attractive
- doubts about your sexuality.

Case study: Relationships

When Leila was at secondary school, she was involved in a rather difficult friendship with another girl who was quite controlling. This led her to worry constantly over whether or not they would have an argument, or if she was doing anything that might upset the other girl. At home, she began to perform some rituals that she felt would stop anything bad from happening – it could be all kinds of things, from staring and blinking at a boy-band poster on her wall to lining up her teddies in a particular order. It gave her a sense that she had some control over the situation with her friend.

Despite these actions, the friendship eventually faded in the way that teenage friendships often do. The OCD also faded and she got on with her life – friends, jobs, boyfriends. Then she met a fabulous guy. She was convinced he was 'the one', and he seemed equally smitten with her. All seemed rosy until Leila began to get persistent thoughts that she needed to be certain that he really was 'the one'. Yet this time, instead of having to do things like keeping her room in order or organizing cuddly toys, she had frequent urges to question him about his feelings for her and to come clean about all of the past relationships (even unrequited crushes) she had ever had. Although her boyfriend really didn't want to hear about them, she felt she had to tell him or else their relationship would be a sham and doomed to failure.

These kinds of thought don't occur only in the context of a romantic relationship, but can also affect friendships, as with Leila, and can occur in relationships with family members. In common with philosophers, poets and writers, Hanif repeatedly questioned what love was and whether or not what he felt about his family – his parents, brothers and sister – was in fact love or something else. And if it was something else, what was it? Rosie and her partner had just had their first baby. Adele was the most gorgeous little thing. Everyone agreed she had the cutest little lips, just like her mother, and luxurious dark eyelashes just like her father. In other words, she was perfect in every way. Yet Rosie would look at this little bundle asleep in her cot and wonder whether she felt the way she should be feeling. Did she love her baby? How upset would she be if this child were taken away from her? She felt terrified and guilty that she didn't seem to feel certain, and even more so should anyone find out that she thought this way.

Case study: Sexuality

At the age of 20, Richard had never had a steady girlfriend. Sure, he had lots of girls who were friends as well as lots of boys who were friends. Sociable and outgoing, he had always been very popular, both at school and at the university where he was now in his final year. He wasn't really sure why he had never been in what he thought of as a 'proper' relationship.

He'd lost his virginity during his first term at university at a drunken party with a girl studying medicine. For a while, he only seemed to get to the kissing stage with some of the girls he'd begun to hang around with, although before long things developed and he had what he described as a 'brief period of popularity' with several opportunities for sexual encounters. Although he found these enjoyable enough, they never turned into anything more than one- (or two- or three-) night stands. He couldn't understand why, and began to wonder if there was something the matter with him that put girls off.

He ran over all kinds of ideas in his head until eventually it struck him that maybe he was gay. After all, gay men often have lots of female friends. Maybe girls had a 'Gaydar' and were able to spot someone who wasn't straight a mile off. To test out his theory, Richard would check out his reaction to the poster of Cameron Diaz he had on his wall to see whether or not he got an erection. Sometimes he did but the more often he looked at it, the less aroused he seemed to get. Was this evidence for what he suspected was true? He needed to be certain and so he began looking on the internet for videos of men having sex with other men, and then became alarmed that he got an erection even at the prospect of watching. Yet he didn't seem to feel attracted to men. What was going on? He just couldn't work it out.

Rules, rituals and avoidance

If doubting plays a significant role in your experience of OCD, it is likely that some or all of the following are things you do either to prevent or to reduce worries or anxiety:

- put off decisions because you never feel certain
- have to repeat things until it feels right
- argue with your thoughts
- review your thoughts and/or actions over and over again
- try to reassure yourself
- attempt to distract yourself.

Put off decisions because you never feel certain

Do you spend so much time worrying about things you need to do that they take a long time to finish? Do you find it difficult to throw things away because you're worried that it might be important? Do you find it hard to make decisions that other people don't think twice about?

Have to repeat things until it feels right

Are there things you have to do over and over again? What about having to reread something several times? Or having to repeat random things, like going in and out of the door? Do you have any rituals involving touching, tapping or rubbing? Or have to 'balance out' something you did with your right hand with an action with your left hand?

Argue with your thoughts

Do you constantly argue with your thoughts? Try to make yourself feel completely certain? Constantly weigh up the pros and cons of situations? Are you always indecisive?

Review your thoughts and/or actions

Do you spend a lot of time reviewing what you've done or thought? Do you go over the same things again and again? Is it hard to let go of thoughts or doubts?

Try to reassure yourself

Are you always looking for reassurance? Maybe looking for information on the internet to put your mind at rest? Do your family or friends get annoyed because you ask them the same questions repeatedly?

Attempt to distract yourself

Do you put lots of effort into trying to do something to take your mind off things, like forcing yourself to watch a film or read a book?

If you answered 'Yes' to any of these questions or doubting takes up a lot of your time or makes you anxious, you may have **doubting** or **rumination** OCD.

Deviant

Doubts about sexuality can take other forms too; worrying about whether you are the wrong gender is an example, as are worries such as whether you are developing the sexual features of the opposite sex. Such concerns can crop up either in combination with obsessions about relationships or on their own. Obsessional fears are often about being deviant in some way. Deviant means straying away from what is acceptable or natural. Even these days, sex can be a taboo subject. It's not surprising, then, that unbidden thoughts about it are extremely frequent OCD concerns. That's especially true of ideas about children, incest or animals.

Jeremy was alarmed by images of getting turned on by his cat. 'This is so sick', he shuddered. He couldn't let anyone know about this. Because most people are familiar with more obvious forms of OCD, such as washing and checking, such involuntary thoughts, images and ideas can easily be mistaken for something else – something more sinister than an anxiety problem.

Case study: Sexual thoughts

Sahib had always been mad on sport and fitness and was thrilled to get his dream job at a gym near his home. His favourite gym activity was the spin class and he loved leading the action at least a few times each day, encouraging his class to go for the burn while he sang along with effortless ease as they sweated away to keep up with his pace. Of course, it was important to cast a watchful eye on those he already considered 'his' class to make sure they weren't slacking.

A few female members of his class enjoyed being on the front row, vying with one another to be the star performer. Sahib hated this because it was impossible not to see down the front of their vest-tops as they bent over the handlebars. At the start of each session, he would cross his fingers that some of the guys would get to those bikes first and do his best to avert his gaze away from the women in the class. He was worried that they would think he was eying them up or (as he called it) being a bit of a 'perv'. That they might think this was really upsetting because he was in a steady relationship and hoped to marry his girlfriend the following year.

Sahib became more and more fixated about not noticing women's chests. And the more he tried not to notice them, the more he seemed to think about them. He became even more convinced that this was wrong and he shouldn't think this way. In an attempt to prevent any misunderstandings, he deliberately avoided looking at female members – not even looking them in the eye, as he still got a glimpse of their cleavage.

So he began focusing on the men in his class instead. This seemed to solve the problem and all was fine until the day a new guy came to join the group. Lycra-clad, he was muscular and fit – clearly a regular at the gym, but not at this class. Sahib gave a quick glance to check out the newcomer's technique in the way he always did with the 'newbies', but almost recoiled when his eyes alighted on the man's groin. To his mind, this could only mean one thing: he really was a 'perv'. But as he thought it through, he began to worry that maybe he was gay. He just knew he had to work it out, and began to check himself for signs that he was becoming aroused when he looked at women. Or men. And the more he tried to work it out, the more confused and worried he became.

Case study: Paedophile thoughts

As a teenager, Mandy drove her mum and dad mad. It took an absolute age for her to get ready for bed: lining up all her cuddly toys in the right order, putting her school clothes out 'just so', and then insisting that her mum and dad kissed her goodnight in a very precise but sing-song way to which she also replied in a similar fashion: 'Nighty, night', 'Same to you', 'Sleep tight', 'Thank you'. If Mandy felt that either the rhythm or the intonation wasn't quite right in some way, she'd get upset until her parents did it again in the right way. As you can imagine, it could sometimes take a while before Mandy was finally satisfied – especially when either of her parents got so annoyed that they couldn't keep the infuriation out of their voice. The longer it went on each night, the worse it got.

In desperation, Mandy's parents took her to a psychiatrist, who diagnosed OCD. With just a little help, she was able to break the habit. That was a long time ago. Now in a long-term relationship with the loveliest, kindest man she could imagine, life should have felt complete as they had a gorgeous little baby. Betsy was the first grandchild in the family and absolutely doted on. But Mandy just couldn't feel joyful. The first time she changed Betsy's nappy, she was horror-struck by an image which came into her head. What kind of person would think about touching a baby in that way? She felt sick and disgusted.

Terrified of having more of these thoughts, Mandy began to avoid nappy-changing and even holding her baby as these images seemed to play at the edge of her consciousness. Why was this happening? She had to work it out and constantly trawled her mind for explanations. 'Maybe that's it!' she concluded, as the memory of playing 'doctors and nurses' entered her head. She'd read somewhere that paedophiles and child abusers often began their sickening ways messing around with other kids. It hadn't crossed her mind that it could be OCD.

Thoughts about being deviant crop up in different ways too. Thoughts and doubts to do with religion, or right and wrong (morality), or committing a crime are common, as are ideas about saying or doing something that might upset other people or cause offence. Angelique struggled throughout services at her church. Because she was terrified that she might blurt out swear words, she would take a swig of water as she went in and hold it in her mouth. If it was still there at the end of the service, it reassured her that she couldn't have opened her mouth at all so there was no chance she had sworn. Except it was really hard not to swallow. Quite often there was very little water left in her mouth. That really bothered her.

The myth of 'Pure O'

Deviant thoughts are frequently found in what is often called 'Pure O'. Although it's a catchy label, it isn't accurate. Earlier in this chapter, we learned that compulsive behaviours are not only physical actions, like washing or turning the taps off. There are lots of compulsions that others can't see – things we do in our head, for example. If most of the action takes place in your head, we call it **rumination**. In a similar way to cows chewing their cud (or ruminating), we chew over intrusive thoughts, doubts and worries again and again.

Rules, rituals and avoidance

If deviant OCD is a problem for you, it is likely that you do some or all of the following things either to prevent or to reduce worries or anxiety:

- try to push thoughts out of your head
- try to problem-solve or work out what these thoughts mean

- avoid anything that triggers thoughts
- attempt to convince yourself these thoughts don't reflect the 'real you'
- think a good thought after a bad thought.

Try to push thoughts out of your head

Do you try not to have particular thoughts? Or try to push them out if they pop into your head? Do you keep trying to push them away even if it doesn't seem to work?

Try to problem-solve or work out what these thoughts mean

Do you spend a lot of time looking for reasons or explanations for why you have these thoughts? Are you convinced that finding the reason for them is necessary? Do you worry that they mean that you're a bad person in some way?

Avoid anything that triggers thoughts

Do you go out of your way to avoid sparking these thoughts off? Are many things difficult to do because you worry that you may act on urges or impulses? Do you steer clear of certain films or television programmes because they might have scenes that could make you anxious?

Attempt to convince yourself these thoughts don't reflect the 'real you'

Do you put a lot of effort into persuading yourself that you're not a bad person? Do you compare yourself to others all the time? Do you look for reassurance on the internet?

Think a good thought after a bad thought

Do you try to think something nice or positive when you have an unwelcome thought? Maybe conjure up a pleasant image to cancel out the bad one?

If you have answered 'Yes' to one or more of these questions, you might be suffering from a type of OCD often called **obsessional rumination**.

35

Something for everyone!

Obsessional concerns can be about anything and everything – it really is a case of 'something for everyone'. As a result, it wouldn't be possible to cover here absolutely everything that anyone could worry about. At this point, you might be thinking 'This book is just like all the others on OCD. It just doesn't tell me much about *my* concerns'.

The categories which we've called the 'four dreads of OCD' seem to cover most OCD concerns, but there's a lot of overlap between them. That's also true of rules, rituals and avoidances. Compulsions can – and do – apply to a whole range of obsessional worries. It's possible that you have a number of different concerns, or that new worries have crept in as old ones have become less of an issue. By 'unpacking' these broad headings, we can find some general principles that will help you to understand your own experience of OCD. There are a few things that don't fit neatly into these categories – order and tidiness, for example, or hoarding. Hoarding is now seen as a separate problem from OCD, although there can be hoarding features in OCD (and vice versa). It's also possible to have both hoarding and OCD at the same time.

OCD and me: Identifying my problem

Maybe you're already confident that the difficulties you've been having are the result of OCD. Whether or not you're sure, the following questionnaire will help you look at different elements that may or may not be part of your experience.

By asking yourself how upsetting or distressing you find each of these elements and giving each item a rating, you can begin to discover whether there is a particular theme (or themes) to your worries. So it's more a measure of *what* bothers you and *how much*.

The total score isn't an important factor in deciding whether or not you have OCD; the score is more helpful as a measure of how much things have changed over a period of time. But it is a good idea to fill in the questionnaire now and add up your scores for each section. This will help you identify areas you need to work on.

Self-assessment

The following statements refer to experiences which many people have in their everyday lives. In the column labelled 'Distress', circle the number that best describes *how much* that experience has distressed or bothered you during the past month.

Give each item a rating from 0–4; 0 = not at all; 1 = a little; 2 = moderately; 3 = a lot; 4 = extremely distressing.

Obsessive–compulsive inventory (OCI)		
		Distress
1	Unpleasant thoughts come into my mind against my will and I cannot get rid of them.	0 1 2 3 4
2	I think contact with bodily secretions (perspiration, saliva, blood, urine, etc.) may contaminate my clothes or somehow harm me.	0 1 2 3 4
3	I ask people to repeat things to me several times, even though I understood them the first time.	0 1 2 3 4
4	I wash and clean obsessively.	0 1 2 3 4
5	I have to review mentally past events, conversations and actions to make sure that I didn't do something wrong.	0 1 2 3 4
6	I have saved up so many things that they get in the way.	0 1 2 3 4
7	I check things more often than necessary.	0 1 2 3 4

(Continued)

8	I avoid using public toilets because I am afraid of disease or contamination.	0 1 2 3 4
9	I repeatedly check doors, windows, drawers etc.	0 1 2 3 4
10	I repeatedly check gas and water taps and light switches after turning them off.	0 1 2 3 4
11	I collect things I don't need.	0 1 2 3 4
12	I have thoughts of having hurt someone without knowing it.	0 1 2 3 4
13	I have thoughts that I might want to harm myself or others.	0 1 2 3 4
14	I get upset if objects are not arranged properly.	0 1 2 3 4
15	I feel obliged to follow a particular order in dressing, undressing and washing myself.	0 1 2 3 4
16	I feel compelled to count while I am doing things.	0 1 2 3 4
17	I am afraid of impulsively doing embarrassing or harmful things.	0 1 2 3 4
18	I need to pray to cancel bad thoughts or feelings.	0 1 2 3 4
19	I keep on checking forms or other things I have written.	0 1 2 3 4
20	I get upset at the sight of knives, scissors and other sharp objects in case I lose control with them.	0 1 2 3 4
21	I am excessively concerned about cleanliness.	0 1 2 3 4

22	I find it difficult to touch an object when I know it has been touched by strangers or certain people.	0	1	2	3	4
23	I need things to be arranged in a particular order.	0	1	2	3	4
24	I get behind in my work because I repeat things over and over again.	0	1	2	3	4
25	I feel I have to repeat certain numbers.	0	1	2	3	4
26	After doing something carefully, I still have the impression I have not finished it.	0	1	2	3	4
27	I find it difficult to touch garbage or dirty things.	0	1	2	3	4
28	I find it difficult to control my own thoughts.	0	1	2	3	4
29	I have to do things over and over again until it feels right.	0	1	2	3	4
30	I am upset by unpleasant thoughts that come into my mind against my will.	0	1	2	3	4
31	Before going to sleep I have to do certain things in a certain way.	0	1	2	3	4
32	I go back to places to make sure that I have not harmed anyone.	0	1	2	3	4
33	I frequently get nasty thoughts and have difficulty in getting rid of them.	0	1	2	3	4
34	I avoid throwing things away because I am afraid I might need them later.	0	1	2	3	4
35	I get upset if others change the way I have arranged my things.	0	1	2	3	4

(Continued)

36	I feel that I must repeat certain words or phrases in my mind in order to wipe out bad thoughts, feelings or actions.	0 1 2 3 4
37	After I have done things, I have persistent doubts about whether I really did them.	0 1 2 3 4
38	I sometimes have to wash or clean myself simply because I feel contaminated.	0 1 2 3 4
39	I feel that there are good and bad numbers.	0 1 2 3 4
40	I repeatedly check anything which might cause a fire.	0 1 2 3 4
41	Even when I do something very carefully I feel that it is not quite right.	0 1 2 3 4
42	I wash my hands more often or longer than necessary.	0 1 2 3 4
	TOTAL SCORE	

From Foa, Kozak, Salkovskis, Coles and Amir (1998).

Scoring

Adding up your score for each item will give you a total score between 0 and 168. You might be bothered by almost everything on the list, or only one or two things. Although a score of 40 or above is considered to indicate OCD, even if it's only a 'little bit of OCD' we should tackle it – so don't get too hung up on your total score.

What kind of overall pattern have you noticed from your scores? Where have you scored the most 3s and 4s? What are your main problems?

You might have spotted that individual questions in the inventory are rather vague and don't mention specific concerns like 'worrying about leaving the iron plugged in' or 'concerns about HIV and AIDS'.

There's a good reason for that – specific obsessional concerns are so individual in terms of their content that it wouldn't be possible to develop a questionnaire that could cover all possible permutations. It includes some questions about hoarding; the questionnaire was developed before hoarding was thought of as a separate problem, and it is still helpful to know if hoarding is a feature of your OCD experience.

Chapter summary

In this chapter we have:

- looked at a range of obsessional thoughts
- identified compulsions that are often used with certain types of OCD
- read about real-life experiences of OCD
- gained an understanding of how OCD affects *you*.

OCD can take on so many different forms. There are probably as many different versions of OCD as there are OCD sufferers – it really is a case of 'something for everyone'. While overt compulsions are what most people connect with OCD, there are so many compulsions that aren't visible to others. Trying to not to have a thought or attempting to work out what certain thoughts mean are very common covert strategies. From this point of view, 'Pure O' is a myth. However, being troubled by unwanted thoughts is just as distressing even if the 'action' (so to speak) is in our heads. Completing the Obsessive–Compulsive Inventory has helped you identify specific areas of concern.

Now that you have a clearer idea of how OCD affects you, are you ready to discover more about OCD? In Chapter 3 we'll find out who gets intrusive thoughts, learn more about what OCD is and why someone might find it hard to seek help.

CHAPTER 3

How does a thought become an obsession?

Overview

We've been looking at the many forms OCD can take. By now, you should have a clearer idea of how OCD affects you. In this chapter you will find out:

- who gets intrusive thoughts
- how thoughts become an obsession
- what OCD is … and what it isn't
- why it can be hard to seek help for OCD.

What is it about some thoughts that turns them into an obsession? After all, thinking is what brains do. They're just a thought machine, churning out thoughts all day (and probably part of the night too, in the form of dreams). Our heads are constantly bombarded with all kinds of thoughts. They can be ideas, opinions, memories, observations. Sometimes thoughts interrupt what we're thinking or doing – in other words, they intrude or interrupt what we're doing.

Who gets intrusive thoughts?

Intrusive thoughts don't only happen if we suffer from OCD. We *all* get intrusive thoughts. It has been estimated that around 40 per cent of the thoughts we have are involuntary. In other words, almost half the thoughts that come into our head aren't things we have deliberately chosen to think about. They're just random things that come into our head and may have no connection at all to what we're doing at that moment.

Intrusive thoughts of the non-OCD kind might include:

- suddenly remembering a funny incident from schooldays
- I mustn't forget to buy milk on the way home
- I could make pancakes at the weekend
- I wonder if those shoes will go with my new dress?
- a song you haven't heard in ages
- That's disgusting!
- remembering a joke
- Does my bum look big in this?
- Mmm ... he's a bit gorgeous
- I forgot to pay that bill!
- What was that noise?
- I hate that colour.

We don't usually tend to consider these kinds of intrusive thoughts as being threatening or dangerous in any way. If we think anything about them, we probably just think of them as being memories, ideas ... in fact, just thoughts that don't really mean much. Sometimes we quite like having these kinds of thoughts because they might give us a nice nostalgic feeling when we recall a distant memory, or look forward to something we might treat ourselves to, or remind us to find a well-loved tune on the internet.

Is it normal to have horrible thoughts?

Of course, not all intrusive thoughts are pleasant ones. Although we've already spoken a lot about intrusive thoughts and the many forms they take, you might be wondering what kind of people get the kind of thoughts you have. Who gets thoughts about losing control and stabbing their partner, or accidentally burning the house down, or shouting out something obscene in a place of worship? The answer (you may be surprised to know) is everyone. Anyone and everyone experiences thoughts that just pop into their head. They may be some strange, unbidden thoughts that just come into our heads when we're not doing anything in particular, or they might be linked in some way to what we're doing at the time.

When prompted, many people who don't have OCD admit that they've had intrusive thoughts about all kinds of things: like acting on an impulse to do something like jumping off a bridge or in front of a train, or pushing someone off the pavement into the path of an oncoming bus. The thing is, they're no different to the kinds of thoughts we discussed in Chapter 2. The only difference is the way in which you *think* about the thoughts. Instead of just shrugging them off as 'just a thought', you have come to label them as being important in some way. So you can see that in many ways these kinds of thoughts are completely normal. We all get them in some shape or form.

What is 'normal' anyway?

Some years ago, a research study was carried out in which a couple of experts on OCD (Rachman and De Silva, 1978) decided to put to the test the idea that there was a difference between normal and abnormal thoughts. They drew up two separate lists of intrusive thoughts. The first list was of obsessive thoughts reported by people with a diagnosis of OCD, and the second list was a list of intrusive thoughts reported by people who didn't have OCD or any kind of anxiety problem. Having jumbled up the lists, they asked a group of experienced mental health professionals to decide which thoughts were those of an OCD sufferer and which those of someone who didn't have an anxiety problem. What do you think they found? That it was impossible to tell.

There's nothing odd about having thoughts that just pop into our heads out of the blue. We all get them, regardless of whether or not we have OCD – fact! Our mind is constantly bombarded by all kinds of thoughts – good, bad, ugly and even indifferent. Who hasn't had thoughts like these?

- an impulse to push someone down the stairs
- a sudden image of your boss naked

- thoughts of losing control when driving
- picturing your father in a coffin
- what if I have a brain tumour?
- an urge to shout or make a noise in a library or other quiet place
- an image of your home burning down.

The only difference between non-OCD intrusive thoughts and OCD intrusive thoughts is how we label them.

If everyone gets these thoughts, why doesn't everyone have OCD?

Thinking is what brains do, and all the time we are bombarded with all kinds of thoughts, urges and images. But even these thoughts don't necessarily come back to haunt us. It's not the thoughts we have that are the problem but the way we *think about* these thoughts – the way we think about our thinking.

In simple terms, whenever we have a thought we have two basic choices about what we think about it: it's either important ... or it isn't.

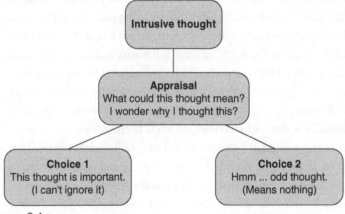

Figure 3.1

It's not simply having a thought (or even how often we have them) that turns an ordinary, everyday experience into a problem. It's how we think about them that's the key. If we label them as 'just a

45

thought', it's unlikely that we would feel particularly bothered about them. However, if we label them as being in some way threatening or dangerous, or as meaning something terrible about us, it will affect the way we *feel*. Our emotional response is likely to be to feel anxious or scared. It isn't the intrusive thought that has made us feel this way, but it's the way we thought about it. This is often called an **appraisal**. If we appraise the thought in a negative way, it is likely to make us feel bad. Some common appraisals of intrusive thoughts include:

● I must be a horrible or dangerous person to think such a thing.
● Because I've thought this, I must want it to happen.
● This could be a premonition.

And, of course, having experienced an intrusive thought and felt distressed or anxious about it, it is likely that you would want to do something that makes you feel better and less worried. An everyday example of this, which we've probably all experienced at some time, occurs when leaving the house. I often find a doubt pops into my head, 'Did I lock the back door?' My thinking goes that if I've thought this, it's possible I have indeed forgotten to do it, and it would be foolish to ignore the doubt because if it wasn't locked and someone came in while I was out and stole my valuables, it would be all my fault – my appraisal – which makes me feel slightly worried. To put my mind at rest and make me feel better, I may choose to take a particular **action** or **behaviour**, which is to check whether or not the door is locked. If I go and check I may well find that the door is locked. Of course, that will stop me worrying and reduce my anxiety and I can leave the house happily. Until the next time I have the doubt. It seems a common-sense thing to do when we get a doubt, and in itself doesn't mean we have OCD ... unless such behaviour begins to take up more and more of our time, or make us feel increasingly distressed and anxious, to the point that checking just once or twice isn't enough to put our minds at rest.

Compulsions refer to the kinds of things you feel you have to do, like checking or washing your hands over and over again, or having to think a 'good' thought after a 'bad' one. Anything you feel you have to do in order to make yourself feel better in such situations is referred to as a **compulsion**.

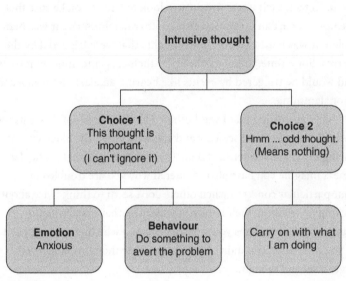

Figure 3.2

Why me? Why now?

In the past, you may have had similar kinds of intrusive thoughts to those that are troubling you now, but not really paid them much attention because they didn't seem important or relevant. What has probably happened is that, at the time the problem started, for some reason you began to pay more attention to a particular thought. Perhaps something had happened that made you notice certain kinds of things more. For example, my neighbours recently had their car stolen. It was parked outside the house on a fairly busy street. Now, living in an area where the sound of house and car alarms is part of the daily din, you get pretty used to hearing them – the sound just fades into the general background hum of urban living. But when I heard about the theft, it made me far more conscious of the possibility of theft. As a result, I began to notice just how many house and car alarms went off during the day and I struggled to ignore them. In fact, I felt it was my duty to look outside to make sure that the noise wasn't an indication that another neighbour's car was being stolen. It was hard to ignore the thoughts that were triggered by the alarms. For a time, thoughts about car thefts became important to me and would be triggered by events like hearing an alarm or even a car door slamming.

It's not surprising that I was bothered by these kinds of thoughts for a while. Notions about security and concerns about the likelihood of having my car stolen sensitized me to the thoughts at that particular time. I imagine you have also wondered why you are troubled by your particular concerns when others don't seem to think twice about locking up, washing their hands, whether they have committed a crime, etc. And perhaps you're wondering too why this has happened to you *now* when you didn't used to give these thoughts, doubts or urges a second thought.

The role of responsibility in OCD

There are many reasons why particular thoughts develop a personal importance for us. Some of the key research into the reasons why some people develop OCD has focused on the concept of responsibility. There are times when we suddenly have a lot more responsibility in our lives. At these times, we become more sensitive to certain kinds of thoughts and situations. Some common events are:

- living away from home for the first time
- getting a promotion at work
- having a baby.

Sometimes other things – perhaps more personal experiences that you have been through – can trigger a greater sense of responsibility. These can include events such as:

- being burgled
- hearing about a hit-and-run accident
- you, or someone in the family, developing food poisoning
- being warned about the importance of infection control in the workplace
- reading that someone was wrongly accused of a crime
- your pet dog getting run over because you didn't shut the gate.

Events such as these can all have the effect of making us feel a personal responsibility to make sure such things don't happen in the future. Sometimes it's because it reminds you that bad things can and do happen – sometimes unexpectedly without any warning, or through a momentary lapse of attention. To have lived through such events can have the effect of sensitizing you to the numerous possibilities of harm in the world. Just because you have had these experiences, it doesn't mean that you have to be troubled by OCD for the rest of your life. As you read through this book and discover more about OCD and how it works, you will begin to understand how you can change your relationship with your thoughts in order to live your life free from OCD.

What OCD is – and what it isn't

So far we've looked at obsessions and compulsions and a number of different ways in which they can be distressing or interfere with our lives. If any of these kinds of thoughts or actions seem familiar to you and have an impact on your life, you've probably wondered what on earth is the matter, especially if you haven't come across explanations of OCD before. Even if you have, you may still be wondering exactly what OCD is. And possibly have fears about what it might be, or hope that it isn't.

What OCD is

OCD is classified as an **anxiety disorder**. An anxiety disorder is a term used to describe several types of difficulties in which anxiety – a feeling of fear or uneasiness ranging for mild to intense – is the main feature.

It can be considered as a psychological problem in that it consists of a pattern of behaviours or psychological symptoms that have an effect on multiple areas of a person's life, often causing high levels of distress.

What is anxiety?

Anxiety is the 'technical' name used by the medical and mental health professions to describe the feelings we get when we feel frightened/scared/fearful. Quite often, anxiety can be referred to as being uptight, stressed, tense, worried. I daresay there are many other ways in which people experiencing anxiety might refer to it.

To think of anxiety as 'worry' is misleading. Anxiety is what we might experience when we get worried – it's a *feeling*. But the worry (or worries, since we often have more than one) are in fact thoughts which then trigger a feeling of anxiety.

Anxiety is a physiological change in our body which leads to a number of physical sensations that we interpret as unpleasant. I say 'interpret' because, interestingly, the same kinds of physical sensations can be interpreted in a different way. Let's have a closer look at what happens when we get anxious.

The most common physical sensations of anxiety include things like a racing heart or palpitations, breathing quickly, feeling hot – perhaps getting sweaty palms – feeling tense or getting butterflies in your stomach. There are many more sensations which you may or may not experience, or you might get different combinations at different times. Often, there are one or two key sensations that you pick up on the moment you begin to feel anxious.

Why do we experience these feelings? Well, it's part of our biological make-up and is something all mammals experience. It's often referred to as the **'fight or flight' response** and it developed as a helpful

Common symptoms of anxiety

Physical symptoms	Psychological symptoms
Pounding heart or palpitations	Feeling nervous
Shortness of breath	Difficulty concentrating
Tightness or pain in chest	Racing thoughts
Sweating	Feeling unreal/detached from your surroundings
Clammy hands	
Diarrhoea	Feeling terrified
Feeling sick (or being sick)	Feeling as if you're losing control/going crazy
Urge to urinate	
Upset stomach	Feeling of dread, like something terrible is about to happen
Tense muscles	
Headaches	Feeling restless
Fatigue or tiredness	Feeling irritable
Insomnia	Feeling constantly 'on edge' Being easily distracted
Numbness or tingling	
Feeling hot	Feeling incredibly alert to things around you
Wobbly legs	
Trembling or shaking	Feeling as if things are happening more quickly or more slowly
Dizzy or light-heading	
Dry mouth	Feeling like you want to run away or escape from the situation.
Trouble breathing or a choking sensation	
Feeling as if you're about to faint.	

automatic response to threats or danger. Our caveman ancestors might not have experienced the sort of stressful situations we face today, but they would have needed to be equipped to deal with a sabre-toothed tiger straying into their midst or a marauding tribe from the other side of the mountain. The fight or flight response creates a surge in adrenalin which helps to activate our bodies, increasing blood flow to the muscles and vital organs (hence an increased heart-rate as the heart pumps blood around the body more quickly, carrying more oxygen to the muscles) to enable us to either fight the enemy or run away. Increased blood flow to those body parts necessary for fighting or fleeing means that less is available for other organs that aren't required at that point, such as the stomach and digestive tract. After all, we'd hardly want to sit down to a delicious meal if we were under threat. That's why it's common to experience some kind of stomach discomfort when we feel stressed or anxious.

But you might have also noticed a lot of psychological or mental symptoms – the way in which your mind responds to this increase in adrenaline. Which of the symptoms on the list above are familiar to you? You probably haven't suffered all of them each time you've become anxious, although you might have noticed many of them at some time . We're all different. Some of us are more keyed into certain kinds of feelings than others. We often find that we have a 'top ten' of signs that immediately flag up to us that we're anxious. Often it's the same kinds of feelings or sensations, although from time to time you may become aware of a symptom you haven't noticed before – this often makes us feel even more afraid because it's unfamiliar to us.

What OCD isn't

Earlier we talked about the way that the idea of being 'obsessed' with something has entered our vocabulary. Being 'obsessed' with Elvis or collecting teapots is not obsessive–compulsive disorder, even if someone describes feeling 'compelled' to buy yet another novelty teapot or Elvis album to add to their collection.

In the same way that the term 'obsession' has been hijacked to explain other conditions or ways of being, so has the term 'compulsion'. You've probably come across descriptions of people as compulsive liars, compulsive gamblers or compulsive shoppers. The main emotion associated with these compulsions is pleasure or excitement – quite the opposite to what you experience as a result of OCD.

OCD is best understood as an anxiety or a worry problem, and we will keep returning to this way of understanding it throughout the book. Someone with OCD is *not* mad or dangerous, and doesn't carry out their unpleasant thoughts. Nor is OCD related to schizophrenia or psychosis. If you suffer from anxiety, it is easy to overlook the fact that *fear* of going crazy is a very common symptom.

Checking and doubting are fairly typical ways in which OCD can affect you. If checking or doubting are key features of your particular worries, it's likely that you might suppose that the problem is a memory problem. You may often feel that your judgment can't be trusted because you're always doubting whether or not you did something correctly, or even whether you did it at all. Well, it might surprise you to know that OCD is not a memory problem.

OCD *isn't* a disease. We can't catch OCD like we might catch a cold. However, there are ways in which we may develop some features of OCD. Sometimes we might hear of something that makes us feel a little worried – perhaps a friend tells us that norovirus has been reported in school. Of course we wouldn't want to get that if we can help it, so we might insist that everyone washes their hands really well before dinner or buy an antibacterial spray to clean the kitchen with the aim of reducing the risk of us getting it. It can also seem as if we've 'caught' OCD by getting involved in compulsive behaviours that people close to us might want us to do. We'll talk about this in more detail in Chapter 15.

Why is OCD such a secret?

Amanda carried a secret around with her for years. She'd never told a soul about it. She never confided in her best friend, her mother or even the lovely man who eventually became her husband. She loved her job as a teacher, adored the kids and everyone told her she was really good at it. 'If only they knew', she thought. If they knew about the dreadful thoughts and the vivid images, she was certain that she would lose everything. No one could possibly want to have anything to do with someone whose mind was full of such sick ideas. The guilt and shame she felt was at times overwhelming.

Fear of what others might think is one of the key reasons why someone with OCD keeps it to themselves. Shame or guilt make it hard to admit that we're troubled by certain kinds of thoughts that won't go away, no matter how hard we try. Jane was too embarrassed to own up to spending so much time washing her hands or showering; instead, she'd fib that the reason her hands were so raw and chapped was because she had a skin condition. She knew that scrubbing her hands with the nail brush was ridiculous, and believed that if others knew she used bleach instead of soap they'd think she was crazy.

Even though Amanda and Jane knew they had a problem, they just couldn't bring themselves to tell anyone – not even their doctor. Worries about being thought mad or weird or sick held them back. Even if OCD isn't an issue for us, any of us would probably find it rather uncomfortable to reveal all of our thoughts, or talk to someone (even if we knew them well) about intimate details of our lives or how we do certain things in a way that might be considered a bit quirky. How much harder, then, when the thoughts you have are about taboo subjects like sex, child abuse, being violent to others or horrible things happening to those you really care about.

We can often see how most people do things like wash their hands, lock their car, keep their children safe or travel on buses or trains, and recognize that they don't seem to do the kinds of things we do or take as much time. We might even have asked the odd question, like 'Doesn't it bother you when your husband comes into the house in his work boots?' or even something more personal, like 'Do you hover when you use the toilet when you're out?' But how can we ask about topics that might be considered unmentionable or offensive? As well as the subjects mentioned above, we're not likely to ask about other intimate acts such as having a bath, wiping your bottom after going to the toilet or nose-picking habits. This means it's difficult to know whether other people have similar thoughts to ourselves, or whether or not what we do is what the average person does.

Added to this is the fear that we would be considered dangerous or crazy in some way. After all, it would be hard to tell your mother that you often had thoughts of stabbing her since she might be both upset that you should think of such a thing and possibly petrified that you might act on these thoughts. And of course, by not telling her you never find out whether she really would react in this way.

There is so much about the private life of our minds that we don't share. While there's nothing wrong with keeping thoughts and ideas to ourselves, it also means that we don't get to discover that what goes on in our own heads is not so different to what goes on in everyone else's.

Fears about seeking professional help aren't that different. If we haven't had the nerve to tell those we usually trust with the most personal and private details of our lives, it's unlikely that we would find it easy to tell someone we know less well. Although we assure ourselves that our doctor, psychologist, health visitor etc. is a professional with training in such matters and has probably heard it all before, it is understandable that we would still be worried about spilling the beans to them … just in case they hadn't, or they confirmed our fears. Widespread reasons for not seeking help include the following.

I shouldn't feel like this – I should be happy

Feeling bad about not feeling good can make us beat ourselves up about the difficulties we have, especially when everything else in our lives would suggest that we should be feeling on top of the world – a great job, lovely partner, opportunities to travel, a beautiful home or other things that people might envy us for.

I need to sort this out myself

We all like to feel we can deal with any difficulties that come along. We might feel guilty if we don't try to do so, or if we have to ask for help.

Chances are that you have tried really hard to help yourself out of this problem but it hasn't worked.

What will people think of me?

Although worrying that others – friends, family, even health professionals – will think badly of you, or view you as mad, bad or dangerous, having OCD (or any other mental health problem) is nothing to be ashamed of. In fact, OCD is considered to be the fourth most common mental health problem in the world. In the UK alone, it's estimated that 1.2 per cent (that's 12 people out of every thousand) are affected by it.

What will happen if I tell?

Often we're afraid that the consequences of telling will be awful, and imagine that people will whisper behind our back, or stop speaking to us. We worry that admitting we have OCD will mean losing our job, partner or even children.

Mental health professionals are a scary and mysterious bunch

Fears about what mental health professionals are like can be another key reason for not seeking help. This is especially true when a person has never had contact with mental health professionals. Sadly, there is still a lot of stigma around mental health and a certain mystique about people who work in that field. The idea that psychologists and psychiatrists can somehow read your mind or are constantly 'analysing' you is widespread.

I'll be locked up

Lack of understanding of services for people with OCD and a range of other mental health difficulties can lead to worries that the only help available is to be placed in a psychiatric hospital, possibly against your wishes. The majority of services for OCD are carried out at GP surgeries or clinics on an out-patient basis.

I don't want to take medication

The most effective type of treatment for OCD is cognitive behavioural therapy (CBT), which is a particular type of psychological (talking) therapy. Although medication might be offered, it is not necessary to take medication for psychological therapy to be effective. Certain types of medication can sometimes be helpful by taking the edge off how you're feeling so that it's easier to make the kind of changes that will help OCD become less of a problem.

Therapy means doing things I'm terrified of

The notion of confronting your fears is widely recognized as a component of therapy for any anxiety. Yet the varying ways in which fears might be confronted are often misunderstood, not least because of the way therapy is often portrayed in the media, with OCD sufferers doing quite extreme tasks without a clear explanation or any background being given.

My doctor won't understand

GPs have an incredible amount of knowledge and understanding at their fingertips and know a considerable amount about a vast number of conditions, diseases and disorders. Of course, they can't be experts on everything and so they are likely to focus their knowledge on certain areas that interest them, like dermatology (skin conditions), respiratory medicine (like asthma or other conditions that affect breathing), or psychological health (such as depression and anxiety). Unfortunately, this can mean that a doctor might not be too savvy about OCD and either not really understand the problem or mistake it for something else, like a phobia or depression, and attempt to deal with it in this way.

Chapter summary

In this chapter you have learned:

- that everyone gets intrusive thoughts
- how thoughts become an obsession
- how to recognize symptoms of anxiety
- why people with OCD don't always seek help.

Thinking is what brains do. We're constantly bombarded with all kinds of thoughts, urges and images. Although we all get intrusive thoughts, we don't usually pay much attention to them. Not all intrusive thoughts are pleasant ones. These can be harder to ignore, but they're no different to other kinds of thoughts. However, if we interpret them as being important or dangerous in some way, we will feel anxious or frightened. We might then do something to reduce our anxiety or minimize the risk of something bad happening. You are less likely to seek help for OCD if you don't understand what it is. Once you understand how the problem works, you can even begin to tackle it by yourself.

Are you ready to find out more? Chapter 4 explains how to give yourself the best start.

CHAPTER 4

Making change possible

Overview

Chapter 3 explained how OCD can develop in response to the kinds of intrusive thoughts that everyone gets. In this chapter, we'll discuss:

- when should you start tackling OCD
- what makes change difficult
- what can make it easier.

OCD is rarely a brief difficulty that we might face for a few weeks or months. And although most of the 'action', so to speak, is in our heads in the shape of thoughts, urges, images or doubts, it isn't self-contained so it spills over into other areas of our lives. Without us even noticing at first, OCD edges its way into our entire lives. It can be very subtle to begin with, but left unchecked it is likely to get worse. Whether you feel that OCD has a major effect on your life or only a little, it is vital to tackle it. If you found even the teeniest bit of dry rot in your house, you wouldn't think, 'Oh, that's not enough to be bothered about'. 'A little bit OCD' is likely to mushroom in a similar way.

The effects of OCD in your life

Whether its effects are small and subtle or large and obvious, OCD spreads into everything. It strikes hardest at the things that are important to us: our relationships, our home life, our work. It hits where it hurts us most. Like Maxine, Carol, Arun, Sahib and the others whose stories we read in Chapter 2, it might start in an innocuous way: Carol switched channels when the news was about to come on, saying she wanted to watch something on the other side; Arun tapped his pocket a couple of times before he left home to make sure he had his keys. It wasn't a problem … to begin with.

Whether OCD affects you a little or a lot, there's no time like now to start working on it. If it's only a minor problem it will be far easier to deal with before it grows. And if it's something you've battled with for a long time … why wait a moment longer?

The 'right time' to change?

We've all been there: I'm going to join the gym (when I'm less busy at work); I'm going to go on a diet (after the party next weekend). We often strive to do things when the 'right time' comes along, but then it never does. There's always something else to keep us busy at work, or another social invitation, holidays, Christmas … . Look at the key themes below. Do any of these ring a bell with you?

Self-assessment

Look at the key themes in the table. Tick any that you can identify with.

Wanting to do things perfectly	
Not feeling in the mood	
Putting off things I don't want to do	
Hoping someone will do it for me	
Other things seem so much more appealing	
Being frightened of change	

Wanting to do things perfectly

If this is our aim, it can seem like we never have a big enough window of time in which to do whatever it is. This also includes making changes that can help free us from OCD. We might kid ourselves that unless we can do whatever it is really well and thoroughly, spending plenty of time in the planning, then it won't be helpful or effective, whereas in reality the smallest changes can make a big difference. Even if there isn't time to have a major clear-out of all the cupboards in the kitchen, in half an hour or so the cutlery drawer could be tidied and given a speedy clean and look so much better for it. And it is a step on the way to the organized kitchen you've been meaning to get around to. Or if you've been putting off writing a letter to an elderly aunt, scribble a quick postcard today. She'll be delighted to get a brief note rather than nothing at all – and you can give yourself a pat on the back for having done a good-enough job of keeping in touch. Working on your OCD is no different. Even if you change just one small thing on one occasion – like not using anti-bacterial gel after going to the supermarket, or leaving the radio on while the newsreader announces an increase in identity theft – it's a step in the right direction. Freeing ourselves from OCD isn't about doing it perfectly; it is about trying.

Not feeling in the mood

In the book *Feel the Fear and Do It Anyway*, the author Susan Jeffers argues that we all spend far too much time trying to get into the perfect mood or frame of mind to feel motivated, rather than just getting on with things. My own experience is backed up by research that if we start doing things despite not feeling like it, our mood actually improves. I have often asserted that the hardest part of starting an activity when we don't feel 'in the mood' is the simple act of getting up and getting on with it. I rather like the quote attributed to Maurice Chevalier: *'If you wait for the perfect moment when all is safe and assured, it may never arrive. Mountains will not be climbed, races won, or lasting happiness achieved.'*

It's a myth that we always need to be in the right mood to do things. If we wait until we're in the right mood or feel motivated, we might wait a very long time. Many things can be done or achieved regardless of how we feel. Getting active often creates motivation – and who knows, we might even feel a bit better when we've done them!

Putting off things I don't want to do

Putting things off is a common human behaviour – especially if we don't want to do something. Remember when you were small? 'Time for bed', yet you'd take an age to put on your pyjamas and brush your teeth, or plead to be allowed just a few more minutes. As adults we're just as likely to put off something we don't want to do, whether at home, in the workplace or in our personal lives. Even though we know doing something is likely to be good for us, we still procrastinate about getting more exercise, flossing our teeth or cutting down on sugary treats. In terms of tackling OCD, you might be worried that it will be too difficult. Putting things off is closely related to wanting to do things perfectly or not feeling in the mood.

Sometimes the problem isn't putting things off because we don't *want* to do them. It may be that you like to do things your own way. If that is the case, you may feel resistant to the advice that self-help books give about the steps required to tackle your OCD. You may or may not believe that a structured approach like CBT can be helpful and bring about the kind of changes you would like. You might have already made some changes and found real benefits but still dismiss the approach as a psychological sticking plaster, considering it to be too superficial. The idea that we need to work out or understand what caused you to have these difficulties (or have these particular intrusive thoughts) in the first place is widespread. It often isn't possible to know for sure why things have turned out the way they have, or why we have particular difficulties. At best we can only guess at it (even therapists who nod sagely and suggest your problem stems from something in your early life or some event you found deeply upsetting but never dealt with). It's possible, but every one of us has encountered difficulties in the past and had experiences that have upset us a great deal. And even if such past events have played a role in the development of your OCD, the good news is that we don't need to look for a cause in order to tackle the OCD.

Hoping someone will do it for me

If you can identify with the points above, no doubt you sometimes wish that someone else could do it for you. It's common for OCD sufferers to involve others in doing tasks which they find difficult. It would be great if someone else could magically make your OCD better, but the truth is that it is something you need to do yourself. You can be encouraged and coached by another person – a partner, friend or therapist – but the only one who can take the necessary steps to overcome your OCD is you. But think of it this way: how satisfying will it be to look back, in the coming weeks, months or however long the journey takes, and to be able to say 'I did it'?

Other things seem so much more appealing

We'd all rather be doing nice things, fun things, stuff we enjoy – watching television, going shopping or to meet friends, taking the dog for a walk, going on holiday. The good news is that you can still do all these things while tackling OCD. In fact, tackling your OCD is likely to make these things more possible and more enjoyable, and it can open the door to doing many more activities that you currently don't feel able to do.

The attraction of more appealing activities can be a particular problem in the early stages of tackling your OCD, when making even small changes can seem very challenging and lead to unwanted increases in anxiety levels. If you believe that the things you attempt should make you feel better straightaway or need to lead to dramatic improvements to be worth doing, you're likely to get distracted by nice, fun stuff. Incidentally, if this is how you tend to think, it's likely that you're a bit of a perfectionist too, thinking 'Unless what I do makes a big difference, it's not working'.

Being frightened of change

Making any change can be scary, but what is it that you're afraid of? Fear of failing is very common, even if we find it hard to admit that even to ourselves. Maybe you've tried to overcome OCD in the past – we'll talk about that shortly. You may have qualms related to your OCD. Are you afraid that your house will burn down, your children will get ill, or other OCD-driven worries?

Change *is* scary. You may fear that you won't be able to keep it up. Even if we're optimistic about making and maintaining changes, the effect on your life may seem daunting. For example, you may want a job once OCD no longer holds you back. And maybe your fear is something more basic: you don't know what you need to do.

When OCD isn't the only problem

We've seen how putting it off or waiting for the 'right time' gets in the way of tackling OCD. Other kinds of difficulties can also make it that much harder. We're only human and don't fit neatly into a diagnostic box. If you have OCD, you may have other problems too. Depression is extremely common, especially if you've had OCD for a long time, as is low self-esteem. Working on your OCD is likely to improve your mood and boost your confidence. If OCD is the most troubling difficulty at the moment, it is a good idea to work on this first.

Previous treatment

For some of you, this book may be your first port of call in your quest to deal with your OCD. But many of you may have had a long battle with the problem. In my clinic, I have met many people who have managed to free themselves from OCD after one or more episodes only to find that the problem has come back. Yet others have struggled in vain ever since OCD began to trouble them and have never managed to overcome the difficulty. No matter what your own personal journey with OCD has been, I am sure you will find both hope and help in this book. But let's look at some of the factors that might account for the fact that OCD is still part of your life despite previous attempts.

Therapy was helpful but you slipped back	Therapy didn't help
OCD has come back in a different form.	Therapy focused on childhood and past events.
Therapy didn't tackle the whole problem.	The therapist didn't really understand OCD.
You stopped working on the problem after therapy ended.	You didn't work on the problem between sessions.
Limited number of therapy sessions.	The techniques used didn't work.
Therapy was partially helpful, but didn't really focus on OCD issues.	You didn't understand what you needed to do.
	You were told to do extreme things for exposure without a proper explanation.
Stressful life event triggered OCD.	
No plan for maintaining progress after therapy ended.	Other issues or life events needed addressing first.
	You didn't complete the course of treatment.

What can make it easier?

While it can never be easy to make changes to free ourselves from problems like OCD, there are some things you can do to help you on your journey. Some of these things are quite small and insignificant, and might not even seem as if they have much to do with the problem. Even so, they can form an important part of your quest to live your life free from OCD. Let's have a look at some of them before we go into more detail.

- Don't wait for the 'right time'.
- Set yourself targets.
- Get support from family or friends.
- Look after yourself.

Don't wait for the 'right time'

As you will recall, there is no 'right time' to get started. Even if you only make a couple of tiny changes right now it will help you on your way. Unfortunately, OCD doesn't go away on its own but it can get better if you deal with it in the right way.

Set yourself targets

It's important to have some targets in mind. Otherwise, how can you know when you've managed to achieve what you set out to do? We'll be looking at goal-setting in more detail in Chapter 7.

Getting support from family or friends

When you have targets in mind, it can be helpful to ask for support from family or friends. If nothing else, it can be helpful at least to explain to one or two people who you feel you can trust the difficulties you've been having. If it feels too difficult to begin a conversation about it, or you just don't know where to start, you could begin by completing the following exercise. If you're feeling brave, you could read it to them. If that feels too much to manage at the moment, you could let them read it for themselves.

Behaviour changing strategy

I need to talk to you about something ...

I don't know if you've noticed that I get really worried and anxious sometimes. There are certain things that upset me like: *(write your OCD concerns below)*

_____

_____

The thing is, I have an anxiety problem. Have you heard of OCD? Lots of people describe themselves as being 'a little bit OCD' because they're neat and tidy, or clean things a lot, or check stuff. But that's not really what OCD is. It can be different things to different people.

Someone who has OCD gets unwanted thoughts, urges or images that keep coming back again and again, even though they try hard not to have them – these are 'obsessions'. And because they seem so scary, it makes you want to do something to stop yourself feeling so anxious – these are called 'compulsions'. It might be something like washing or checking, but it can be all kinds of things – sometimes just things you do in your head, like trying to persuade yourself that everything's OK and nothing bad will happen.

We all get weird thoughts from time to time. Have you ever stood on a bridge and thought you could just jump off? Or push someone under a car? Even though you know you wouldn't do that kind of thing. Sometimes the thoughts can be really weird and horrible. It doesn't mean you want to have them; they just happen.

Well, my problem is a bit like that.

	Tick all that apply
I worry a lot about dirt and contamination, and have to wash and clean a lot.	
I worry a lot about harming others/abusing others, which really upsets me because I'm not really like that.	
I worry that I might be responsible for a fire/flood/burglary and check a lot.	
I get really horrible thoughts that I find hard to ignore.	
I have to do things in a certain way/repeat things/count because I'm scared something terrible will happen if I don't.	

It might sound really crazy, but I find it hard to ignore the thoughts/stop doing what I do. It makes me really unhappy and gets in the way of me living my life how I want to.

I just wanted to explain it to you because you might have thought I was doing some odd things. I'm using this book to help me overcome the problem.

Getting help or support from family and friends doesn't mean they have to be involved in the things you are doing. It doesn't (and shouldn't) take up a lot of time. It's simply about having someone that you can talk to about what you're trying to achieve, someone who can perhaps give you a bit of praise for something you've managed to do, or give you a word or two of encouragement when things seem a bit of a struggle. At various points throughout the book we'll talk about the role of family and friends.

Practical advice ⇨

OCD, you and your relationships

OCD can put a lot of strain on personal relationships. Although it's possible that you feel you're on your own with your OCD, all too often the lives of others are drawn into our personal struggles. The notion of OCD as 'something for everyone' also applies to partners, family and friends. Even if you have kept the problem to yourself, it still has an effect. The effect may be subtle – you seem to spend a long time in the bathroom, or seem uncertain and ask a lot of questions about certain things. The more severely OCD affects you, the more your family or friends are likely to be involved.

OCD might affect your relationships with other because you may:

- always be late because of compulsions
- insist others follow OCD 'rules'
- get upset, angry or frustrated if they refuse
- repeatedly ask the same kinds of questions
- limit what you can do or where you go together
- avoid physical contact or intimacy
- get them to do things that you find difficult
- seem distant or upset but not want to explain why.

OCD might affect their relationship with you because they:

- get upset, angry or frustrated with you
- tell you to pull yourself together
- feel worried and upset about you

- avoid spending time with you
- feel stressed because of having to take on extra tasks
- can't understand the problem
- feel offended when you can't accept their help or hospitality.

OCD can seem terrifying or confusing for those close to us. A better understanding of what it is will help. If you haven't already, perhaps suggest they read this book. The good news is that OCD can be overcome.

It's difficult to see someone we love and care for struggling against their own personal demons. As a parent, I find myself repeating what my mother often said when I was poorly or battling with revision for a dreaded exam: 'If only it was me instead of you' –possibly yours did this too. But as much as we want to help take away the pain, the sad fact is that we cannot. It doesn't stop us trying. And this is one way in which OCD entangles us.

Although we can't 'fix' OCD for someone else, we can support and encourage them. It's hard to know what to say or do, but a hug and kind words go a long way. There will be more tips on how to help in later chapters.

Look after yourself

If you were planning to run a marathon, you wouldn't just turn up on the day without having done any training or prepared yourself mentally for the task ahead. We tend to ignore our bodies. After all, they're just kind of *there*. When you wake up in the morning, there it is … waiting to go. And our bodies generally seem to oblige us by moving, looking, thinking, hearing and so on without us putting any effort into it. Actually, it isn't only that we tend to ignore our bodies. We often mistreat them too, not getting enough exercise, not getting enough sleep, eating too much of the wrong kinds of food.

I'm not going to nag you with the criticisms that we seem to get almost daily in the media about our society heading for an 'obesity epidemic', or urge you to get more exercise or eat your 'five a day'.

But the old saying about healthy minds and healthy bodies shouldn't be ignored. Our bodies are rather like high-performance motor cars. You can just get into a car and keep driving until it breaks down, but you will get far more out of the car if you look after it with regular servicing and topping it up with the correct fuel on a regular basis. If you are already a regular gym goer, cyclist, hockey player etc., that's great. But if you recognize yourself as a bit of a couch potato, making small changes to your daily routine so that you take some light exercise will pay off. In the longer term you may find it helps you to get a bit trimmer and improve your overall fitness levels. In the short term, becoming more active can help you to use up some of the adrenaline your body has been producing when you get anxious. Exercise releases endorphins in the brain and these help us to feel calmer. Endorphins are hormones which reduce the sensation of pain and give us a feeling of well-being.

We mentioned the importance of putting 'fuel in the tank' on a regular basis. There might be several reasons why you've been neglecting your diet. It might just be general bad habits like the ones many of us fall into – it's quicker to grab a packet of crisps and a bar of chocolate instead of making a sandwich to take to work. Or it might be that OCD makes it hard for you to prepare a meal or a snack for yourself because of worries about contaminating the kitchen, or that it's easier not to cook because it takes so long to clean up afterwards. Perhaps you are afraid to eat or drink away from home for various reasons. Even if you generally have quite a healthy diet, there are certain vitamins and nutrients that are really important for a healthy nervous system and maintain the right balance of neurotransmitters – chemicals that send messages from nerves to our brains. It's a good idea to review your diet if you have any kind of anxiety disorder. Fluctuating blood-sugar levels as a result of not eating regularly, or eating too many sugary foods, can lead to bodily sensations very much like those of anxiety.

Practical advice

Helpful habits I: Healthy eating

Follow these simple suggestions to improve your diet.

- Eat regular meals
- Have a balanced diet
- Know the five food groups to avoid
- Don't get thirsty
- Limit alcohol.

Eat regular meals

While three meals a day – breakfast, lunch and dinner – is the traditional idea of having regular meals, you don't have to stick to this routine. In fact, it has been suggested that we should eat smaller meals more often during the day. This isn't always easy to do, depending on demands from work or home. Still, it is good for our health to make sure we eat at regular intervals throughout the day. Although you may hear people say, 'Oh, I never eat breakfast', or 'I'm just not hungry when I get up', it really isn't a good idea to skip breakfast. It helps to start the day with a decent breakfast. After all, your body hasn't had anything to sustain it during the night and a healthy breakfast will help get you started for the day

A few small snacks in between meals help keep our blood-sugar levels steady and reduce tiredness. Choose from healthier options, such as a piece of fruit, some nuts or a low-fat yoghurt rather than biscuits or chocolate.

Have a balanced diet

For a healthy balanced diet, we should aim to eat:

- Lots of fruit and vegetables – at least five portions a day according to current guidelines, with more vegetables than fruit.
- Lots of starchy foods, such as pasta, rice, potatoes etc. – and it's better still if we make that wholemeal pasta and bread, and potatoes with their skins on for added fibre.
- Some protein foods, such as meat, fish, eggs, pulses (like lentils and beans) and nuts – protein is important for building and repairing bones and tissue in the body as well as making hormones, antibodies and other chemicals that keep us healthy.

- Some milk and dairy products, such as cheese or yoghurt – they are an important source of protein and calcium, which are vital for healthy bones and teeth, but it helps to choose low-fat versions, such as skimmed milk, and not to eat too much cheese, which is often very high in fat.
- Very few fatty or sugary foods – while sweet things are nice to eat, having them as an occasional treat will help cut down the amount of sugar and fat you consume. Be aware, too, that many processed foods like sausages, burgers and ready meals often contain a lot of fat and many have hidden sugars too.

Know the five food groups to avoid

While fast foods, ready meals, takeaways, cakes and confectionary are tempting, they should be an occasional treat. In fact, they often have many of the features of five food groups that we should try to avoid:

- brown
- sugary
- salty
- greasy
- crispy.

Don't get thirsty

It isn't only our 'fuel' we need to keep topped up. We need to make sure we have enough fluid during the day. Don't let yourself get thirsty. By the time we actually feel thirsty, our bodies are already on the way to becoming dehydrated. Thirst isn't a reliable indicator of when we should drink. It's fairly easy to train ourselves to want less to drink. Maybe you limit the amount of fluid you have during the day because of your OCD difficulties, particularly if you don't like to use toilets when away from home. Limiting our fluids isn't good for us. Even mild dehydration can lead to:

- headaches
- tiredness
- feeling dizzy or dehydrated.

All of these can make any anxiety we experience as a result of our OCD seem even worse. All non-alcoholic beverages help maintain our fluid levels, although water is probably the best.

Keep alcohol within recommended guidelines

Current guidelines from the NHS recommend:

- no more than 3–4 units per day for men
- no more than 2–3 units per day for women
- avoiding alcohol for 48 hours if you've consumed more than the recommended amount in one day.

A pint of beer (or can of lager) contains around 2 units of alcohol. A small glass of wine (125ml) has 1.5 units and a bottle (750ml) contains 10 units.

Using alcohol to numb feelings of anxiety or to dull down thoughts is not helpful and can add to your problems in the long term.

Chapter summary

In this chapter we've considered:

- whether there is a 'right time' to change
- why we often put off making changes
- what can make tackling OCD more difficult
- how we can make it easier.

We've learned that there's no such thing as the 'right time'. But even when we're desperate to free ourselves from OCD, several things may hold us back. We may be disheartened if previous attempts either didn't last or didn't seem to work. We may have other problems that make it slightly more difficult. Setting targets and getting support from friends and family is a helpful way to get started. Our guide to opening up the opportunity to talk about OCD will help if you've tried to hide your problem. And although we don't need to be exactly 'match fit', adopting a healthier lifestyle can get us into better frame of mind to get started.

Since there's no time like the present, are you ready to learn more about how cognitive behavioural therapy (CBT) can help you tackle OCD?

PART 2

Tackle

Get to grips with what you need to do to make a change

CHAPTER 5

What can I do about it?

Overview

Chapter 4 encouraged you to put aside any excuses and stop waiting for the 'right time' to start tackling OCD. In this chapter you will find out:

● what CBT is
● what Third Wave CBT can add
● how CBT for OCD can help.

There's no miracle cure for OCD and you should steer clear of anyone who suggests there is. Yet it is true that you can free yourself from the tyranny of OCD using a systematic approach. Every journey begins with the first step. In the words of the writer Antoine de Saint-Exupéry: *'What saves a man is to take a step. Then another step. It is always the same step, but you have to take it.'*

Even if they are only small steps, as long as you keep taking them you will get to where you want to be (even if occasionally you take a few steps backwards).

Part 2 of this book aims to give you the tools to help you make the changes necessary to overcome obsessive–compulsive disorder.

Introducing CBT

People are always talking about 'CBT'. It sounds a bit confusing and mysterious, doesn't it? However, there's no mystery to it when you know what it stands for:

Cognitive = how we think
Behavioural = how we act
Therapy = how we can change

Cognitive behavioural therapy (CBT) is based on the principle that the way we think affects how we feel. But what we think and how we feel also has an effect on what we do – on whether we decide to take any action as well as on what kind of action.

Picture the scene: you wake up with a start because you've heard a noise. Your heart is pounding, and you're wondering what it could be. What might you make of it?

a   I must have been dreaming. It's ages before the alarm's due to go off …
b   Blast the neighbours! Do they have to bang around in the night?
c   Burglars!

What would be the consequences of thinking in those ways? How would you feel? What would you do?

If your first thought was (a), you might just sigh and turn over, contented at the prospect of a bit more sleep. You might feel a bit annoyed if you thought it was (b), your noisy neighbours, but probably drop off again after you'd knocked on the wall and yelled at them to be quiet. However, if you thought it was (c), you would probably lie awake listening for other sounds indicating a break-in, at the same time deciding whether to hide under the covers or go and investigate.

So the same situation can make us feel very different, depending on how we interpret or think about it. And what we thought and felt would mean that we behaved in very different ways. Although it's a simple example, we can see how the theory behind OCD works for all of us.

How CBT works

CBT is based on five key principles that provide you with the tools you need to change. CBT is:

● educational
● focused on the present
● skills-based

- goal-oriented
- practical.

Educational

CBT provides us with a new way of looking at our problems. It is very helpful if we tend to get stuck in unhelpful patterns of thought, feelings and behaviour. By learning to identify these, we can take a more balanced view and change what we do in a way that breaks the cycle. CBT gives us confidence to challenge our usual way of processing information.

Focused on the present

CBT can help us to understand what keeps the problem going rather than looking for a cause. Do we need to know what caused someone to break their leg in order to be able to fix it? While it doesn't focus on the past, CBT can help us understand how life experiences may contribute to unhelpful beliefs and behaviours that are keeping us stuck today.

Skills-based

Above all, CBT encourages us to try out new ways of doing things to help us break out of unhelpful patterns of behaviour. By changing what we do, we gradually develop a new way of thinking about things – different beliefs about ourselves, others and the way the world works.

Goal-oriented

Clear goals for what we want to achieve help us work out what steps we need to take to get there. And, of course, we can also look back to see how much progress we've made.

Practical

CBT provides us with ideas that we can work on ourselves and put into practice every day. In fact, regular practice of new skills – ways of thinking and new behaviours – is encouraged. Developing new habits takes time.

Combining all of these principles, CBT helps us develop flexible attitudes and more helpful beliefs about ourselves, others and the world around us.

Basic principles of CBT in relation to OCD

According to theory, obsessional problems occur when we interpret certain thoughts as threatening or dangerous in some way. We discussed this in detail in Chapter 1, but let's recap briefly.

It's not the thoughts themselves that are the problem, it's what we make of those thoughts and how we respond to them that keeps the problem going. After all, everyone has intrusive thoughts. It's just that sometimes certain thoughts come to mean something important to us. If we label them as important or dangerous in some way, we will feel anxious or frightened. We might then do something to reduce our anxiety or minimize the risk of something bad happening. CBT for OCD helps us develop a less threatening view of what thoughts mean.

Responsibility

Sensitivity to responsibility plays an important role in OCD. Doing something wrong or failing to act to prevent something terrible happening are common themes. Responsibility leads us to take extra care, even if we don't have OCD.

Have your neighbours ever asked you to do them a favour? Maybe asked you to feed the goldfish or water the plants while they're away for a few days? Or just be around to accept a delivery while they're at work? They've given you a key to their house. You do these kinds of things all the time for yourself, yet it seems different somehow. What effect does it have? Why do you think that is?

It's quite likely that you tend to be more careful or vigilant when looking after someone else's home. It often applies if you've borrowed something from a friend – a book, a tool or a handbag, for example. It seems more important to make sure everything is all right. We suddenly feel more responsible for anything that could go wrong, get broken, stolen or spoiled. It seems worse somehow if it happens to someone else's property than to our own. Responsibility can seem a burden.

There's been a lot of research investigating the role of responsibility in OCD. This has found that people with OCD share similar ideas which make them sensitive to responsibility. Examples of responsibility beliefs in OCD (from Salkovskis, Wroe, Gledhill, Morrison, Forrester, Richards, Reynolds and Thorpe (2000)) include the following.

- Thinking bad things is as bad as doing them.
- Not acting to prevent harm is as bad as making it happen.
- I must protect others from harm.
- I often feel responsible for things that go wrong.
- If I don't act when I foresee danger, then I am to blame for any consequences if it happens.
- I often take responsibility for things that other people don't think are my fault.
- If I know that harm is possible I should always try to prevent it, however unlikely it seems.
- Other people shouldn't rely on my judgement.
- If I take sufficient care, I can prevent any harmful accidents.

If we feel responsible, we're more likely to act on doubts and fears.

Red alert!
OCD threatens you with the message that your thoughts signify who you are, that your feelings reflect the truth and that you should do everything in your power to get rid of both or risk terrible consequences. It puts us on the look-out for any signs of danger and

convinces us that we need to make sure our worst fear doesn't happen. To put it another way, we feel responsible.

Each time we act on a thought, urge or impulse it can seem as if we've had a narrow escape. Carol reckoned that the only reason she hadn't acted on thoughts of hurting her daughter was because any potential weapons were kept out of easy reach and she was never alone with her daughter. It didn't occur to her that she wouldn't have done it anyway. OCD convinced her that she was dangerous and not a gentle, loving person who cared about her family.

Imagine that a car alarm suddenly sounded outside your house. What would you do? Maybe you'd check that no one was trying to break into your car (or your neighbour's). Imagine that the alarm has gone off again. In fact, it has gone off several times but each time you went to check, everything was fine. What would you think? What would you do next time you heard the alarm? Might you just ignore it, thinking it was faulty – that it was oversensitive and going off for no good reason?

Each time we act in response to a thought (neutralize), these particular situations or thoughts become the focus of our concerns. They become linked with these ideas of danger or threat although they could just be like that oversensitive car alarm: i.e. activated for no good reason. These thoughts and our responses become a habit.

Habits of thinking and doing

In OCD, we have developed the habit of responding to intrusive thoughts as if they're a sign of imminent danger. We lose the capacity to experience cognitions (thoughts) as mental events, viewing them instead as reflections of objective 'truth' or 'me'. This works in a similar way with feelings. If we have experienced a particular feeling in a similar situation that we'd previously judged as dangerous, we're more likely to react in the same way in the future – even if there's nothing else to suggest that it's a risky situation.

Reviewing behaviour

Task

Picture these scenarios.

Situation 1

You've never had any major problems with OCD or anxiety in the past. You wake up one morning feeling a bit on edge for no particular reason. As you leave the house, you get a sense that something could go wrong. You've no idea what – it's just a vague feeling.

- What would you do?
- How likely are you to dismiss it as an odd feeling that doesn't mean anything? (Remember, this is something new to you.)

Situation 2

You've struggled with OCD on and off for some time. You wake up one morning feeling a bit on edge for no particular reason. As you leave the house, you get a sense that something could go wrong. You've no idea what – it's just a vague feeling.

- What would you do?
- How likely would you be to dismiss the idea?
- How likely would you be to try to work out what it might mean?
- Or become more anxious because you've been stuck checking your front door in the past?

Is this pattern familiar to you? If we've felt or thought like this before, we're likely to respond to it in the same way. It becomes a habit. Obsessional concerns have a tendency to shift and change. Something that used to bother us might no longer be a problem as other worries replace them.

OCD and Third Wave CBT

The term 'Third Wave CBT' is used to describe therapies that integrate techniques that weren't previously considered therapeutic. They draw on ideas from spirituality, acceptance and personal values, and use them to explain how psychological problems result from attempts to avoid, struggle with or attempt to control thoughts and emotions. Because CBT is based on both theory and research, it continues to evolve. What can be considered 'traditional' CBT (as developed by Aaron Beck or Albert Ellis) grew from treatments which were based solely on changing behaviour.

	Focus for change		Outcome
First Wave	Behaviour	$\Longrightarrow$	Reduce anxiety
Second Wave	Thoughts	$\Longrightarrow$	Reduce anxiety
Third Wave	Relationship of thoughts and feelings	$\Longrightarrow$	Accept thoughts and feelings

Various forms of Third Wave treatments have been developed. They are all based on the idea that emotions such as fear and anxiety are natural and that to try to control thoughts and feelings or to get rid of them is unhelpful and makes them worse.

Here are brief summaries of some of the main Third Wave CBT approaches. Although this book draws on a few ideas from these approaches, we do not focus on them.

Acceptance and commitment therapy (ACT)

This approach proposes that we accept thoughts and feelings for what they are, rather than what we *think* they are, i.e. thoughts and feelings that will never go away. It focuses more on what we *do* and less on what we think or feel. We should neither avoid nor attempt to control uncomfortable experiences: if we let intrusive thoughts and anxiety come and go, they stop interfering with our lives. Compulsions are a way of trying to 'fix' anxiety and discomfort. By constantly avoiding strong emotions, our lives become extremely limited. The fixes we have that prevent us feeling anxiety eventually become the problem. At the same time, we are encouraged to commit to living our lives according to our personal values.

Has your life become more rewarding and satisfying as a result of trying to control anxiety or obsessions with compulsions or avoidance? If not, might this be because these behaviours interfere or stop you doing the things you really value and want to have in your life?

Dialectical behaviour therapy (DBT)

The core principle of DBT is to accept unwanted thoughts and feelings. By just allowing them to be there without battling against them, we can live the life we want rather than the life OCD insists that we have.

For anxiety, DBT emphasizes the importance of tolerating uncomfortable feelings. By being mindful of our distress but not attempting to change it, we can improve the moment. Like ACT, the idea is that acceptance increases tolerance of distress.

Mindfulness

Have you ever found yourself 'on autopilot'? For example, you intend to eat a few squares of chocolate but before you know it, all that's left is an empty wrapper. You were distracted by the busy-ness of your mind taking you away from the present moment, the moment in which you were eating the chocolate. The central message is that we do not have to accept thoughts as facts: they are opinions and ideas. We can choose whether or not we want to attend to them.

Mindfulness doesn't try to make you feel 'better'. What it does is to teach us that we don't have to engage with every thought that comes into our mind. It encourages us to become an impartial observer. For example, 'I'm observing that I'm having intrusive thoughts and I'm still going to carry on' or 'Here's one of those urges' and choosing not to act on it. It helps us to recognize and step away from habitual ways of thinking, feeling and doing.

When you're distressed, you may feel there's another 'present' that you'd like to be in but you're not. Most likely this would be a present that is free of doubt and anxiety. If we accept being in the present with dissatisfaction, we can act in different ways

Mindfulness does not run counter to CBT but works at a **metacognitive** level. That means it's thinking *about* thinking. So as in traditional CBT for OCD, it works with beliefs *about* thoughts rather than the thoughts themselves.

Compassion focused therapy (CFT)

The focus in CFT is to help a person to develop their capacity to adopt a more compassionate way of relating to themselves (and others). In my work I have often come across people who feel terribly guilty, sometimes in relation to their OCD and sometimes in relation to past events. This can sometimes feed into their OCD, for example reinforcing the person's view of themselves as a 'bad' person who is undeserving. If you identify with being highly self-critical, with a tendency to feel guilty or ashamed, then you may well benefit from some compassion-focused work aimed at helping you to develop your capacity to treat yourself with the same respect, kindness and consideration that you probably find it easy to feel for others.

CFT also helps us to understand that the feelings of anxiety and danger that we experience are not our fault – that the 'primitive' part of our brain is designed for self-preservation – which can help us to understand why we may find ourselves getting caught up in a cycle of compulsions.

Learning to treat ourselves with kindness and compassion can help us to disengage from our 'safety behaviours' (typically driven by our threat system), which otherwise keep us locked in a pattern of overestimating threat and overly reliant on adopting a 'better safe than sorry' approach in life, which can restrict what we are able to do.

Practical advice ⇨

Helpful habits II: A good night's sleep

In Chapter 4, we talked about the importance of looking after ourselves. Here's the next instalment of helpful hints. Follow these tips to help yourself sleep better.

Improve your sleep environment

- Make your bedroom a calm, relaxing haven.
- It's much nicer to get into a tidy bed with plumped up pillows.
- Make sure the room is not too hot or too cold: we sleep best in a cool bedroom.

Create a bedtime routine

- A soothing routine gets us ready for sleep.
- Put your clothes out ready for the next day, or set a tray for breakfast.
- A warm bath or shower can be relaxing.
- Set an alarm if OCD keeps you up.
- Enjoy the feeling of snuggling down in bed.

Eating and drinking

- Avoid big meals and rich or spicy food in the evening (perhaps cheese does make us dream more!)
- Don't go to bed hungry or thirsty.
- Cut out caffeine; replace coffee, tea or cola with herbal tea or a milky drink.
- Alcohol can make us restless … and need the toilet.

Early to bed … early to rise

- Our body-clock runs on a roughly 24-hour cycle called **circadian rhythm**.
- Keep to a regular bedtime as far as possible.
- There's some truth in the saying 'an hour's sleep before midnight is worth two after'.
- Most of us function best on seven to nine hours sleep each night.
- Stick to your routine, even at weekends – you can always enjoy sitting in bed with a cuppa and the newspaper.

Suitable activities before bed

- Don't exercise for at least two hours before bedtime.
- It's fine to make love – and the hormones produced (e.g. prolactin) help us relax.
- It's OK to read a book, or listen to music or some other relaxing pastime.
- But avoid looking at your phone, laptop or other mobile device.

Relax

- Enjoy the feeling of being in bed.
- If you often feel tense, progressive muscle relaxation can help. (You can find instructions on the internet.)
- Mindfulness meditation can ease an over-active mind.
- Have a really good stretch – doesn't that feel good?

Turn down the light to have a good night

- Soft lighting during the evening helps us wind down to sleep.
- Bright light from a television, computer or mobile phone screen prevents production of the sleep hormone melatonin, so avoid them in the bedroom.
- A dark bedroom improves sleep.

Reduce noise

- Make your bedroom quiet and peaceful.
- Try earplugs if outside noise or a snoring partner disturbs your peace.
- Developing a mindful relationship with external noises can even help us drop off to sleep.

Medication

- Improving sleep using natural behavioural methods like these takes time; new habits need practice.
- Medication should only be used as a last resort and for a short time only.
- Poor sleep can be a symptom of depression as well as anxiety; it might be helpful to discuss this with your doctor.

Don't worry about not sleeping

- The major cause of not sleeping is *worrying* about not sleeping.
- Don't look at the clock if you wake in the night.
- There's no need to put the light on to go to the toilet – you know the way!
- If you had a bad night, don't try to catch up or have a nap in the day; just go to bed at the normal time.
- Don't focus on worries or concerns about the day before, or the next day.
- Don't lie in bed getting anxious if you don't go back to sleep after a few minutes.
- Don't worry about whether or not you'll get to sleep OK tomorrow night.

    Sleep tight!

Reviewing behaviour

Task

We can all benefit from getting a better night's sleep, whether we're poor sleepers or not. What will you do?

Write down two things you will start to do or do more of (e.g. 'I will go to bed before 11 p.m. Sunday to Thursday' or 'I will get myself a new pillow') and two things you will stop doing or do less of (e.g. 'I will stop taking my phone to bed' or 'I won't stay up after midnight if I have to work next day').

What I will start doing/do more

1 _____

2 _____

What I will stop doing/do less

1 _____

2 _____

Chapter summary

In this chapter you have learned:

● CBT helps us understand links between thoughts, feelings and behaviours
● OCD results from interpreting certain thoughts as threatening or dangerous
● Third Wave CBT focuses on thinking about thinking.

There's a strong relationship between thoughts, feelings and behaviours. OCD develops if we label certain kinds of thoughts as threatening or dangerous in some way. If we spend a long time thinking about those thoughts – or doing things to prevent harm – it keeps those ideas on our mind. The more often we have these thoughts, the more likely we are to keep believing that they're important in some way. We overlook the fact that what we do fuels the problem.

By using a CBT approach we can:

● reduce the significance of thoughts, doubts, urges and impulses
● alter our behaviour – what we do in response to thoughts
● change our beliefs.

Third Wave CBT emphasizes changing our relationship with our thoughts and feelings: thoughts are just thoughts; feelings are just feelings. Learning to accept uncertainty and tolerate discomfort enables us to live the life we want, not the one OCD chooses. It works from the outside in: if we change our behaviour, belief-change follows.

Are you ready to find out how OCD traps us in a cycle of thoughts, feelings and behaviours? In Chapter 6 you will learn how a formulation shows the way it all fits together.

CHAPTER 6

Making sense of your experience

Overview

In this chapter you will learn:

- how what you think, feel and do fit together to keep OCD going
- how different types of OCD problems can be understood in the same way
- how to draw your personal experiences of OCD as a model that helps explain what keeps the problem going.

No matter what kind of problem we're faced with, the vital ingredient for solving it is to have a thorough understanding of what is going on. OCD can seem so random and senseless to us that we're left puzzling over what it all means. To add to our confusion, we might find it hard to understand why we just can't stop doing the things we do even though we can see that they're excessive or that others deem them unnecessary. A couple of real-life examples are given to explain the process. Using step-by-step guidelines you can develop your own **formulation** to show how the different aspects of your OCD keep the problem going. Understanding the maintenance cycle is vital to breaking the cycle.

What is a formulation?

A formulation is a diagram or structure which illustrates how different things are related to each other. A vicious circle is a simple example. As human beings, we're never very straightforward and it's often the case that there might be more than one vicious circle in operation at any one time. We can fit them together into a bigger picture called a formulation. This is something that psychologists and psychiatrists generally do: they piece together various types of information, such as symptoms, behaviours, stressful events that might have triggered a current problem or difficult experiences in the past, and draw them together to create a **hypothesis**. A hypothesis is a scientific term for an explanation for something – like OCD, for example. And it isn't just helpful because it offers an explanation: it is an explanation that can be tested to see whether or not it really is a satisfactory explanation.

The OCD Vicious Flower

The good news is that we don't need to start from scratch to build a formulation. There has been extensive research into OCD and how it works, so psychologists have already come up with a formulation we can use to understand our own individual experience.

If the Vicious Flower is looking rather complicated and scary, don't despair. 'Vicious flower' is just the nickname given to the OCD formulation because it looks rather like a flower. It's not difficult if we take it one step at a time. Looking at the whole diagram (Figure 6.1), can you see how the 'petals' are in fact a number of separate vicious circles?

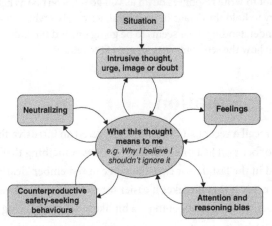

Figure 6.1: The OCD Vicious Flower.
(After Salkoviskis, Richards and Forrester (1995))

We're going to go through the process step by step in the way we would if we were working together in a therapy session, using the version of the OCD Vicious Flower shown in Figure 6.2: My Vicious Flower. In this version, you will see that there is a number for each of the headings. This is to make it easier to follow the order we're taking. At each stage there will be questions to guide you and case studies as examples, and then we will fit it all together.

Surely we need to know what caused OCD first? A common mistake is to try to work out why you got the problem in the first place. You've possibly spent a lot of time considering the many possibilities. Has this helped you get rid of OCD? I thought not! In Chapter 7 we'll look at this approach again but in the meantime, let's focus on what keeps the problem going. It should soon begin to make sense.

Reviewing behaviour

Make a copy of the basic Vicious Flower diagram (Figure 6.2: My Vicious Flower). It will be easier to have it on a separate sheet of paper so that you can add to it as you read through the chapter. It's important to write responses down as you go – it won't be as helpful if you try to hold the details in your head. Remember what we said about understanding what seems to be going on, and the importance of knowing how the separate parts seem to fit together?

Step 1: Situation

Can you recall a recent **situation** that triggered an intrusive thought? It's best to focus on just one situation for now, something that happened in the last day or two that you can remember clearly. The reason for this is that it makes it easier for us to recall the details and to reconstruct what was happening – a bit like a detective trying to piece together evidence.

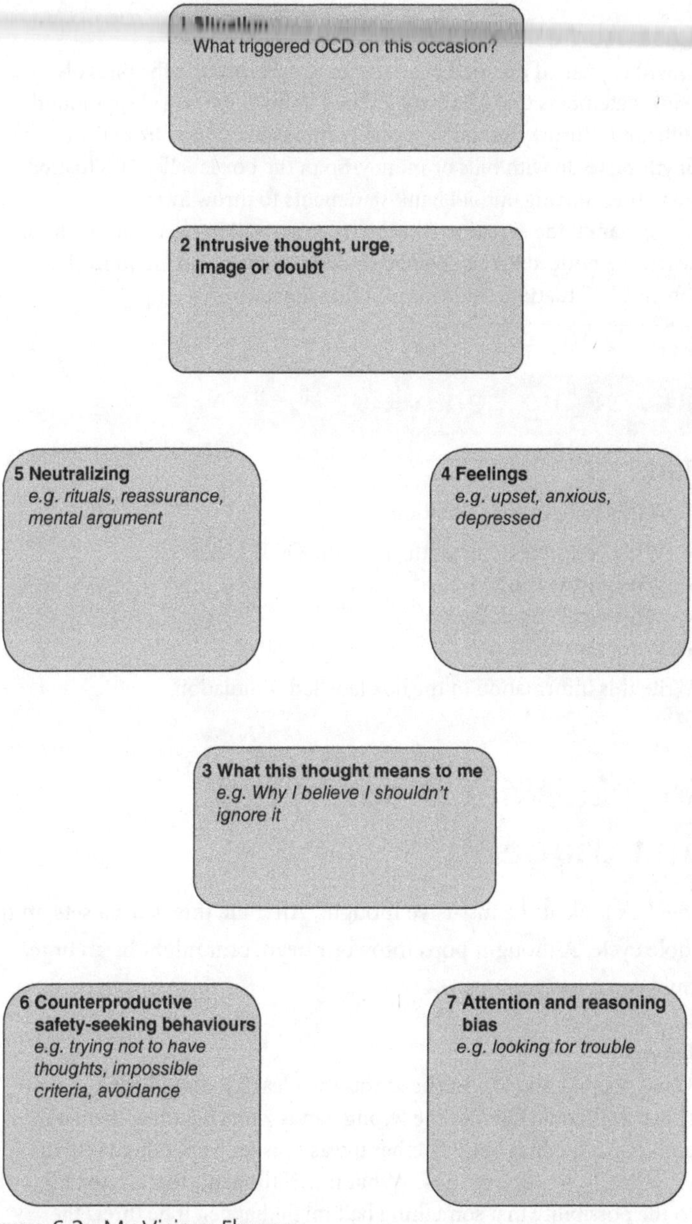

1 Situation
What triggered OCD on this occasion?

2 Intrusive thought, urge, image or doubt

5 Neutralizing
e.g. rituals, reassurance, mental argument

4 Feelings
e.g. upset, anxious, depressed

3 What this thought means to me
e.g. Why I believe I shouldn't ignore it

6 Counterproductive safety-seeking behaviours
e.g. trying not to have thoughts, impossible criteria, avoidance

7 Attention and reasoning bias
e.g. looking for trouble

Figure 6.2: My Vicious Flower

Case studies

David explained that he'd been trying to sort through the piles of bank statements that had accumulated in his room. He always found it difficult to throw stuff out, especially things like letters from the bank or anything to do with bills or money. So in the box labelled '1 Situation', he wrote: 'Sorting out old bank statements to throw away.'

For **Janet**, the situation was that she was walking her son to school when she noticed that a dog had fouled the pavement. So in the box labelled '1 Situation', she wrote: 'Seeing dog poo.'

Reviewing behaviour

Task

Now think about *your* situation.

- What you were doing at the time the OCD kicked in?
- Where were you?
- What were you doing?
- Who were you with?

Write this information in the box labelled '1 Situation'.

Step 2: What thought did that trigger?

Now let's look at the intrusive thought. After all, this is what sets off the whole cycle. A thought pops into your head, or it might be an urge, a doubt or an image.

David

What popped into David's head was the idea that his old bank statements could fall into the wrong hands when he threw them out, along with doubts about whether it was sensible to put them into the recycling. It was one of those 'What if ...?' thoughts that alerted him to the possibility that something bad might happen if he threw the statements out. So what David enters in the box labelled '2 Intrusive thought, urge, image or doubt' is: 'This might fall into the wrong hands' (Figure 6.3).

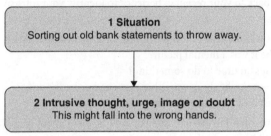

1 Situation
Sorting out old bank statements to throw away.

2 Intrusive thought, urge, image or doubt
This might fall into the wrong hands.

Figure 6.3: David's Step 2

Janet
Janet explained how she'd developed a knack for walking along with one eye constantly on the ground. Although the dog mess that she spotted was quite old and dried up, a sense that it was dangerous still came into her head. She said it didn't really feel like a thought as such. Nevertheless, the idea was enough to trigger the urge to do something to protect both herself and her son from potential danger. Janet added to her formulation in the box labelled '2 Intrusive thought, urge, image or doubt': 'This is dangerous' (Figure 6.4).

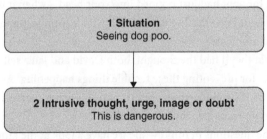

1 Situation
Seeing dog poo.

2 Intrusive thought, urge, image or doubt
This is dangerous.

Figure 6.4: Janet's Step 2

Reviewing behaviour

Task

Let's go back to your recent experience to identify your intrusive thought.

- What was the idea that popped into your head at that time?
- Maybe it was a mental picture?
- Perhaps an urge to do something?
- Maybe a doubt about something you had or hadn't done?
- Or just a vague sense of some kind of danger?

Remember that intrusive thoughts might be ideas about something that could happen in the future, or about something that happened in the past (or something that you fear could have happened in the past if you hadn't been careful). The vague sense of danger often occurs when we've become so used to having a particular thought or concern that we don't even need to spell it out any more.

   Add this to your formulation in the box labelled '2 Intrusive thought, urge, image or doubt' and link it with an arrow, as in the examples above, to show that the situation was a trigger for your intrusive thought.

Step 3: What did the thought mean to you?

When the thought had just popped into your head – when it was still fresh – what did you think it meant? Why did it seem so important to you at that moment?

   Now that they'd had the thought, both David and Janet felt responsible for preventing these terrible things happening. As we saw in Chapter 5, a heightened sense of responsibility is a characteristic of OCD. Do you recognize this in yourself?

   Keep the questions in mind while we have a look at the kinds of meanings that David and Janet came up with.

David

Whenever David was faced with a pile of papers he always ended up worrying that he might throw something away that he'd later discover he needed, and often felt uncertain about whether or not a particular letter or piece of information that he'd been sent was something important that he needed to keep. And he was always hearing and reading about identity theft, it felt like something that could happen to him at any time if he wasn't careful.

Although he tried not to think about it too much, in his darker moments he imagined having every last penny taken from his account – money that he'd worked hard to save. It wasn't just that he worried about mistakenly throwing away something he would later need; he didn't trust his judgment about anything – even something that should be really simple, like filing at work. His constant doubting affected many aspects of his life (Figure 6.5).

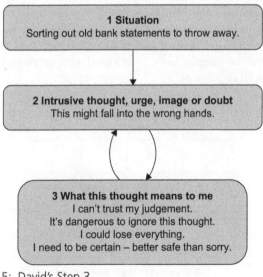

Figure 6.5: David's Step 3

Janet

Janet's son had been such a longed-for baby that he was the most precious thing in the world to her. She wanted to do everything in her power to protect him, keeping him healthy and safe. She'd always been a bit of a 'clean freak', as she called it, just a bit on the house-proud side but nothing major. With a new baby she reckoned it was even more important to keep her home clean and germ-free.

When he was a tiny babe in arms it was relatively easy, but once he was able to walk it became so much harder – his little hands were into everything, crawling around on the floor and then sticking his thumb in his mouth. Although Janet had wondered about disinfecting his thumb, she dismissed the idea as ridiculous. She'd have to constantly wipe it, it probably would taste awful (making him cry) and it would possibly be harmful to him. So she reasoned that it would be best if she just made sure that everything he had contact with was kept hygienically clean. Now he was bigger, the task of keeping him clean and safe was harder as there were even more dangers he could come into contact with. Especially picking up a parasite from dogs. And dog faeces seemed to be everywhere – even in their garden, where foxes seemed to leave their calling cards on a regular basis. To be a good mum she needed to be really careful (Figure 6.6).

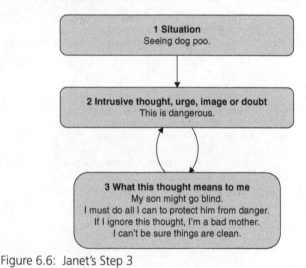

Figure 6.6: Janet's Step 3

Sometimes we're not aware that we've made an interpretation of our thoughts at the time they come into our heads. We don't always consciously consider what these thoughts mean or why we'd had them at all. Our brains are amazing. They process huge amounts of information in milliseconds. Much of the time, we don't even have to get our brain to do it; it just happens automatically. We manage to do all kinds of things on autopilot, especially things we do a lot. We very quickly stop consciously making an appraisal of the intrusive thoughts: OCD becomes something we might do on autopilot.

Reviewing behaviour

Task

Now picture yourself in your situation again.

- What did you think it meant when that thought popped into your head?
- What did you believe would happen right now if you ignored it?
- And in the future?
- In what way did it seem dangerous or risky to let the thought go?
- What would it mean about you?

Add this to your formulation under heading '3 What this thought meant to me', and link it with an arrow as in the examples above to show that the intrusive thought seemed significant or important to you because of the meaning you attached to it.

Step 4: How did it make you feel?

Even if you weren't aware of the meaning, how did you feel when you'd had the thought?

Most likely when the intrusive thought popped into your head it seemed to make you feel really uncomfortable. The feelings we have can be:

- emotional – affecting our mood, e.g. anxious, angry or depressed
- mental – e.g. stressed, doubtful, threatened, apprehensive, a sense of doom (as if something terrible is about to happen)
- physical – e.g. tense, jittery, hot, racing heart or a mixture of bodily sensations.

Mood plays a number of roles in OCD. Just having unwanted thoughts makes us feel anxious, stressed or worried. Struggling to be free of the problem makes us feel down or depressed, especially if we've battled against OCD for a long time.

Whatever our mood, we tend to pay more attention to the kinds of thoughts that fit with the way we feel and also the way we do certain kinds of things. For example, when I'm in a happy mood I'm likely to put on some upbeat and cheerful music and might even start dancing around while I do the ironing. Even though it might be more helpful to do that when we feel really down, we're more likely to be drawn towards the kinds of activities that reflect how we feel – moping around, perhaps not even bothering to get dressed when (if?) we get out of bed, and listening to songs that seem to exactly describe the pit of despair we've found ourselves in (an old song by the Smiths seems to sum it up: 'but heaven knows, I'm miserable now'). We'll talk about the role of attention again shortly.

David

Not only did David's constant doubting affect almost every aspect of his life – driving him to check everything he did and keeping him uncertain of his abilities so he was afraid to progress in his career – but it kept him in a permanent state of anxiety. The non-stop worrying made him feel so tense that his neck and shoulders ached. And the more tense and anxious he felt, the more doubtful he became. And the more true it felt (Figure 6.7).

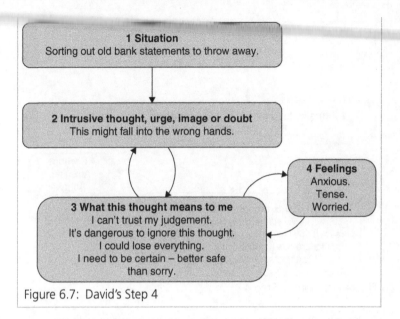

Figure 6.7: David's Step 4

Janet

When she saw what was on the pavement, Janet's initial response was anger: 'Why does everyone think it's all right to let their damn dog crap in the street and just leave it there?', swiftly followed by a flood of physical sensations. A rush of heat from her stomach upward caused her head to throb as if it was shouting 'Danger! Danger!', fuelling her anxiety. But when she wasn't faced with what seemed like the imminent danger of contamination with faeces, what she felt was despair and depression.

She could see that her efforts to keep her son safe seemed to cause almost as many difficulties as they prevented, as her husband frequently pointed out to her in the heat of the moment. She felt hopeless ... and a complete failure. All she wanted to be was a good mother but it seemed as if the harder she tried, the more she failed (Figure 6.8).

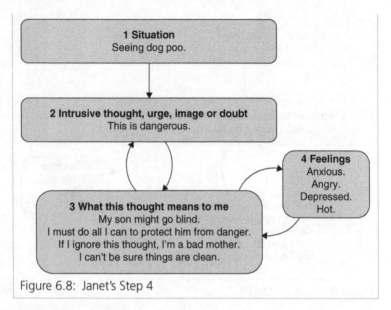

1 Situation
Seeing dog poo.

2 Intrusive thought, urge, image or doubt
This is dangerous.

4 Feelings
Anxious.
Angry.
Depressed.
Hot.

3 What this thought means to me
My son might go blind.
I must do all I can to protect him from danger.
If I ignore this thought, I'm a bad mother.
I can't be sure things are clean.

Figure 6.8: Janet's Step 4

Maybe you felt it as stress or anxiety, or perhaps your mood took a dip, making you feel down or depressed. The trouble is that when we feel stressed or down, we're more likely to have unpleasant thoughts or worries come into our heads. And because we seem to be getting even more of these unwanted ideas, the more likely we are to jump to the conclusion that we need to do something about them.

If we feel fearful or anxious, we're more likely to make a threatening appraisal. It's that old idea that 'there's no smoke without fire'. In other words, if I feel so scared it must be true.

Reviewing behaviour

Task

So let's reflect on your emotional response at this time.

- How did it make you feel?
- What did you notice first?
- What happened to your mood when you had this thought?

- Did you notice any physical sensations? What were they?
- When you felt these sensations, how did you feel?
- What effect did it have on you mentally?

Add this to your formulation under the heading '4 Feelings'. Link it with arrows:

- from the 'Meaning' box to the 'Feelings' box
- from the 'Feelings' box to the 'Meaning' box.

This shows that the meaning you attached to the thought (even if it wasn't actually at the front of your mind at that time) affected the way you felt at that time. It also shows that how we feel has an effect on how we interpret experiences.

Step 5: What did you want to do to help yourself feel better?

Because you felt this way, no doubt you wanted to do something to make the feeling (and the thoughts) go away. Neutralizing reduces the discomfort from the thoughts and also reduces the feeling that we're somehow to blame if we just ignored the thought. What we mean by 'neutralizing' is anything we do to try to counteract or cancel out the thought, or our efforts to make things safe.

Yet another vicious circle is created when we believe that it is what we did that prevented the feared catastrophe. In turn, it makes it seem as if it was something we really needed to do. Maxine was convinced that she was on the brink of becoming dirty, smelly and unacceptable and only her extreme cleaning routines saved her. Arun could never put into words exactly what he believed would happen if he didn't tap, touch or repeat. Yet it seemed to him that he'd averted some dreadful fate. In this way, neutralizing strengthens some responsibility beliefs.

Quite often, the only thing that neutralizing prevents is our anxiety increasing. But as we saw in Chapter 3, this is only a quick fix. In fact, what we have now is another vicious circle.

David

Sitting on his bed amidst piles of papers that he had dug out from drawers and boxes in his room, David felt quite overwhelmed. He had tried to sort the statements into just two piles: one for keeping and the other for getting rid of. The thing was, he found himself spending ages checking each letter or statement, reading it over and over while debating in his head whether or not it was something he should keep. And each time he felt he had made a decision about whether it was to be kept or thrown away, another doubt crept in. So he started a third pile – the 'maybe' pile – which soon became the one with the most in it.

To try to set his mind at rest, David decided to ask his mother to have a quick look through and tell him whether he should be keeping anything in the 'out' pile. When he also asked her to look at the other piles, he ended up with yet more doubts when she suggested that most things needed to be discarded. Not only did it make him feel more tense and worried because he felt he had to go through this new pile of stuff his mother said he should get rid of, but it intensified his belief that his judgment couldn't be trusted (Figure 6.9).

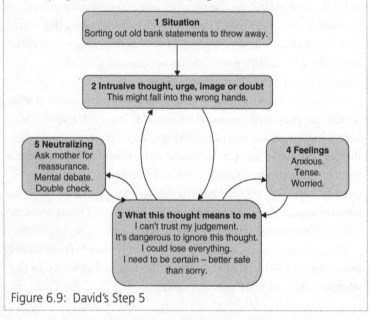

Figure 6.9: David's Step 5

Janet

'Just don't think about it', Janet kept telling herself, trying to stop herself thinking about all the awful things that germs from dog faeces could cause. The thoughts still came into her head, making her wrinkle her nose in disgust and hold her breath to prevent breathing in anything that might be harmful. She didn't know whether or not bacteria from excrement floated around in the air, or any dust from the surface of old deposits on the pavement, but she wasn't going to take any chances. Of course, she'd make sure that she had a really good wash when she got home and change her clothes.

She kept her outdoor clothes – coats and gloves – in the garage, which her husband teasingly called the 'decontamination chamber'. She always wore a coat and gloves to go out, and tried to insist that the rest of the family did. The world was a dirty place and she didn't want that filth in her home, thank you very much. Even with gloves on (and the promise of a wash) Janet found it reassuring to carry some antibacterial hand gel with her wherever she went, just in case she needed to take her gloves off. 'Thank goodness for antibacterial cleaners', she mused, 'I'd never manage without them' (Figure 6.10).

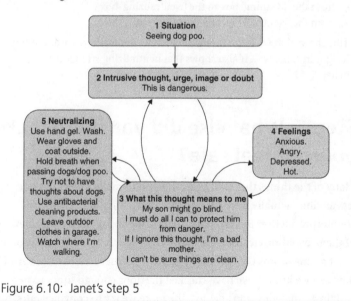

Figure 6.10: Janet's Step 5

Reviewing behaviour

Task

Now think about your response to these worries.

- What did it make you want to do?
- Was it a physical ritual – something that other people could see, like washing, checking, repeating an action?
- Or was it a covert ritual – something you do in your head, like thinking a good thought after a bad one, or having a mental debate with yourself?
- Do you have 'rules' about the way you (or others) should do things?
- What else did you feel you needed to do to put the thought right, or make yourself feel better?
- And, even if you didn't do it on this particular occasion, what else do you sometimes do to make yourself feel less stressed or anxious when you have this thought or in a similar situation?

Add this to your formulation under the heading '5 Neutralizing'. Link it with arrows:

- from the 'Meaning' box to the 'Neutralizing' box
- from the 'Neutralizing' box to the 'Meaning' box.

This shows that what the thought meant to you made you want to put it right in some way. It also shows that neutralizing strengthens your belief.

Step 6: What else did you do to make yourself feel safe?

Many of the things that OCD gets us to do to make us feel safer or less anxious actually have the *opposite* effect. They are essentially counterproductive. By trying *not* to have the thoughts, we get more of them; avoiding cleaning the bathroom because we're worried about toilet germs means the bathroom gets even dirtier from neglect. And how can we know if we have checked the door enough times to be certain an intruder won't get in? The more we try to convince ourselves that we're safe, clean or certain, the more doubts we get. And we're back to square one. You know what this is another example of? That's right – a vicious circle.

Why can't I *not* have these thoughts?

Try *not* to think of a purple giraffe … try *really* hard. Have you managed *not* to picture it, or is it wandering through your mind as you read this? Trying not to have a thought doesn't help at all. In fact we tend to get even more of them. This becomes more of a problem when we're attempting not to have thoughts about something that didn't happen. Mandy tried desperately not to picture herself touching her baby's genitals. The more effort she made, the more the thoughts would come and the less certain she was that it hadn't happened.

Thought suppression is unhelpful in a number of ways.

- We have to tell ourselves which thought we don't want to have …
- … and so it pops into our head.
- It increases the number of unwanted thoughts we have …
- … and we conclude that maybe this is because we want to have these thoughts or that we're a bad person …
- … so we become even more convinced that it's dangerous to ignore them.

Thought suppression is a form of **avoidance**. Even distraction – trying to deliberately take our mind off OCD by doing something else – is a type of avoidance.

Why is avoidance unhelpful?

You may deliberately avoid situations or activities that might trigger thoughts. Although it may reduce your anxiety to begin with, the effects don't last. Shiralee went out of her way to avoid triggering memories of her time at the coffee shop. She stopped shopping on the high street. This helped for a while, but since the well-known chain was everywhere it proved hard not to spot a branch. In fact, seeing any café was enough to set it off.

Avoidance is unhelpful because it:

- keeps the thought in your mind
- increases its importance
- leads to further avoidance.

As Shiralee found, seeking to avoid certain coffee shops led her to notice them everywhere. She also didn't want to think about 'that man' (as she referred to him). It was impossible, too, not to hear or see the name 'Steve', since it is hardly unusual. In fact, the more she tried to avoid hearing it, the more she seemed to notice it.

Am I trying to achieve the impossible?

Perhaps, like Shiralee, you are also trying to achieve the impossible. We've seen several examples of **impossible criteria** already. How else does this show itself in OCD? Striving for complete certainty in what you do is a key example. Attempting to:

- be completely certain and doubt-free
- eliminate all risk
- be perfectly clean/safe/sure etc.

David

In order to prevent any personal or financial information falling into the wrong hands, David tended to put off throwing things away. That way, he could avoid making mistakes – and also avoided the horrible feelings of doubt that niggled away at him whenever he tried to make decisions about what was unnecessary or no longer needed. However, he even got in a state about junk mail and ended up keeping this too since much of it seemed to be addressed to him by name and had his address on it. After all, even if it didn't actually have his bank details

---

on it, some fraudster could use it to steal his identity. To prevent this possibility, David got himself a shredder. However, his doubts meant he rarely used it as he never seemed to feel certain enough to throw much away despite getting his mother to check (Figure 6.11).

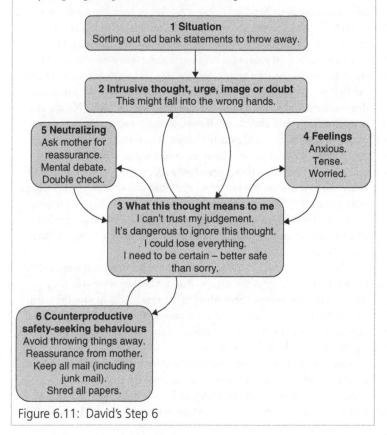

Figure 6.11: David's Step 6

Janet

Janet had developed an extensive repertoire of actions and avoidances to manage her fears. They'd become such a part of her life that it often didn't seem as if concerns about contamination with animal faeces was an issue. A bottle of hand gel in every pocket or handbag meant she didn't have to remember to take one with her. Friends were amused by her vintage-style coat and gloves combinations, with lightweight macs and pastel-coloured gloves for summer comfort (as well as avoiding suspicion about the true reason for dressing this way). Janet always did her best to avoid going anywhere that she might come across dogs and dog-walkers. 'I'm just not the outdoors type', she'd reason. 'Nature just doesn't do it for me', she'd laugh if anyone suggested a walk in the park or the countryside … and swiftly change the subject.

To Janet, the expression 'The world and his dog' seemed to sum it up in one. It seemed as if everyone had a flipping dog these days, so she often had to cross the road to avoid any close encounters. Blasted things were so unpredictable and always seemed to come sniffing or jumping up at you. Yuck! Since cats and foxes often seemed to use the garden as a lavatory, Janet had taken to drying the washing indoors even on a sunny day.

It hadn't been too difficult to persuade her husband and son to leave their outdoor clothes in the garage. And while they were at it, they may as well strip off out there when they came in just to save her a trip upstairs to fetch the dirty laundry. Of course, there never seemed to be any since it went in the washing machine the moment she, her son or her husband came in from outside.

Janet enjoyed family life, shutting the door on the outside world and spending time with her husband and son, just the three of them. She didn't feel the need for the company of friends these days, which was just as well since many of them seemed to be getting pets (Figure 6.12).

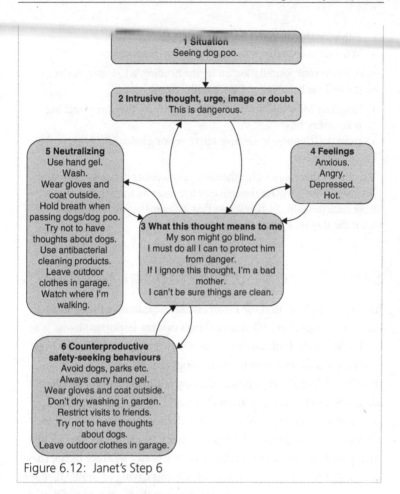

Figure 6.12: Janet's Step 6

Reviewing behaviour

Task

Take in to account all the things you did to bring down your anxiety.

- What else did you do to make yourself feel safe?
- Did you try to suppress thoughts or take your mind off them?
- Was there anything you avoided doing?

- Either on this occasion or at other times?
- What do you do that may be chasing the impossible?

Add this to your formulation under the heading '6 Counterproductive safety-seeking behaviours'. Link it with arrows:

- from the 'Meaning' box to the 'Counterproductive safety-seeking behaviours' box
- from the 'Counterproductive safety-seeking behaviours' box to the 'Meaning' box.

This shows that there were other things you either did or avoided doing because of the intrusive thoughts, or because you were trying not to have such thoughts. It also shows that it can make your appraisal of what the thoughts mean seem even *more* true.

Step 7: Are you looking for trouble?

It's easy to see how all these factors make the intrusive thoughts seem even more important. We notice things that are important to us. We tend to be on the look-out for them. This is known as **attention bias**.

Our attention is drawn towards things that are relevant to us at that time. We're all very good at filtering out information that doesn't seem relevant to us at any given moment. I'm sure you'll have had such experiences. Say you've gone out clothes shopping, looking for a T-shirt in a particular colour (a blue one). It seems like you can just stick your head in a shop and immediately notice whether or not they have T-shirts in the colour you want without having to shuffle through everything hanging on the rails. Is it because there are more of that colour ... or is it that you've just noticed it more because blue T-shirts have a personal relevance for you at that time?

Mood also plays a role in attention bias. If, for example, we've experienced a bereavement or relationship break-up, we only seem to notice things that fit in with how we feel – it's as if every song on the radio seems to know how we feel, and the television and magazines are full of deaths or divorce.

The effect is even more noticeable with something that is not only important but threatening. Not only would we be constantly on 'red alert' for upsetting thoughts, but also for potentially dangerous situations. So what happens as a result? If we're looking for trouble, we invariably find it – with knobs on. Attention bias explains why Shiralee was alert to the name 'Steve', Sahib noticed low-cut necklines and Stefan saw the number six everywhere he looked.

How else can being on the look-out for trouble feed OCD? If we notice more 'danger signs', we might also conclude that bad things are even more likely to happen. This is an example of **reasoning bias**. Other examples include:

- I wouldn't get so many thoughts if it wasn't true/dangerous/risky
- I must be a bad person if I think this way
- because I feel so bad it must be true.

Reasoning biases make us jump to conclusions without considering other evidence.

David

David noticed news items about identity fraud all the time: it was in the newspapers, on the television, everywhere. And whenever he withdrew cash from the ATM machine, he was conscious of the reminder to be careful that no one was looking over his shoulder at his PIN. He overheard someone on the train one morning telling another passenger about how his brother or somebody was having a battle with the bank over £3,000 that had been withdrawn from his account. 'Yeah, he reckons someone hacked his details off the internet', he heard them say.

The world really seemed like a very dangerous place. Despite all his efforts to cut out the risk, David still felt full of doubts. In fact, he never seemed to feel completely certain of anything, no matter how hard he tried. And because he felt so uncertain and so anxious, it really felt as if it was true (Figure 6.13).

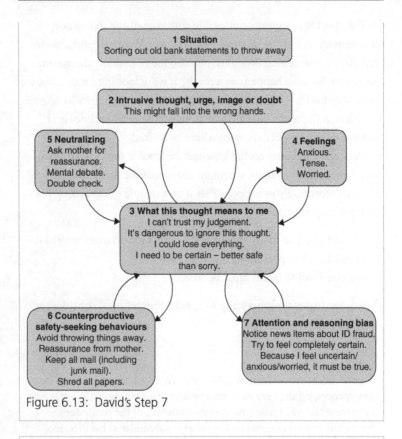

Figure 6.13: David's Step 7

Janet

Janet saw dog-related danger everywhere. Whenever she left the house, she'd see dogs. You couldn't walk more than a few steps without seeing dog poo. It wasn't always new (by crossing over whenever there was a dog in sight she could usually avoid this 'pleasure') but there were crusty, dried heaps all over the place, even tucked away under hedges and bushes at the edge of the path. What she hated most was seeing brown smears on the paving slabs where someone had clearly trodden in it, or chunks that had been kicked accidentally by an unsuspecting pedestrian.

Because no one seemed to clear up after their dogs, Janet would constantly look down as she walked. She noticed brown marks everywhere. Never wanting to leave it to chance, she avoided stepping on anything that triggered even a hint of a doubt. She kept clear too of anyone who might keep pets, scrutinizing strangers' clothing for signs of animal hairs. Janet couldn't understand how why no one else seemed to be as careful as she was. Unless she felt completely clean, she simply couldn't relax (Figure 6.14).

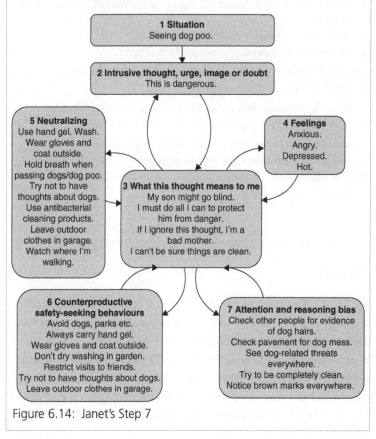

1 Situation
Seeing dog poo.

2 Intrusive thought, urge, image or doubt
This is dangerous.

5 Neutralizing
Use hand gel. Wash. Wear gloves and coat outside. Hold breath when passing dogs/dog poo. Try not to have thoughts about dogs. Use antibacterial cleaning products. Leave outdoor clothes in garage. Watch where I'm walking.

4 Feelings
Anxious.
Angry.
Depressed.
Hot.

3 What this thought means to me
My son might go blind.
I must do all I can to protect him from danger.
If I ignore this thought, I'm a bad mother.
I can't be sure things are clean.

6 Counterproductive safety-seeking behaviours
Avoid dogs, parks etc.
Always carry hand gel.
Wear gloves and coat outside.
Don't dry washing in garden.
Restrict visits to friends.
Try not to have thoughts about dogs.
Leave outdoor clothes in garage.

7 Attention and reasoning bias
Check other people for evidence of dog hairs.
Check pavement for dog mess.
See dog-related threats everywhere.
Try to be completely clean.
Notice brown marks everywhere.

Figure 6.14: Janet's Step 7

Reviewing behaviour

Task

Spend a moment or two considering how attention and reasoning biases contribute to OCD for you.

- What kind of things are you on the look-out for?
- What kinds of situations seem risky or dangerous to you?
- What was it about how you felt that made it seem risky or dangerous?
- What are the effects of the things you do?
- What kinds of reasoning biases might you have?

Add this to your formulation under the heading '7 Attention and reasoning bias'. Link it with arrows:

- from the 'Meaning' box to the 'Attention and reasoning bias' box
- from the 'Attention and reasoning bias' box to the 'Meaning' box.

This shows that the *meaning* we give to something gives it personal importance. It also shows that we pay more *attention* to those things. We can misinterpret the *reason* for this as a sign that it is more significant than it really is.

Is this what keeps the problem going?

Our Vicious Flower provides an explanation of how OCD takes hold and keeps hold. We can see that each individual 'petal' forms a vicious circle of its own and strengthens our belief in the significance of the intrusive thoughts. So we can see that OCD isn't random or senseless. In fact, if anyone believed that intrusive thoughts should not be ignored and that they were responsible for preventing harm or danger, they would no doubt do exactly what you do: they would have OCD.

The final step is to draw an arrow from the 'Meaning' box to the 'Intrusive thought' box. Now there are arrows:

- from the 'Meaning' box to the 'Intrusive thought' box
- from the 'Intrusive thought' box to the 'Meaning' box.

This final petal shows how labelling intrusive thoughts as meaningful is what keeps the whole cycle going.

Chapter summary

In this chapter you have learned:

- how what we think, feel and do fits together to make a vicious circle
- how OCD is made up of a series of vicious circles that create a Vicious Flower
- that the same formulation can explain different kinds of OCD worries
- that the meaning or interpretation we attach to intrusive thoughts keeps the problem going
- how to draw your own personal formulation.

A formulation is a diagram that shows the relationship between different aspects of OCD. What keeps the problem going is more important than looking for the cause. We can see how what we do in an attempt to feel better or prevent harm often fuels our worries further and strengthens unhelpful beliefs.

You now have a formulation that shows the factors that keep OCD going for you. Are you ready to discover how to break those vicious circles? Chapter 7 will offer you a less threatening way of making sense of intrusive thoughts and help you understand what you can do to free yourself from OCD.

What do I need to change?

Overview

Chapter 6 outlined how the *meaning* we attach to an intrusive thought affects the way we feel and what we do. You also learned how our responses to these thoughts create a series of vicious circles which keep the problem going. In this chapter we'll be asking:

- is there a less threatening way of looking at the problem?
- does this way of looking at the problem need a different solution?
- what can we learn from the individuals in our real-life examples?
- what does this mean for you and your OCD difficulties?

By following the guide in Chapter 6, you have grown a Vicious Flower of your own which illustrates how the meaning you attach to intrusive thoughts sets up a number of vicious circles which act together to keep the problem going. We have no control over what thoughts come into our mind. We don't have much influence over how we feel. And it's difficult to persuade ourselves to believe something else. So the only thing that we *can* change is what we *do*. The key to breaking the vicious circles is to do things differently.

Centuries ago, there was a widely held belief that the Earth was flat. Because of this, sailors were understandably cautious when they went to sea. To minimize the risk of inadvertently sailing off the edge of the world, they used certain strategies to keep themselves safe, like trying to stay within sight of land or not sailing any further than seagulls would fly, to reassure themselves that all was well, and they avoided setting sail if there was any hint of bad weather. Of course, storms at sea sometimes caught them by surprise in the midst of even the calmest days, and they'd be so afraid of being blown off-course and dropping off the edge of the world. Who knew what kind of purgatory would be down there? And then astronomers started to insist that in fact the Earth was round, not flat, so there wasn't the slightest chance of going over the edge. Do you think the sailors just slapped their thighs in a jolly way, exclaiming 'Oh, silly us!' and sailed blithely off towards the distant horizon? Probably not. No doubt they were scared to change their ways because they still didn't believe it. But until they took that leap of faith and started to *act* as if this new theory was true, they were unlikely to change what they believed.

This story has two important messages for tackling any anxiety problem.

1 If we always do things the same way, we don't make new discoveries.
2 If we change our behaviour, belief-change follows.

In other words, if we continue doing all the things that we believe keep us safe we will never discover how necessary these behaviours really are. What we need to do instead is to act as if we have confidence in our judgment and walk away from the door without checking the lock, or as if our hands are clean enough, or as if thoughts about harming our child aren't important. These less threatening ideas gradually become the way we really do see the world. By changing our behaviour, we change our beliefs: we develop a new theory about how the world works.

How does this apply to OCD?

The key to understanding OCD and what keeps it going is the *meaning* we attach to certain kinds of thoughts when they come into our heads – the 'four dreads'. The cause of the trouble is when we accept what we believe the thoughts to be as true. Mandy believed that her childhood games of 'doctors and nurses' meant she was in danger of becoming a child molester. David believed that his lack of certainty meant that his judgment was poor. They have each developed a theory about what their problem is, as have all the others whose OCD stories we have read. Let's call this **Theory A**. The key theme we can identify from each of their theories is that something bad could happen if they ignored the thoughts. It's not surprising that they would want to do something to prevent these bad things from happening, and have developed various behaviours and strategies to avoid their feared outcomes. If any of us saw a danger that we could prevent, it's likely that we too would want to do something about it.

	Theory A
Maxine	My problem is that I'm dirty and smelly.
Tadeusz	My problem is that my home will be burgled/burn down/flood.
David	My problem is that I have poor judgement.
Sahib	My problem is that I'm a pervert.

What do we need to do if Theory A is true?

Looking at the problem in this way suggests that there are certain things we should be doing to solve the problem, whether it's a problem of dirt, danger, doubt or deviance. After all, it makes perfect sense that if our hands are dirty the way to 'solve' that dirt problem is to wash them, or if someone was a murderer it would make sense to keep them away from other people and anything that could be used as a murder weapon. As you can see from their belief ratings below, Maxine and the others all held a strong belief in their Theory A; even Sahib's slightly more doubtful 50 per cent at times rose to 75 per cent, making it seem too chancy to take the risk.

Maxine

Theory A: My problem is that I'm dirty and smelly.

Belief: 100%

What I need to do to solve this problem:

Wear clean clothes every day.

Have a bath or shower if I've done anything that might make me smell.

Make sure I use lots of toilet paper (and wet wipes) after a 'number 2'.

Clean my flat really thoroughly.

Use lots of nice-smelling cleaning products.

Throw out anything that can't be washed.

Avoid eating smelly foods like fish, garlic, curry.

Don't cook anything at home to prevent smells getting into my things.

Wipe my mouth after every mouthful to prevent my face absorbing horrible smells.

Hold food with a napkin so it doesn't get on my hands.

Tadeusz

Theory A: My problem is that my home will be burgled/burn down/flood unless I'm really careful.

Belief: 85%

What I need to do to solve this problem:

Check doors, windows, gas, electric, taps.

Check again if I feel uncertain.

Never leave electrical things plugged in.

Turn all lights and appliances off before going to bed or leaving the house.

Use a wind-up alarm clock instead of a clock-radio.

Check things in a systematic way.

Repeat things like 'window, window' so I can feel sure I've checked it.

Take photos of the kettle, taps, door on my phone so I can check that they're OK if I get worried when I'm at work.

Don't use the kettle, toaster or anything else that might get hot before I go to work in the morning.

Always wait until the cooker or other appliances have cooled down before going to bed or leaving the house.

Put sink plugs on the window ledge so they can't fall in and cause a flood.

David

Theory A: My problem is that my judgement is poor.

Belief: 99%

What I need to do to solve this problem:

Read and reread everything until I feel certain.

Avoid making decisions about important things, e.g. anything work or finance related.

Keep all mail (including junk mail).

Never throw anything out unless I'm certain it's not important.

Shred anything with personal details or things to do with money, e.g. till receipts.

Always double-check with my mother before shredding.

Sahib

Theory A: My problem is that I'm a pervert.

Belief: 50–75%

What I need to do to solve this problem:

Avoid looking at women at the gym.

Try not to notice women's breasts.

Avoid looking at men's groins.

Take my contact lenses out before a gym class so I can't see details.

Avoid using the changing rooms.

Get changed in the staff toilet and shower at home.

Concentrate on looking only at men's faces.

Try to convince myself I'm not gay.

Think about my girlfriend whenever I get thoughts about being a pervert.

Check to see if I'm getting physically aroused when I see women, e.g. on television.

Is there another way of looking at it?

But maybe there's a different, less threatening way of looking at the problem? Just because we believe something doesn't necessarily mean it *is* true. Sahib, David and the others have developed opinions or ideas about what their unwanted thoughts mean. Perhaps OCD has conned them into believing these things about themselves and, more importantly, persuaded them that they need to do certain things to prevent their worst dreads happening. Could it be possible that their problem isn't in fact danger but *worry about* danger. We called their original theory Theory A; let's call this alternative explanation **Theory B**.

Now let's compare this alternative with each of the 'four dreads' using our real-life examples.

	Theory A	Theory B
Maxine	OCD says that I'm smelly and dirty	My problem is that I worry that I'm smelly and dirty
Tadeusz	OCD says that my home could be burgled/burn down/flood	My problem is that I worry that my home could be burgled/burn down/flood
David	OCD says that I have poor judgement	My problem is that I worry that I have poor judgement
Sahib	OCD says that I'm a pervert	My problem is that I worry that I'm a pervert

Reviewing behaviour

Task

Now that you've seen some examples of Theory A/Theory B, how would we word Theory B for other people in our examples: Carol, Janet, Stefan, Arun and Mandy?

	Theory A	Theory B
Carol		
Janet		
Stefan		
Arun		
Mandy		

Here's what they wrote:

	Theory A: OCD says ...	Theory B: My problem is ...
Carol	I am a dangerous person who could lose control at any moment.	I worry that I am a dangerous person.
Janet	Dog poo is dangerous.	I worry that dog poo is dangerous.
Stefan	Certain numbers are unlucky.	I worry that certain numbers are unlucky.
Arun	Bad things will happen unless I do things in a certain way.	I worry that bad things will happen unless I do things in a certain way.
Mandy	I'm a child molester.	I worry that I'm a child molester.

Reviewing behaviour

Task: What does your Theory A/Theory B say?

What would you say *your* Theory A is? And what would be another way of thinking about it? In other words, what does Theory B say the problem is?

Fill in the first row of the table here or on a copy of the Theory A/Theory B worksheet, or under headings written on a sheet of paper. We'll be developing the Theory A/Theory B idea further throughout this chapter.

My personal Theory A/Theory B	
Theory A: OCD says my problem is _____ **Belief:** _____ %	**Theory B:** My problem is _____ _____ **Belief:** _____ %
Evidence for Theory A: **Belief:** _____ %	**Evidence for Theory B:** **Belief:** _____ %
What I need to do to solve this problem:	**What I need to do to solve this worry problem:**

What's the evidence?

Pause for a while and consider your experience of OCD. Each of our real-life examples has based their Theory A conclusion on evidence from their own experience, and no doubt you have too. Perhaps you haven't thought of it in terms of Theory B before – that it's a worry problem. Which of the two theories seems the most likely? They can't both be true. Now, it wouldn't be reasonable to expect you to just accept this new idea. It makes sense to look for **evidence** for both. Shall we see what kinds of evidence the individuals in our real-life examples came up with?

	Theory A: OCD says my problem is …	Theory B: My problem is …
Maxine	I'm smelly and dirty.	I worry that I'm smelly and dirty.
	Evidence for Theory A: My things have a funny smell that other people are bound to notice. I can smell my armpits when I get too hot. I seem to get BO all the time.	**Evidence for Theory B:** Other people don't wash or clean as much as I do yet they don't seem to smell bad. I've always been sensitive to smells. I seem to get sweatier when I'm really worried. All the things I do make me worry more, not less.
Tadeusz	My home could be burgled/burn down/ flood.	I worry about my home being burgled/burning down/flooding.
	Evidence for Theory A: A house burned down in the neighbourhood when I was young.	**Evidence for Theory B:** I never used to worry about these things – it started when I got a place of my own.

	I read somewhere that electrical appliances cause fires and that they should be unplugged.	I see danger in everything
		My friend leaves his computer switched on and his phone charging all night and seems to think it's fine.
		I have to check more when I'm under a lot of stress.
David	I have bad judgement.	I worry that I have bad judgement.
	Evidence for Theory A: I have doubts about everything I do, so it must be true.	**Evidence for Theory B:** I've always been a worrier.
	I get really anxious when I have to make decisions, especially at work.	When I get anxious I find it harder to concentrate and that makes me more doubtful.
	My manager was annoyed when I couldn't find the file she wanted.	I'm very sensitive to people getting annoyed with me since being bullied at school.
Sahib	I'm a pervert.	I worry that I'm a pervert.
	Evidence for Theory A: I always notice parts of peoples' bodies that I shouldn't.	**Evidence for Theory B:** I don't suppose I'd be upset by these kinds of thoughts if I really was a pervert.
	I get so many of these thoughts it must be true.	The guys at work often make jokey comments about each others' bodies and just laugh about it.
		There's been such a lot in the news about TV presenters and sexual abuse that I've found it hard not to think about it.

Carol admitted that she didn't really have any hard evidence that she was a dangerous person. She'd never harmed anyone in the past – she just *felt* dangerous, partly because she got lots of thoughts that upset her. Similarly, Arun's only 'evidence' was that it felt wrong to ignore these urges. He went on to say that he thought superstitions were rather silly and sheepishly suggested that maybe what *he* was doing was just a kind of 'home-made' superstition. From all the things she'd read on the internet and in magazines, Janet knew there were all kinds of dangers from faeces. What's more, dogs seemed to foul everywhere. She'd never known anyone personally who'd gone blind or become seriously ill, although an old boyfriend had got an infection in a wound when he'd skidded on his knees when playing rugby. Although she wasn't sure, she thought it was from some dog faeces. But it had cleared up easily with a course of antibiotics. She agreed that she might have a tendency to over-react to these things since she hadn't used to be so worried before her son was born, and there probably wasn't any more dog mess around these days.

Reviewing behaviour

Task: What's your evidence?

Go back to your personal Theory A/Theory B and ask yourself what evidence you have for each of the theories.

- Think about your experiences, the things that have happened to you.
- How do other people behave in similar situations?
- Is your evidence based on facts or just how you feel?
- Have you always had these concerns?
- If you didn't get anxious or distressed, would you still do things in the same way?

Add your evidence to your personal Theory A/Theory B table and re-rate your belief in light of this evidence.

Finding the right solution to the problem

Have you noticed how looking at evidence for both theories has already led to a shift in how much Maxine and the others believe Theory A? Considering any evidence they have has already helped to open them up to other possible explanations for the thoughts they've been having. Of course, we wouldn't expect them to suddenly accept this alternative view. At this point, you don't need to make a decision either about which of the two theories is likely to be correct. However, we do need to consider whether or not the strategies that might be helpful if Theory A is true would help us to solve a problem of a different kind – a **worry problem**.

Let's take another look at Maxine's problem. OCD is telling her that she's dirty and smelly. If indeed that was the case, it would make sense for her to be extra careful to keep herself clean and fresh. It might even be a good idea to avoid eating food that has a lingering smell to make sure she doesn't cause offence to others. But if the problem is really that she is someone who worries a lot about being clean and fragrant, what is likely to happen if she tries to deal with it using the strategies listed for Theory A? Will it make her feel more worried or less worried in the long term?

There are several ways in which it is likely to keep going her worries about being dirty and smelly. For one thing, Maxine would always have to be on the look-out for potential problems. That would keep the concern about smells on her mind all of the time. In order to deal with this worry problem, Maxine needs to stop using Theory A solutions and take another approach to dealing with the problem. Take a look at what she needs to do to solve Theory B.

Maxine	
Theory A: OCD says I'm dirty and smelly.	**Theory B:** My problem is that I worry that I'm dirty and smelly.
Belief: 50% (previously 100%)	**Belief:** 100 %
What I need to do to solve this problem: Change into clean clothes several times a day. Keep clean and dirty things separate/in bags. Have a bath or shower if I've done anything that might make me smell. Make sure I use lots of toilet paper (and wet wipes) after a 'number 2'. Clean my flat really thoroughly. Use lots of nice-smelling cleaning products. Throw out anything that can't be washed. Avoid eating smelly foods like fish, garlic, curry. Don't cook anything at home to prevent smells getting into my things. Wipe my mouth after every mouthful to prevent my face absorbing horrible smells. Hold food with a napkin so it doesn't get on my hands.	**What I need to do to solve this worry problem:** Allow thoughts and worries about being dirty or smelly come and go without washing, cleaning, etc. Treat these concerns as worries and not facts. Eat whatever food I fancy without washing or changing my clothes. Put clean clothes on in the morning. Wear some items of clothing several times without washing them, e.g. coat, jeans. Keep clothes in the wardrobe. Put dirty clothes in the laundry basket. Bath or shower a maxiumum of once a day. Stop using wet wipes. Clean my flat once a week. Just use a damp cloth for wiping up spills. Stop using air-fresheners. Eat sandwiches and chips with my bare fingers. Cook a curry at home.

What kind of things would Tadeuz be doing to tackle his problem as if it was a worry problem?

Tadeusz	
Theory A: OCD says my home will be burgled/burn down/flood unless I'm really careful.	**Theory B:** My problem is that I worry that my home will be burgled/burn down/flood unless I'm really careful.
Belief: 50% (previously 85%)	**Belief:** 90%
What I need to do to solve this problem: Check doors, windows, gas, electric, taps. Check again if I feel uncertain. Never leave electrical things plugged in. Turn all lights and appliances off before going to bed or leaving the house. Use a wind-up alarm clock instead of clock-radio. Check things in a systematic way. Repeat things like 'window, window' so I can feel sure I've checked it. Take photos of the kettle, taps, door on my phone so I can check that they're OK if I get worried when I'm at work. Don't use kettle, toaster or anything else that might get hot before going to work in the morning. Always wait until the cooker or other appliances have cooled down before going to bed or leaving the house. Put sink plugs on the window ledge so they can't fall in and cause a flood.	**What I need to do to solve this worry problem:** Ignore thoughts about bad things that could happen. Don't check anything more than once even if I feel uncertain. Leave things like the microwave, kettle, TV, clock-radio, computer plugged in all the time. Just close windows I know I've opened without checking the others. Turn taps off with a gentle twist. Stop taking photos on my phone. Have coffee and toast for breakfast before going to work. Make a hot drink before bed. Leave a casserole to cook in the oven while I go to the shop or for a walk. Leave plugs on the sink, wash basin and bath.

And how about David?

David	
Theory A: OCD says my judgement is poor.	**Theory B:** My problem is that I worry that my judgement is poor.
Belief: 60% (previously 99 %)	**Belief:** 50%
What I need to do to solve this problem: Read and reread everything until I feel certain. Avoid making decisions about important things, e.g. anything work or finance related. Keep all mail (including junk mail). Never throw anything out unless I'm certain it's not important. Shred anything with personal details or things to do with money, e.g. till receipts. Always double-check with my mother before shredding.	**What I need to do to solve this worry problem:** Treat these worries as just worries. Read things only once. Keep on reading without going back, even if I'm not sure whether or not I've understood it. Throw junk mail out straightaway. Throw away till receipts unless they're for expensive items or things with a guarantee. Keep bank statements and share certificates. Throw away the letters that come with them (in the bin!). Only use a shredder for bank/credit card statements. Don't ask my mother for reassurance. Daily filing at work (don't let it build up). Decide for myself where things should be filed. Allow myself to make some small mistakes with filing.

Let's have a look at Sahib's Theory B solutions.

Sahib	
Theory A: My OCD says I'm a pervert.	**Theory B:** My problem is that I worry that I'm a pervert.
Belief: 25% (previously 50–75%)	**Belief:** 100%
What I need to do to solve this problem: Avoid looking at women at the gym.	**What I need to do to solve this worry problem:** Ignore the thoughts.
Try not to notice women's breasts.	Wear my contact lenses.
Avoid looking at men's groins.	Look around at everyone in my class.
Take my contact lenses out before a gym class so I can't see details.	Allow my gaze to drift wherever it chooses.
Avoid using the changing rooms.	Use the changing rooms.
Get changed in the staff toilet and shower at home.	Stop monitoring my body.
Concentrate on looking only at men's faces.	Don't keep questioning myself.
Try to convince myself I'm not gay.	Don't think about my girlfriend just because I've had an unwanted thought.
Think about my girlfriend whenever I get thoughts about being a pervert.	Treat worries as worries.
Check to see if I'm getting physically aroused when I see women, e.g. on television.	

Reviewing behaviour

Task

What ideas do you think Carol, Janet, Arun, Stefan and Mandy came up with in order to tackle their problem according to Theory B – a worry problem?

- What would their Theory B say?
- What kind of things do you think they need to do?

You can either use this table to write down your ideas or put them on a sheet of paper.

	Theory B: My problem is …	**What I need to do to solve this worry problem**
Carol	I worry that …	
Janet	I worry that …	
Arun	I worry that …	
Stefan	I worry that …	
Mandy	I worry that …	

How do your ideas compare with what they came up with? What do you think about their ideas? Did you come up with something different?

	Theory B: My problem is …	**What I need to do to solve this worry problem**
Carol	I worry that I'm a dangerous person.	Treat the thoughts as 'brain spam'.
		Keep sharp knives in the kitchen drawer.
		Use sharp knives for preparing food even if family are in the kitchen.
		Watch soaps and dramas on TV.
		Read the newspaper.
		Take the dog for walk with my daughter.
		Visit my family.
Janet	I worry that dog poo is dangerous.	Don't change clothes when I (or family) come in the house.
		Go out without a coat or gloves (apart from in the winter).
		Invite friends to the house.
		Hang washing out on the clothes line.
		Go for a walk in the park.
		Stroke friendly dogs.
		Ditch the hand gel.
Arun	I worry that bad things will happen unless I do things a certain way.	Do things, e.g washing hands, only once.
		Don't check keys or phone.
		Keep walking even if I get a 'bad' thought.
		Treat thoughts as worries, not real dangers.
		Stop tapping and touching things.
		Allow myself to feel doubtful – the feeling won't last forever.

Stefan	I worry that certain numbers are unlucky.	Ignore thoughts about numbers.
		Buy things in packs of four.
		Sit with my mates at work, no matter how many are at the table.
		Stop doing sums! Don't deliberately look out for number plates.
Mandy	I worry that I'm a child molester.	Change Betsy's nappy.
		Give her a bath.
		Play cuddling and tickling games with her.
		Don't keep trying to work out why I'm having these thoughts.
		Thoughts are just thoughts, not a sign of danger.
		Enjoy doing all the things mums do.

Reviewing behaviour

Task: Are you using the right solution to your problem?

In our various examples, we've seen that the kinds of things that we would need to do to solve a danger problem are different from the things that would help to solve a worry problem.

So far you've been treating your problem according to Theory A. Make a list of all the things that you currently do that fit with this way of viewing the problem. Write them in the last row in the left-hand column of the table, just beneath your Evidence for Theory A. These might be sensible precautions if your problem was danger. But the same precautions wouldn't be at all helpful to deal with a problem of worrying about danger. What would be a more helpful way of dealing with these worries?

Write your ideas down in the last row in the right-hand column, under the heading 'What I need to do to solve this *worry* problem'.

Chapter summary

Now that you've finished this chapter, you have:

- developed a less threatening way of looking at the problem
- discovered that there might be a more helpful way of tackling your problem
- drawn up your personal Theory A/Theory B.

In this chapter, we explored the possibility that there is a less threatening way of thinking about your problem: that it's a problem of excessive worry rather than one of danger. These two very different problems require different solutions. But which of them is most likely to be true? Maybe OCD conned you into believing your problem really is that you're dirty, dangerous or deviant or that there's good reason to doubt. As a result, you developed strategies for dealing with the problem you believed you had. Using the wrong solution to the problem will make us feel *more* worried rather than less worried. There seems to be far more evidence for OCD as a worry problem. Has the way in which you've been trying to deal with OCD helped so far? Maybe it's time to change what you're doing.

Are you ready to try out the ideas you developed for tackling OCD as a worry problem? In Chapter 8 you can find out how to make change possible and use these ideas as the start of your action plan.

Practical advice ⇒

How to make the most of this book

This might seem like an odd point at which to first make some practical suggestions about how you can make the most of this book. I make no apology for this. Many of my clients have come to me following numerous attempts at 'self help' using books like this one and have become frustrated and disheartened when all their reading hasn't brought about the changes they hoped for. They have read so much, eagerly bought every OCD book they could find and yet they still struggled with OCD in their lives. The reason is often this: they have focused on *reading* the books, and although they may have gone through the exercises these books usually contain, they have done so in their heads while continuing to read. I wonder if this is what you have been doing? If not – fantastic! I'm really pleased that you have taken the time to complete the written exercises and make notes. I hope that this is beginning to pay off in terms of helping you to better understand OCD and how it works, and encouraging you to make the necessary changes to break free from OCD. Some of the following ideas and suggestions may further enhance the benefits of following this self-help programme.

Don't be embarrassed, though, if you have simply read through to this point. You're in good company, and it is often helpful to go through the book before returning to the beginning and *working* your way through the exercises and practical suggestions. It's a bit like getting a new gadget (in this case, it's the book that's the gadget); you're so keen to get it going that you're too impatient to read the instructions and then find you can't get it to work properly. At this point, you might choose to continue to read to the end to get an idea of what tackling OCD is all about, or you might decide to finish reading the hints and tips in this chapter and then make a start in a more effective way.

In order to make the most of using this self-help book, I recommend that you follow these suggestions:

- make some notes
- complete all the exercises
- record yourself
- listen to your recordings.

These recommendations are based on my many years of clinical practice. I've found that those clients who have made the most improvement, and (perhaps even more importantly) managed to maintain these improvements long after we stopped meeting, have approached therapy in a systematic and orderly manner. Self-help books are therapy too, but in some ways it's even more important to be disciplined in the way you work on your difficulties. After all, you haven't got a therapist to nag or remind you.

Make some notes

It seems obvious, but note-making is helpful in so many ways. For a start, most of us aren't blessed with an amazing memory so when we read we tend to forget most of it instantly. By making your own notes, you can focus on those things that you have found especially interesting, useful or relevant to *your* experience of OCD. That's often a criticism of self-help OCD books: they discuss many different types of obsessional difficulties but only some of it fits your individual problem, or perhaps it doesn't really refer to your own concerns, although you find the general discussions helpful. If you've found there is little or no mention of your specific concerns here, you can rewrite some of the things you've read to include them. Because OCD is so idiosyncratic, it's impossible to make the whole book completely relevant to each person who reads it. However, the general principles will apply even if the examples given do not. The tasks and exercises throughout the book are intended to help you in creating your own personalized treatment handbook.

I would also encourage you to write some brief summaries of where you're at with your OCD at various times, particularly at the start when your OCD is probably pretty bad. Make some (detailed) notes of things that you are concerned about, the kind of things you feel compelled to do and things that you avoid doing or struggle to do because of the problem. Very often, as things improve you may lose sight of just how difficult things had been. In part, it's because we often just take what we're able to do now for granted and forget how hard it may have been to reach this point. For example, following an operation you may have been unable to lift anything heavier than a bag of sugar for some time. Eventually, you regain the ability to lift heavier things. It will probably have been a gradual change, but you have slowly rebuilt the necessary muscles until you can happily lift a couple of heavy shopping bags without giving it a second thought.

A notebook is a better idea than loose bits of paper. It means that notes won't go astray, or end up in the wrong order. Don't worry about your handwriting or spelling, or even writing it 'properly'. It's for your eyes only, and as long as you can read it and it makes sense to you, that's fine. However, it is better to explain things clearly rather than just put a few words, or you may return to notes some months later and puzzle over what you actually meant by one or two cryptic words. You can also use your notebook to 'guide' your reading. Just reading is a bit like revising for an exam. It's hard to know whether or not we have learned or understood something without knowing what the question is that we're trying to answer. So before you sit down to read a chapter, take a few moments to jot down two or three short questions that you would like to know the answer to. For example, 'Why doesn't reassurance make me feel better for longer?' or 'What steps can I take to get a better night's sleep?' Then after you've read the chapter, write down an answer to these questions. Try it from memory first – you can always go back to the relevant sections to add to your notes if you need to (be careful that it's not just an OCD doubt that is tricking you into thinking you haven't understood it). The idea is that you can build up your own personalized 'treatment manual' which also includes a diary of your progress. You can use this to refer back to in the future, either to remind yourself of how far you've come in combating OCD or to zap any blips that might occur along the way.

Record yourself

I know what you're thinking but don't just skip to the next section – this really can be helpful. And now that we have so much technology at our fingertips it can be very straightforward. Most phones are able to do voice recordings; have a look in your apps, or find a free download to enable you to make a recording. I always encourage my clients to record our sessions each time we meet and to listen to them before our next meeting. There are some good reasons for doing this.

- What we can remember of the session is limited. It's hard to remember everything that we spoke about and easy to forget details that we thought were really interesting and/or important at the time. Even if you believe you can recall most of what was said, there will most likely be things that you had forgotten or simply missed.
- It's a very different experience when you're there 'in the moment', trying to talk, think, listen and remember, with the added complication of how you might be feeling at that particular point. For example, if you're feeling anxious or upset at the time it makes it much harder to do any of those things.
- We get a completely different experience. We can gain some 'emotional distance' when we listen to the recordings, as we're likely to be in a different frame of mind or mood. It can be like listening to someone else talking about their experiences on a radio programme,

or hearing a friend explain how they have been feeling. Although you might be able to empathize with what they are experiencing, you are likely to feel less emotionally caught up in what is being said and so take a calmer and more balanced viewpoint.

Of course, making a recording might seem as if it makes more sense when a therapist and a client are in a real-life therapy session. But it is possible to put recordings to good use when using a self-help approach. It can be a particularly useful strategy if you find it hard to write detailed responses to the exercises in the book. Try some of these suggestions.

- Imagine you're talking to a therapist or a supportive friend. If it feels too weird talking out loud to no one, you could try 'talking to' a photograph, a soft toy or even a pet (although pets have a tendency to walk away when we're in mid-sentence without so much as a by-your-leave – not an ideal quality in a therapist, either real or imaginary!) Tell them about your OCD difficulties, the way it affects you in your everyday life. Explain the kinds of things you feel you have to do, and any activities or situations that you have to avoid because of your difficulties. You won't be interrupted by someone telling you all about *their* troubles in return or told to 'pull yourself together'. It may well be the first time you've ever voiced your concerns aloud, and that can feel very uncomfortable for many reasons; you might feel embarrassed or ashamed, for example. Or giving voice to your concerns might make your worries feel more real, triggering more intrusive thoughts. Or maybe verbalizing them makes them sound silly or pathetic.
- Record yourself when carrying out rituals. Again, you can use your phone for this – on many mobile phones these days it's easy to make video recordings, although an audio recording is fine too. Explain what triggered off the need to carry out a ritual, describe what you're doing and in what way it seems to be helpful, define how you decide when it's OK to stop doing whatever it is that you're doing, and so on.
- Make sure you make time to listen to your recording before making the next one. This is the advice I always give to clients who are working directly with me. It's far more helpful to make use of the recording before the next 'session' (or, for the purposes of this self-help

book, before moving on to the next step or chapter). Human nature being what it is, we tend to put off things we don't really want to do, and there may be reasons why you would want to put off listening. A common defence is not wanting to hear your own voice. It *is* a peculiar experience and everyone tends to cringe when they hear themselves for the first time – 'Please tell me I don't really sound like that!' is a plea I often hear. Even after many years, hearing my own voice in recordings can make my toes curl. I tend to notice every little flaw or hesitation, every cough or 'um ..' as well as features of my accent that seem to shout which part of the country I'm from. But although you will find yourself paying attention to these things yourself, if you keep listening despite your 'inner critic' picking up on all of these things, it will get easier and you will find yourself listening increasingly to what is being said rather than how you're saying it. It's another example of how you can unhook yourself from how it feels to hear yourself. After all, if you heard someone with a similar accent to yours on the TV or radio, would you stop watching or listening?

When you listen, imagine that you are listening to a friend telling you about the difficulties he or she has been experiencing. Pretend that you haven't heard what they are saying before, and jot down any questions that you would want to ask for clarification. Maybe you would like to be able to ask more about what they feel, or what makes them believe that they need to carry out certain actions to prevent bad things from happening.

Once you have some additional questions, spend some time answering them. Again, it can be helpful to do this aloud and to record your response. Most people find that they can go into a lot more detail and give fuller explanations of what they think, feel or do if they just talk about it. You could then write it down in your notes so that you can look at it again in the future, and use the information for exercises and tasks that you come across later in the book. By the way, it probably isn't the best idea to think that you could just listen to it all over again. It would take a lot of time, and be very difficult to find the exact bit you were looking for. Far better to write a few notes in which you summarize the key points and then if you choose to keep the recordings, you will have a better idea where to find what you wanted to hear again.

PART 3

Escape

Learn how to let go of intrusive thoughts and replace old behaviours with more helpful ones

CHAPTER 8

Getting to where you want to go

Overview

In Chapter 7, you discovered another (less threatening) way of looking at OCD and how different strategies are needed to deal with it. In this chapter, we're going to look at how you can make possible and look at:

- why goals are important
- the features of clear therapy goals
- how our case studies tackle their OCD
- where to begin when setting your own goals.

Now that we've begun to take a different view of what OCD actually is – that it is a *worry* problem rather than a danger problem – you may already be considering what might be a more helpful way of approaching it. Even when we have decided that 'Yes, things need to change …', we often still feel uncertain about whether we're doing the right thing. And it's common to wonder what the 'right thing' is, let alone how we're going to manage to do it. No matter what we want to do or achieve, it always helps to have a plan. This is especially true when we want things to be different. Wishing, hoping and dreaming for things to be different isn't enough to bring about changes. Our hopes and dreams can provide a starting point, but without taking some action they will remain just that. To make change not only possible but also manageable, there are three things we need to identify:

1 Goals – what do you want to achieve?
2 Objectives – how can you break this into smaller steps?
3 Strategy – where should you start?

Goals and their importance

Goals are important because they give us an idea of what we want and what we need to do in order to reach them. Although we might not realize it, our everyday lives are driven by lots of goals. They might be big goals or small goals. Wanting to get dinner ready by one o'clock, saving up for a holiday, training for a marathon – these are all examples of goals. Even choosing to read this book can be seen as a goal-driven behaviour: wanting to learn more about OCD or finding out how to overcome it. Yet it is even more important to have goals to help us achieve our bigger aims in life, like pursuing a career. Or tackling a problem like OCD that has had a major impact on your life.

Good goals get us where we want to go. We can think of goals as a destination: it's a place we want to get to. It's not enough just to know where we want to go; we also have to know how we will get there. To do this, we need to plan our route. First, we need a rough idea of the direction we should be going: north or south? Which major towns or cities will we pass through? And then we might want to schedule a coffee break or a stop for lunch, but we wouldn't want that to be just minutes after we've set off or within a mile of our destination. It needs planning with some clear objectives, e.g. estimate where we'll be after an hour or so, where the closest services would be, whether we're likely to need another stop etc. We might even make some alternative plans in case we hit a traffic jam or make such good time that we could fit in a spot of sightseeing on the way.

When clients come to see me, I always ask what they hope to achieve from therapy. In other words, what goals do they have. Mandy wanted to 'get rid of OCD 'and enjoy being a mum to Betsy. David said he'd like to 'feel better' and keep on top of paperwork, both at home and at work. While these wishes certainly tell us what we want to be different in our lives, they don't help us to know what we need to do to make it possible. In other words, they don't tell us which way to go.

Although our principle goal is to overcome OCD, we need to understand what this means for us individually. What would you be doing if you *didn't* have OCD? If you can't imagine what your life would be like without OCD, what do other people (friends, family, colleagues) do that you would like to be able to do or find it difficult to do?

● What do I need to do more of?
● What do I need to do less of (or stop doing)?
● What do I need to do differently?

David needed to throw out junk mail and other papers more often, and do the filing at work without allowing it to build up, Tadeusz needed to stop checking and taking photos on his phone, and do the kinds of things that most people do at home, like making a cup of tea before work and leaving the television on stand-by. Sahib needed to act in a relaxed and friendly way with people in his spin class, and allow his gaze to fall on any part of their body. Maxine needed to cook and eat all kinds of dishes, whether or not they made things smelly. Breaking these individual goals into smaller steps or **objectives** gives us a clearer idea of what we need to do. Together, they make up a **strategy**, or plan.

Most of our goals, whether they are goals to challenge our OCD or more general life-goals, can't be achieved in just one simple step. We often need a strategy or plan made up of several smaller steps or objectives. By tackling smaller steps one at a time, not only does it help us to move towards our objective in a graded way but helps us to gain confidence as we begin to achieve more and more. It's a bit like learning to drive: our ultimate goal might be to drive on the motorway, but if we've never even sat behind the steering wheel of a car before, the prospect would seem rather daunting. If instead we break it down into smaller steps with clear objectives for what we will do by the end of the first lesson up to when we take our driving test (and then beyond that) it will seem far more 'do-able'.

Our 'Theory B' approach (which we developed in Chapter 7) begins to give us some ideas about the kinds of goals that might be helpful – 'What do I need to solve this worry problem?' – but doesn't necessarily give us enough information about how that general aim might be achieved.

SMART goals

How can we make sure that our goals for tackling OCD will get us to where we want to go? What we need are some **SMART** goals. SMART goals have five features; they are:

Specific
Measurable
Achievable
Realistic
Timely.

Specific

It's important that your goals are specific. This will help you to know exactly what you need to do in order to reach that goal. While our Theory B ideas are a good starting point, they may not be specific enough to help us plan a good strategy for tackling OCD. They might be too vague. Let's have a look at some of them.

	Vague	Specific
Mandy	Enjoy doing all the things mothers do.	Change Betsy's nappy. Give her a bath. Play cuddling and tickling games with her.
David	Keep on top of the filing. Don't let letters accumulate at home.	Throw out junk mail straight away. Keep on reading without going back, even if I'm not sure whether or not I've understood it.

	Vague	Specific
Maxine	Allow thoughts and worries about being dirty or smelly to come and go without washing, cleaning etc.	Eat sandwiches and chips with my bare fingers. Wear some items of clothing several times without washing them, e.g. coat, jeans.
Tadeusz	Ignore thoughts about bad things that could happen.	Have coffee and toast for breakfast before going to work. Make a hot drink before going to bed. Leave a casserole to cook in the oven while I go to the shop or for a walk.
Carol	Watch the TV. Read the newspaper.	Keep sharp knives in the kitchen drawer. Use sharp knives for preparing food even if family are in the kitchen. Look for stories about murders etc. in the newspaper. Watch soaps and dramas with violent scenes.
Janet	Don't change clothes when I (or family) come in the house. Go for a walk in the park.	Hang washing out on the clothes line. Use a dog photo as a screensaver on my phone and laptop. Stroke friendly dogs.
Stefan	Ignore thoughts about numbers.	Buy things in packs of four at least five times each week.

		Sit with my mates at work, no matter how many are at the table.
Arun	Disregard urges to repeat actions.	Leave the room at least once during a meeting so I can practise walking in without repeating.
		Take keys and phone out of my pockets whenever I'm in a place for more than five minutes, e.g. car, restaurant, office, barbers.
Sahib	Just let the thoughts come.	Look everyone on the front row bikes up and down at the start and end of each class.

So you can see that most of the people in our case studies have a mixture of vague and specific goals. With a little tweaking, even their vague goals can be turned into something specific. We'll come back to that shortly.

Measurable

It's much easier to stay on track when you measure your progress. It will give you a far better idea of how well you're doing and how far you have progressed on your personal journey. Useful questions to ask yourself are:

● how much?
● how many?
● how will I know when I've achieved it?

Tadeusz planned to have coffee and toast for breakfast three times a week. Arun would make an excuse to leave the room at least once during a meeting. Stefan would buy lots of things in packs of four until it no longer bothered him to do so.

It can give you a real sense of achievement to be able to look back at the things you have done and be able to say, 'I did that'. It also helps to identify what you might need to do next to increase your success.

Achievable

Without a clear understanding about the nature of thoughts and OCD, a common goal is to 'stop having these thoughts'. If that's still your main goal, it might be a good idea to have another look at Chapter 3, to recap on why this is not a helpful goal to have. To have a chance of success in meeting our goals, we need to make sure we're not attempting something impossible. An impossible goal might be things that no one could ever achieve, such as never having intrusive thoughts, or being certain that nothing bad will ever happen to us at any time in the future. It can also be things that are too big a step for us to work on right now. It doesn't mean we shouldn't have big goals; it just means we have to think carefully about the steps we need to take in order to increase the likelihood of having success with it.

For Janet, it was too big a step for her to stroke a dog after years of avoiding anything remotely dog-related. Similarly, Maxine hadn't done any cooking in her home, let alone strongly aromatic dishes like curry or fish, so it made sense to start with something less challenging.

Another way to think about the 'A' in SMART is that not only should the goals be achievable, but they should be **active**, i.e. things you will *do*, rather than what you won't do or plan to stop doing. It's easier to motivate ourselves to do something rather than to stop doing it. For example, if you're trying to lose weight you're more likely to stick to a goal such as 'Eat an apple when you feel peckish' rather than 'Don't eat chocolate or cake'. It gives you an alternative – something you can do instead. And that is a message that is at the heart of learning how to live your life free from OCD: we have a choice.

Realistic

Part of what makes a goal achievable is that it is also realistic. Since Maxine hadn't cooked anything at home, a realistic goal for her to begin with was to cook some less aromatic foods. Notice that Tadeusz didn't aim to make toast and coffee every day of the week: he sometimes had to leave early for meetings so didn't have time to sit down for breakfast, preferring to grab something at the station. It wouldn't have been realistic for Mandy to change Betsy's nappy every time it needed changing as her grandma enjoyed looking after Betsy whenever she came to visit. And of course, Stefan couldn't guarantee that three of his mates would already be seated by the time he went to join them.

As well as being realistic, goals should also be **relevant**. We're more likely to stick to a relevant goal. If Maxine hated curry, she would hardly be bothered to cook it. Nor would Mandy consider taking up football. It's important too that the goals are relevant to the problems you identified in Chapter 3.

Timely

While we could make one big list of goals to work towards, a better strategy is to arrange them in a timely way. Having a clear timescale helps us to work towards our goals. If we don't set ourselves a timescale for working on particular goals, it's all too easy to put off whatever we'd planned to do – most of us are excellent procrastinators! You might have come across the sceptical retort, 'This year, next year, sometime, never' to a half-hearted promise to get something done.

To make timely goals, try breaking them into short-, medium- and long-term goals. Ask yourself what you would like to achieve:

- in the next month
- in the next three months
- in the next year.

Some of your goals, especially the medium- or long-term ones, may include more general life-goals, although they should consist mainly of

OCD-related goals. It's harder to be really specific about medium- and long-term goals because we cannot know for certain what kinds of activities or situations will still be a challenge for us once we've already made some changes.

GOALS	Short-term	Medium-term	Long-term
Mandy	Change Betsy's nappy. Give her a bath. Play cuddling and tickling games with her.	Help my friend bath her baby (due in 11 weeks).	Let Betsy run around without a nappy. Have another baby. Become a child-minder.
David	Throw away till receipts, e.g. for magazines, groceries. Do the filing each day, even if I have doubts. Read the newspaper for 15 minutes every day; keep reading even if I have doubts.	Throw away junk mail as soon as it arrives. Put non-confidential papers in the recycling bin. Read a book for 30 mins or more at least four times a week.	Apply for promotion.
Maxine	Keep the same clothes on all day, even after eating. Eat a sandwich with my bare fingers.	Wear the same jeans for three days. Eat 'smelly' sandwiches, e.g. tuna or salami, with bare fingers without washing afterwards.	Have a friend to stay. Get a lodger.

	Use a paper napkin to wipe my hands instead of a wet-wipe. Cook beans or egg on toast (or similar) five times a week. Wipe visibly dirty surfaces or spills with a damp cloth only.	Eat a takeaway at home. Cook a curry. Invite a friend round (either for curry or the next day).	
Tadeusz	Iron my shirt before going to work. Turn taps off gently. Leave a light on while I am out. Leave appliances plugged in all the time (kettle, TV, table lamps, radio-alarm, etc).	Leave the iron plugged in and the fire on while I go for a walk. Leave the plugs in the sink and bath. Set the automatic timer to cook a meal ready for when I come in from work.	Go on holiday for two weeks.
Carol	Keep sharp knives in the kitchen drawer. Use a sharp knife for peeling veg. Knit while I watch my favourite soap (at least three times week).	Use sharp knives for preparing food even if family are in the kitchen. Walk the dog with my daughter (and carry the lead while the dog has a run).	Babysit my nephew and niece.

GOALS	Short-term	Medium-term	Long-term
	Stick up names of killers in the kitchen, bathroom and bedroom. Visit my brother and his family on Saturday.	Watch a murder film with my husband. Read a thriller where the killer is a woman. Spend an hour alone with my granddad on Tuesdays and Fridays.	
Janet	Go to the shops without a coat. Keep the same clothes on indoors after going to the shops. Go for a walk in the park twice a week. Use a dog photo as a screensaver on my phone and laptop. Let my son wear his dirty football kit while he sits with a drink in the kitchen.	Hang washing out on the clothes line. Lie on the bed in my 'outdoor' clothes. Sit on a park bench. Walk behind a dog-walker. Let my son get undressed upstairs and put his dirty kit in the washing basket.	Go for a picnic and sit on the grass. Stroke a dog. Be on the rota for washing the whole football team's kit.
Stefan	Buy things in packs of four. Wear a football shirt with '4' on the back.	Invite three friends home to make a foursome.	Book a flight home on 6/6.

	Sit with my mates at work, no matter how many are at the table.	Buy three six-packs of lager to share with my mates.	
Arun	Keep walking even when I get a 'bad' thought. At meetings, leave the room at least once so I can practise walking in without repeating. Take keys and phone out of my pockets whenever I'm in a place for more than five minutes, e.g. the car, restaurant, office, barbers (and don't check after I've put them back).	Agree with my 'bad' thoughts instead of arguing with them. Deliberately think a 'bad' thought as I walk into the room (do the opposite of what OCD is telling me).	Run a half-marathon.
Sahib	Look gym goers in the eye when I speak to them. Purposely look at strangers on the bus or in the street and imagine them naked.	Look everyone on the front-row bikes up and down at the start and end of each class.	Get married to my girlfriend next April.

GOALS	Short-term	Medium-term	Long-term
	Agree with thoughts, e.g. that I'm a perv or don't love my girlfriend.	Watch *Brokeback Mountain* with my girlfriend.	

Planning your goals

It's a good idea to begin with the short-term goals that will get you moving towards living your life free from OCD. Have a look at your Theory B to get you started.

It might sound weird, but to start with something slightly challenging can be easier to tackle than something that seems really easy and straightforward. Goals that are too low often lower our motivation. It's better to aim high and miss than aim low and achieve our goal … or is it? Although we shouldn't set our goals so low that we don't get a sense of achievement when we've stepped up to the challenge, it's equally important not to set the bar so high that it seems impossible. If some of your Theory B goals seem too much, ask yourself what you are prepared to do. What else could you do then to stretch you that bit more? Just because a goal seems too much of a challenge doesn't make it impossible – it only needs to be broken down into more manageable stages.

Every journey begins with the first step. Even if the steps are only small ones, as long as we keep taking steps in the same direction, we will get to where we want to go.

To get you started, here's a reminder of the three things you need to know.

1 Goals – what do you want to achieve?
2 Objectives – how can you break this into smaller steps?
3 Strategy – where should you start?

And consider also the magic wand question. Imagine that during the night a fairy waved her magic wand over you and sprinkled some magical fairy dust while you were asleep. When you woke up in the morning, you no longer had OCD. What kinds of differences would you notice that would make you think that something magical had happened?

- What would you do differently?
- What would you be doing more of?
- What would you be doing less of, or have stopped doing?

Sadly, it's highly unlikely that a good fairy will wave her magic wand over us. But just supposing she did:

- What would be the first thing you'd want to do in your new OCD-free day?
- How often does that happen now?
- What kind of steps could you take to make it happen more often?
- If you kept taking those steps, what effect would that have on your life?

Reviewing behaviour

Task: Identifying my goals

What are my main goals? What are the key things I would like to do?

1 _____

2 _____

3 _____

4 _____

If you have more than four main goals, that's fine. Just add them to your list.

Planning the strategy for reaching your goals

Now that you have some goals, how are you going to achieve them? Think about the main goals you have just made a note of, and take into account your answers to the 'magic wand' question. What are the individual steps or objectives that will help you work towards your main goals? Here are some questions to help you.

- What can I do today to tackle OCD? Or even right now?
- What could I do to challenge OCD just a bit more?
- What can I do in the next month?
- What could I do in the next three months?

These objectives form part of your **strategy** for tackling OCD in a systematic way.

Behaviour changing strategy

Task

Now that you have identified some of your goals, write them down. Vague goals are unachievable. Writing them down stops the goals being vague. It also means we won't forget what we are working towards and that we won't keep moving the goalposts (in either direction).

You can either use the goals list here or make a copy of it. Or if you prefer, you can write your goals down in a notebook, on a large sheet of paper or on your smart phone or computer. But make sure that you can look at the list regularly.

Finally, are each of your goals and objectives SMART enough? How well do they stand up against the requirement to be: **S**pecific, **M**easurable, **A**chievable, **R**ealistic and **T**imely?

My main goals or aims	Short-term (e.g. what I will do today and this week)	Medium term (e.g. what I will do this month)	Long-term (e.g. what I would like to do in the next three/six/12 months)
1	1 2 3 4 5 6	1 2 3 4 5 6	
2	1 2 3 4 5 6	1 2 3 4 5 6	
3	1 2 3 4 5 6	1 2 3 4 5 6	
4	1 2 3 4 5 6	1 2 3 4 5 6	

You don't have to have six objectives for each goal, although it is important that you work on several things at a time rather than just one or two. The more things you can do to challenge OCD *each day* the better. You will make progress far more quickly than if you only do a couple of things every now and again.

Chapter summary

Now that you've finished this chapter you have:

- understood why goals are important
- written a clear list of goals for yourself
- developed a strategy for tackling your OCD with manageable steps.

Having clear goals for tackling OCD means we know *where* we want to go and *what* we need to do to get to there. Asking ourselves the 'magic wand' question helps us identify the kinds of changes we need to make and what we should prioritize. Using 'SMART' principles for setting our goals is a great way of boosting our motivation: they are stepping stones towards achieving even bigger goals. Making sure each step seems manageable gives us hope and boosts our confidence to try new challenges. Don't view not reaching a goal as a failure. It just means we need to find a new way of achieving that goal, a different way to approach it. Asking ourselves, 'What can I do *right now* to challenge OCD?' and then doing it, is a step in the right direction. Remember, no matter how small the steps are, as long as we keep taking them in the same direction, we will get to where we want to go.

Your goals will help you with the next step of discovering how to live your life free from OCD. Are you ready to get the benefits of doing things differently and changing your relationship with your thoughts?

CHAPTER 9

Changing our relationship with our thoughts

Overview

In Chapter 8, you found out why goals are important and drew up your own strategy for tackling OCD with manageable steps. In this chapter you will:

- learn how a shift in your thinking can change your life
- develop a new way of understanding your thoughts and feelings
- get started on your goals.

What does change involve? Is it a matter of doing something different on just one occasion? While taking another approach on only one occasion will, of course, create a different outcome, more lasting changes occur as part of a process during which we keep doing things differently. This applies to both thinking and behaviour.

Our relationship with our thoughts

In order to live life free from OCD, we need to develop a different relationship with our thoughts and feelings. It isn't only with OCD that we misinterpret thoughts and feelings in a more threatening way; it's a common phenomenon in all kinds of problems. For example, people suffering from conditions such as panic, health anxiety and depression often have an unhelpful relationship with their thoughts and feelings too. So in what way do we need to develop a different relationship with our thoughts and feelings? Put bluntly, we need to view thoughts as just thoughts, feelings as simply feelings. Mindfulness and other Third Wave therapies are based on this very principle (see Chapter 5).

We have already seen how interpreting the thoughts that pop into our heads unbidden in a threatening or scary way leads to us trying to control them in some way – trying to **suppress** or block the thoughts. Or we might try to put them right in some way – **neutralize** the thoughts or carry out a compulsive behaviour. Even trying to avoid triggering thoughts in the first place is problematic as it makes us focus on them even more, and often increases the number of worrisome thoughts we have because we're always on the look-out. In other words, it keeps the problem going.

Are thoughts important? How much do our thoughts really reflect reality? Or what we're really like as a person? Could they simply be our interpretation of events? Or creative ideas? Many fiction writers describe the most gory and horrendous scenes in their novels. What does that mean about them? Are they like the characters they portray or just people with incredible imaginations?

Thoughts are just thoughts, but all too often we accept thoughts that come into our mind at face value. This is especially true when they're part of a familiar pattern, like OCD thoughts. They've probably been around for a while in some shape or form, and although they're neither pleasant nor welcome they've become an everyday feature of our mental life. We've got used to them being around, and often respond to them on a kind of autopilot. The OCD bully says 'Jump!' (or more usually 'Wash!', 'Check!', 'Be certain!') and we do it without question because it's what we do.

OCD thoughts have become part of the constant chatter that our brains create, and when this is punctuated by thoughts we perceive as dangerous, we hear them loudly above the general background noise (like the way that traffic alerts or urgent news bulletins cut in over the sound of our favourite radio station).

Labelling thoughts

Instead of trying *not* to have the thoughts, try taking a different approach. Learning to label our thoughts *as* thoughts helps us recognize them for what they are: they're opinions, not facts.

Instead of just accepting thoughts as they come into your head, identify them as a thought by giving them a label in the following way.

That could be dog poo.	My mind sent me the thought that it could be dog poo.
My baby could die.	My mind sent me the thought that my baby could die.
What if I'm a child molester?	My mind sent me the thought that I'm a child molester.
The number 4 is unlucky.	My mind sent me the thought that the number 4 is unlucky.
I don't love my girlfriend.	My mind sent me the thought that I don't love my girlfriend.

Get the idea?

Reviewing behaviour

Task

Now try this with your own thoughts. It doesn't have to be with your OCD thoughts to begin with. Perhaps try it with thoughts like feeling hungry or tired, or wanting a cup of coffee. Or things that you notice around you.

Try it for several minutes, just allowing thoughts to come into your head as and when they do.

What have you noticed? Before you begin to answer this, perhaps you could begin your reply with 'My mind sent me the thought that …'.

When we label thoughts in this way, it enables us to put some distance between the thought and the (often instant) emotional response. You could describe it as a kind of emotional bungee elastic. To begin with, allowing OCD thoughts to come into our minds in this way immediately 'pings' the elastic so strongly that we are catapulted at full force into feelings of anxiety. However, repeatedly stretching this imaginary bungee elastic to gain emotional distance from the thoughts that are 'just thoughts' causes it to become permanently stretched and far less likely to ping back with a violent snap.

It takes a bit of practise getting into the habit of labelling thoughts in this way, but the more we do it the better we get at it. I don't expect you to do this all the time but as a strategy it can help us become more mindful. By the way, it isn't meant as a method of neutralizing in order to reduce your anxiety. Once we have learned to recognize OCD thoughts, urges and impulses for what they are we can recognize what we need to do. Instead of automatically falling into our old knee-jerk habits, we can make wise choices.

Just let it go

There are a number of ways in which we can think about intrusive thoughts. One is that it's like living next to a busy road with lots of lorries going by. You might not like having so many lorries going passed. If every time you heard one coming you jumped up and shouted 'Go away' from your window, what effect would this have? Would it reduce the number of lorries that passed, or would it simply make you even more aware of them?

We can also use a computer analogy, seeing unwanted thoughts as like spam emails or those irritating pop-up adverts that float across our screens; we don't have to read them to know that they're not important and we can happily ignore them.

Don't use the wrong tools

Learning to label our thoughts can be helpful in getting us on our way to freeing ourselves from OCD, but it's only one of the things that we need to change.

The dangers of thinking too hard

Trying to think our way out of problems is something that we all do. In fact, being good at solving problems or considered to be a 'good thinker' or having an analytical mind has long been seen as a desirable quality in our society and in many civilizations. Nevertheless, in OCD the use of 'thinking solutions' is very much a part of the problem. Most people with OCD spend far too much time on thinking solutions.

This is particularly the case with 'Pure O' where intrusive thoughts tend not to lead to the kinds of compulsions that can be seen by others (like cleaning excessively, spending a long time checking that doors and windows are closed or that the tap is off). The kinds of compulsions that accompany 'Pure O' often can't be seen by others because they're something that you do in your head, sometimes called **covert neutralizing** (if you need a reminder, have a look at Chapter 1). One of the most commonly used covert neutralizing strategies is the use of these kinds of thinking solutions, where you attempt to solve the problem by thinking your way out of it. This is often referred to as **ruminating**.

While trying to solve everyday problems in this way can be a good idea, it's not helpful in dealing with OCD problems for a number of reasons.

- Often it's used to try to solve problems that can't be solved or answer questions that can't be answered, e.g. 'Will I burn in hell for all eternity?', 'How can I be certain that I really love my partner?'
- Ruminating often leads to further worries that you hadn't thought of before, and can create even more 'What if ...?' questions in your mind ...

- … which you then try to answer, thus making the process take even longer.
- It makes you feel worse because you can't find the right answer.
- It leads to feelings of hopelessness and despair, e.g. 'Unless I can work it out once and for all, I'll never have peace of mind.'

The whole process becomes one big vicious circle leading to increased frustration and low mood, as you become caught up in an increasing vortex of questions which you strive to answer, failing miserably despite your best efforts (it's that 'who wins when you play Noughts and Crosses with yourself' scenario). Although you might believe that you will never feel better until you get The Answer, it is in fact *trying* to work it out that is one of the key behaviours that keeps the OCD going. It keeps you locked into your own internal world of thoughts and prevents you from taking real action and living in the 'real world', just getting on with things.

Case study

'I was furious!' fumed Philippa. The shop assistant in the tiny shop had promised to keep an eye on the pushchair while she popped through to look at baby clothes in the back room. The assistant had carried on straightening displays and didn't appear to be watching her son as he slept peacefully. Although no one had come into or left the shop, Philippa's mind was full of 'what if' questions.

It was only later, while she was telling her husband, that she realized what had gone on. Thoughts and reality had become fused together. 'By stepping back, I can see that nothing actually happened.' She could see how looking in on ourselves and our feelings means we don't see things as they really are.

The likelihood is that the assistant would have noticed if a customer had come in and stopped what she was doing, shifting her attention to what was happening at the time. She didn't need to constantly watch the door to know whether that was the case. The assistant was paying attention to what was needed in the present.

I need to work out why I keep getting these thoughts

Another way in which we might try to use thinking solutions is by trying to work out why it is we keep getting these thoughts (looking for another version of The Answer). You might find yourself endeavouring to find some explanation from your early experiences that could account for being troubled by them.

If any previous counselling or therapy you've had took a theoretical approach other than CBT, there may have been a strong focus on the past and your childhood. Even if you haven't previously had therapy, there's a widely held view that any difficulties we suffer today have somehow been caused by something damaging or traumatic. From a CBT perspective there is a different view, which is that it's what we *do* in the 'here and now' that keeps the problem going.

Later in this book, we will touch on how beliefs about ourselves, the world and other people have been shaped by past experiences. But for now, it isn't helpful to try to work out the relationship between intrusive thoughts, what they mean or where they've come from. Thinking is simply what brains do – our brains are just thought factories, churning out thoughts all day and all night. However persuasive the urge to uncover historical reasons for your current difficulties or the kinds of things you worry about, it is not the key which will magically set you free.

Living in our heads

An unintended consequence of spending time, effort and concentration on trying to apply thinking solutions to our difficulties can lead us to feeling a bit detached or separated from the outside world. It's like living in our own little bubble – one of those snow globes which, when you shake it up, causes glittery stuff to swirl around in the globe until it gradually settles again. The glittery bits are like our thoughts. Some of them are pretty and nice to look at. But the trouble is that there are others we don't like: tarnished and drab, spoiling the landscape of our snow globe. By thinking too much we're constantly shaking it up, and inevitably we'll stir up all the unwanted bits too.

By spending too much time 'living in our heads', thoughts and reality become fused together, as we saw in the last real-life example. To break these apart, we need to shift our attention *outside* ourselves into the real world. Constantly looking in on ourselves and our feelings often means we don't see things as they really are and get entangled in an internal world that seems fraught with dangers and threats. Transferring our attention to what is going on around us is a vital step towards changing our relationship with our thoughts and feelings. No matter how insistent we may feel the need to stay focused on our thoughts or feelings, we can choose to focus our attention on the wider environment. It may feel really hard to resist shaking up the snow globe, but when we do the tiny particles gently drift to settle on the bottom again.

Some people think that this is just an emotional sticking plaster: 'It's not getting to the bottom of the problem.' Nevertheless, it gives your mind a chance to rest and recover. We described earlier how thinking patterns in OCD can be so ingrained it becomes a habit to automatically respond in that way. What neurological research has shown is that repeated actions (both thoughts and behaviours) strengthen and reinforce neural pathways. This becomes a kind of 'super-highway' which will automatically be chosen as the main pathway unless we choose to over-ride it. Doing and thinking things in new and novel ways helps to build new neural pathways.

Case study

After Richard gave up checking his reactions to Cameron Diaz and gay porn films, he found he seemed far less bothered by thoughts about his sexuality. In fact, he realized just how much time these compulsions had taken up. He now had more leisure time, so joined the film club and started playing badminton. He enjoyed talking to the other members – he didn't give a thought to what gender they were, they were just people who shared his interests.

He met up with some of his new friends at other times too, and after several months he moved in with his badminton partner. She admitted she'd fancied him from afar but he'd always seemed so aloof. It hadn't occurred to Richard that OCD might give others a completely different impression of him.

I need a better strategy to deal with these horrible feelings

Another common misconception about tackling OCD is the idea that you could stop your compulsions if only you knew how to get rid of your anxiety. Anxiety isn't a nice feeling. It can feel really awful. It can seem as if it will keep on getting worse and never go away unless we do something about it. Anxiety is a big con – it might tell us that we won't feel better until we do something about it but, like any feelings we have, it will pass in time ... as long as we don't try to 'fix' it.

To be human is to experience different moods. Anxiety, like depression, is a mood. Our mood can change for no apparent reason. We can wake up in the morning feeling in a particular mood without knowing why. It might be because of a dream we've had, but actually it doesn't matter whether we work out why we feel the way we do (in the same way that we don't need to work out why we've had particular thoughts, as we discussed above). In fact, the more we try to work it out, the more likely this mood is to linger. If we just carry on doing what we planned to do – get up, shower, dress, have breakfast and get on with the tasks of the day – it is likely that the mood will change (and even if it doesn't, we'll have done the things we intended to and got on with our lives). Remember the task you did in Chapter 5?

But there's another way in which we can benefit from changing our relationship with our feelings/mood/emotions. The term 'anxiety' is an interpretation of a number of physical sensations and bodily changes, such as a tight chest or dizziness (see Chapter 3). We could possibly include some mental changes too, such as the sensation that our brain is a bit sluggish or foggy.

In the same way that we can misinterpret thoughts that come into our mind, it is also possible to misinterpret physical sensations. When Maxine became anxious, she felt a rush of heat through her body. Because she was always worried about smelling, she misinterpreted the physical sensation as a sign of this.

Should we trust our gut reactions?

Let's pause for a moment. Have you ever had a scary thought or felt anxious or guilty, only to find there was no need? Such as putting your hand in your pocket to get your purse or wallet and experienced that lurch in your stomach because it wasn't there? And then found it in the *other* pocket? Or how about driving along and spotting a police car in your rear-view mirror and suddenly feeling guilty for no good reason?

Reviewing behaviour

Task

Think of a time when you've had a scary thought or felt anxious or guilty, only to find there was no need.

- What did it feel like?
- How did the physical sensations you had affect what you thought?
- Did how you felt make you believe that something bad had just happened?

People often talk about having a 'gut reaction'. What do we mean by that? The term is used to describe a physical feeling, often felt in the stomach or gut, as a reaction to something. It can trigger powerful emotional reactions … even when it's completely wrong. It is:

- an immediate, felt response
- a response you don't think about rationally
- an emotional response to something like danger or disgust
- often felt over-responding to something.

Janet's nausea when she saw or thought about faeces literally gave her a gut reaction: danger! Gut reactions aren't generally based on any rational decision making process, but are often referred to as intuition – a felt sense. Although they can be a positive feeling, like trust, OCD leads us to respond to negative ones, such as feeling uneasy.

When this way of reacting has become a habit, it will always take you in the wrong direction – it's that knee-jerk reaction again. In these situations, we need to do the *opposite* of what 'intuition' is telling us. If we always trust our gut, we'll often make bad decisions. We need to choose wisely.

When it comes to choosing wisely with OCD, we need to take that leap of faith and do things differently, just like those sailors in Chapter 7. Are you ready to start doing instead of thinking?

Where should I start?

In Chapter 8, you wrote out your personal goals list. Have a look at your list of short-term goals. This is a good place to start – they may seem a challenge but not too difficult. If they do seem too hard, try breaking them down into smaller steps. You could choose one or two things that you feel you could manage just to build your confidence, but you will make more rapid progress by taking on more OCD challenges. It's a bit like going on a diet: we can cut out crisps and chips, but if we're still eating sweets and chocolates we won't lose weight so quickly.

Whatever your concern, you need to stop doing things the old OCD way and begin to do the things we'd do if we didn't have the problem. More importantly, you need to drop your safety behaviours *despite* thoughts coming into your head. In fact, the more you can allow worries to come in and carry on regardless the better. Let's have a look at a few examples.

Tackling contamination concerns

- Janet stopped wearing gloves and a coat when she went out, stopped using antibacterial gel and only washed her hands after going to the toilet or before eating.
- Although she felt really anxious at first, she found that the anxiety calmed down after a while.
- After a few days, she chose to challenge herself a bit more … and sat in the lounge after coming back from town without changing her clothes.

Tackling checking

- Tadeusz stopped checking before leaving for work.
- He made himself coffee each morning and drank it while ironing a shirt.
- When a doubt came into his head, he just agreed with it: 'Yeah, maybe I left the taps on.'
- He used his radio-alarm to wake him in the morning.

Tackling doubting

- David threw away till receipts straightaway.
- At work, he spent 15 minutes twice a day on filing. He had lots of doubts to begin with that slowed him down but he found that if he just filed a letter and moved on to the next one, and then the next one, he soon forgot about the doubts.
- Even though it was one of his medium-term goals, he decided to have a go at throwing out junk mail.

Tackling harm

- Mandy spent time on her own with her baby instead of going to her mother's every day, or getting her husband to take time off work.
- She began to change Betsy's nappy at least three times each day and let her kick her legs about for a while after she'd cleaned her up.
- She gave Betsy her bath while her husband washed the dishes downstairs.

Tackling rumination

- Sahib chose to look everyone in the eye when he spoke to them. He found that his eyes naturally just wandered from their faces to other places – on their body, or straight past them. Wherever his eyes went, he just allowed them to stray.
- Whenever intrusive thoughts popped into his head, he just let them be there.
- At the gym, he decided he should do what the other instructors did: have a good look at everyone in the class during the session.

Big steps or little steps?

Taking the first step, resisting compulsions, is always the hardest. It's very likely that you will have lots of thoughts about catastrophes and believe you need to prevent them. Although it may seem as though smaller steps would be easier for us to begin with, doing it this way still buys into Theory A (that the problem is danger or harm). By tackling OCD as the worry problem that it is, we choose to respond differently to all situations despite feeling anxious. You will feel uncomfortable – after all, you've had lots of experience of feeling uncomfortable. But you might not know what happens next when you stop doing things the OCD way.

Big steps, little steps or any size in between: the most important rule is that you take lots of them, frequently and repeatedly. Learning to live your life free of OCD is a journey. By taking many steps each day, you will get there.

Chapter summary

Now that you've finished this chapter you have:

- discovered how labelling thoughts changes our relationship with them
- understood how thinking too much plays a role in OCD
- learned that accepting our gut reaction prevents wise choices
- learned that working on our goals is a process that needs practice.

While our mind constantly steers us towards 'thinking solutions', anxiety cons us into believing we need to fix it. Neither of these are effective strategies for tackling OCD. Thoughts and feelings can't be trusted as accurate representations of reality. We can resist carrying out a compulsion, but we cannot refuse to think an obsessive thought. Confidence comes from doing things differently *despite* how we feel. While choosing less challenging goals to start with can boost our confidence, dealing with OCD as a worry problem means we should encourage obsessive thoughts and feelings of anxiety. After all, the best strategy for dealing with anxiety is to allow it to just *be*. By dropping our safety behaviours and neutralizing, we can learn something new about the problem.

A shift in your thinking is all it takes to change your life. But how can you be sure that it's the right thing?

Can fear of uncertainty be another OCD trap? Chapter 10 looks at how trying too hard to eliminate doubt feeds the problem.

Living with uncertainty

Overview

In Chapter 9, you began to understand how a shift in our thinking can allow us to make wiser choices to combat OCD. This chapter explains:

- how to live with uncertainty
- why trying too hard is a problem
- what happens when we stop trying to fix anxiety.

You might have heard OCD called the 'doubting disease'. Doubt is what fuels the problem. It creeps up on us unawares as we try harder to satisfy that niggling feeling. Everyday actions turn into a magic charm to ward off uncertainty and doubt. Even when it no longer works, we are conned into wondering just how much more awful we would feel if we hadn't applied the 'magic' of our compulsions.

The frog and the piece of string

Once upon a time a very poor man was walking along the road when he suddenly spotted a frog sitting on the ground in front of him. Being kind, the man picked it up and placed it safely on the grass verge.

Instead of hopping away, the frog just sat and looked at the man. In the way of these kinds of stories, the frog was (of course) a magic frog. 'Young man, I am so grateful to you for you have indeed saved my life,' the frog exclaimed. 'As your reward, I will bestow on you great wealth and a magnificent mansion as your home since I know that poverty has been your lot.' Of course, the man was delighted with this unexpected turn of fortune, even when the frog announced that there was a condition attached to his bequest. 'But I must advise you that in the small room at the top of the highest turret of the west wing of the mansion there is a piece of string suspended from the ceiling. Under no circumstances whatsoever must you – or anyone else – ever touch that piece of string.' And with that ominous warning, the frog disappeared in a puff of smoke.

'Well,' thought the man, 'That's a small price to pay for all this wealth.' He looked around at the magnificent tapestries and antiques which adorned his palatial residence. Although he had no idea what fate might befall him, he decided that a lock on the door would be a sensible precaution to put his mind at rest. Yet he still worried. As he implemented more and more security measures in order to prevent anyone from gaining entry to the forbidden room, he found himself confined to a single room in the east wing.

The man continued to live in this very restricted way until he was very old indeed. Then one day, he wasn't feeling too well and called for his physician. The physician examined the old man carefully, and informed him that he had but a few days to live. After the physician left, the man reflected on his life and how it had turned out. Being wealthy wasn't the joyous experience he'd hoped for, and he'd constantly been troubled by fears about the piece of string that he'd been warned to stay clear of. He'd never known the reason *why* no one should ever touch it, but thought it was a small price to pay in exchange for his wealth. But what did he have to lose now?

With trepidation, he made his way to the west wing. He unlocked the door. It creaked open, and there in front of him hung the string, laced with dusty cobwebs but still intact. With his heart in his mouth, he reached up slowly and gave the string a sharp tug … and nothing happened.

And the moral of the story?

We can live our lives in fear of some unknown outcome, taking all kinds of precautions to prevent the dreaded thing, whatever it might be, from happening. Or we can live our lives in a way that is consistent with our values and goals in life. What's the saying: better to travel hopefully?

While he was rich beyond measure, the man was unable to find any pleasure in life as he spent all his time worrying about an ill-defined catastrophe that might happen if he wasn't careful enough. Does this sound familiar to you? OCD works in a similar way: we spend a long time stressing and worrying about something that may not even happen. It robs us of our lives and dictates how we should do things. What a shame the man in the story waited until his life was at an end before daring to take a chance and pulling on the string!

Making changes in our lives, especially the kinds of changes we need to make in order to tackle our OCD, is always a challenge. But it would be such a shame if you continued to live your life in fear of some dreaded outcome which may or may not happen. Perhaps, as in the story, nothing will happen when you begin to do things differently. You may have come across the wise words of Winnie-the-Pooh in a story by A. A. Milne. While he was walking in the woods with his friend Piglet (who was a huge worrier), Piglet asked, 'What if a tree falls on our head while we're underneath it?' to which Pooh replied, 'What if it didn't?'

Anxiety and worry make us waste a lot of time and energy trying to solve a problem that doesn't even exist.

Is it possible to rid ourselves of doubt?

Whatever form OCD takes for you, **reassurance** is a common compulsion. It can take various forms. Checking is an attempt to reassure yourself, and even if we don't do so physically, we are likely to have carried out some kind of mental assessment. Janet spent hours looking for information to put her mind at rest: reassurance again. These days, the internet is an infinite source of reassurance. No matter what the question, it will provide many answers. And with its many answers, it will fuel many more questions.

Throughout our lives, we build our confidence by looking to others whose decisions we trust. In time, our self-assurance grows so we are less reliant on others. OCD saps our confidence, making us believe our judgment cannot be trusted. Do you repeatedly ask questions? Have friends or family become irritated because you ask the same thing on several occasions? Are you aware of sneaky ways you have of seeking reassurance: 'I haven't upset you, have I?' 'Do you think it's OK to …?' 'Is it normal to …?' While everyone uses reassurance sometimes, if it becomes a habit – especially if you already suspect what the answer is – it's part of OCD.

But I *need* to know …

The effects of reassurance-seeking are short-lived. OCD will never be satisfied, no matter how much reassurance you get. It's an example of impossible criteria (which we'll look at later in this chapter).

Often, you will only stop your search for reassurance when you find some information that does the opposite of what you wanted: then you are even more anxious than before.

Friends and family (even therapists!) can accidentally get drawn into providing reassurance. After all, if someone asks us a question we just answer it without considering the motive of the person asking. Since reassurance-seeking plays a major part in keeping OCD going, it's important that we don't play the game. A 'tough love' approach is needed – after all, you wouldn't give alcohol to an alcoholic. Refusal doesn't need to be brutal with a different strategy.

It could be reassurance if:

- they keep asking the same (or a similar) question
- your answer leads to more questions
- you get lots of phone calls asking for advice
- you often have to repeat what you've said to make sure they understood
- you're asked to write things down so they don't forget

- quootlono are unanswerable, e.g. 'Are you sure this couldn't cause a fire?'

What you can do.

- Ask how difficult it would be *not* to know? Remind them that it's a sign of OCD and not a genuine need for information.
- Gently remind them that they've asked this before … and that they know your answer.
- Reassure the person rather than reassuring the OCD, e.g. 'You seem to be struggling with your OCD at the moment; let me give you a hug.'
- Don't try to answer unanswerable questions, e.g. 'It's hard, but we have to live with not knowing.'

It's hard work keeping up this approach, especially if we're busy or tired. Don't beat yourself up if you bought into the reassurance trap, whether accidentally or out of exasperation. We're only human!

How can I live with uncertainty?

Uncertainty is one of life's certainties. We might not want to accept the truth of this – and OCD constantly tells you to doubt it – yet it is true. No one can guarantee that bad things won't happen if you stop carrying out compulsions. What is guaranteed, though, is that if you continue to do all the things you have been doing, you will continue to be plagued by OCD. Of that, there is no doubt.

The key to living with uncertainty is being able to allow the uncomfortable feeling to stay with you. Even though it seems to you that the last thing you want is suffer that horrible feeling of uncertainty, remember that the way you have tried to fix it in the past hasn't worked for you either – trying to reassure ourselves in some way just keeps the doubt cycle going. Trying to get rid of the doubt simply leads to more doubts.

> ### Case study
>
> Tadeusz struggled to leave for work without doing his round of checks. 'Even if I'm uneasy doing what I'm doing now, and feel more uncomfortable than I want to feel, I'll keep doing it.' Why? 'Because I will miss so much more in the future if I don't tackle OCD now. It's worth the discomfort.'

Even if bad things happen, we have to find a way of carrying on. Most people have coped with upsetting events like a relationship breaking up, losing a pet or getting turned down for a job. We find a way of coping. Accept less satisfaction now for a better life tomorrow.

The dangers of trying too hard

As we've already seen, one of the major themes that drives OCD is the fear that you might cause something really awful to happen. It's understandable that, once you've thought of some dreadful calamity, you would want to try very hard to prevent or ward off such an event. What you might not realize, however, is that trying too hard can create even more problems. It's not just that, say, washing or checking so much swallows up time you would prefer to have free for work, family, hobbies or just having fun. What seems to happen in many cases is that the goals we sometimes set ourselves are downright impossible, even though we firmly believe that achieving this goal will guarantee that catastrophe is less likely to strike. We don't always realize that the task we have set ourselves is impossible. Often we become increasingly distressed as we fail to achieve it, try even harder, and so on.

> ### Case study
>
> Whenever Maxine had put some rubbish in the bin, she washed her hands very thoroughly. She wanted to make sure her hands were completely clean and that there was no risk of any smelly 'bin juice'

lingering that could get on to other things in her flat. Despite using perfumed hand wash and scrubbing her hands and forearms for several minutes, she still didn't feel certain she was clean enough, so she scrubbed them again, this time using disinfectant as well. Although sometimes she washed for half an hour or more, she couldn't get rid of the doubt that her hands might not be clean enough.

Trying to get rid of the doubt is often the reason that rituals become longer and longer, and more and more upsetting. Let's have a look at the kinds of things you might find yourself doing and whether or not you are in danger of trying too hard.

Goal	Why it is impossible
Not have a particular thought.	You have to tell yourself *which* thought not to have, so then you've thought of it anyway.
Remember every detail of a scene or event, or even of a whole day.	Our memories aren't big enough. Instead, they are cleverly designed to pick out the noticeable things we need to remember and forget the rest.
Feeling totally, totally sure.	The harder we try to feel certain, the less certain we become.
See a clear mental picture of something not being there or not having happened.	This is a bit like not having a particular thought. In the back of your mind, you have to have an image of the thing being there so that you can check *your* image to make sure it isn't. No wonder you end up confused, and as far from clear as can be.
Have a totally clear mental picture.	This one is a bit like being totally sure.

Goal	Why it is impossible
Stare harder and harder at the light switches/my hands etc. to make myself believe they are off/ clean etc.	Again, this is like trying to make yourself totally, totally sure. A further snag is that staring at something for a long time often leads to what are called **feelings of dissociation** – feeling distant or unreal – and of course these sorts of feelings (although they're perfectly normal) are probably the total opposite of the down-to-earth, unquestioning acceptance of reality that you're seeking.
Do the 'perfect' check/wash, etc.	Is anything ever completely perfect?
Do 'everything I can' to be safe/ clean etc.	How long is a piece of string? Can we ever do everything possible?

It's striking that many of the impossible tasks that we might set ourselves in our quest to solve our OCD problems involve trying to *consciously* control mental processes which (naturally) occur *automatically*. Processes such as remembering things are rather like breathing or balancing: although we might occasionally become aware of them, there's no need to concentrate on them for them to happen as they should: they just do. Indeed, there's a limit to how much we can actually alter them through conscious control. Did you ever try to stop yourself breathing when you were a child?

So trying to apply too much conscious control over such processes is rather like trying to change gear manually in a car which is designed to do it automatically. A familiar example is when you stare harder and harder, longer and longer, at a word you know perfectly well. What happens? Often what you experience is that the word suddenly looks strange or unfamiliar. You might even feel like you don't recognize it or as if you've never seen it before. You might wonder if it's spelt wrong, or have doubts about what it means. Yet this is a perfectly ordinary word which you have read dozens of times and have no problems using day to day. Part of the reason for this odd experience is that recognizing the look and meaning of a written word is, for the practised reader, an automatic process. This is just as well since our conscious attention is limited and it's better to use it for understanding the story rather than for working out what the words are. If you're trying too hard in response to OCD concerns you may well be doing much the same thing as the person staring too long at a word, but (to make matters worse) you may have fallen into the trap of mistakenly believing you need *more* conscious effort to give you the confidence that only accompanies the automatic process.

The solution to trying too hard

The solution is first to identify what impossible goals you may be setting yourself in your attempts to prevent your feared catastrophe, and then to replace them with more realistic and appropriate goals.

One way of identifying these sorts of impossible goals is to ask yourself:

- What am I looking for to know when I can stop my ritual?
- How will I know when I have done enough?

You may find that you've come up with one of the answers we have already described. It's particularly helpful to ask yourself these questions when you are in a situation where you have the urge to carry out a compulsive action or ritual. Sometimes it's only then that it becomes clear what you have actually been expecting of yourself.

Reviewing behaviour

Task

Make a note of any impossible goals you catch yourself setting. To give you an idea, here's what Maxine wrote.

Goal I set myself	To have perfectly clean and unsmelly hands.
Why it's an impossible goal	There's no such thing as perfect. I can never be certain that my hands are 'perfectly' clean. Even clean hands have an odour.
What should I do instead?	Wash my hands quickly with only a little soap (or just rinse them with water). Let myself feel doubtful. Accept that my hands might not be clean.

Learn how to urge surf

By relying on rituals to make you feel better, you need more of a 'fix' to get the same sense of relief. Trying too hard and striving for certainty mean you never find out what happens to your anxiety or doubt.

Behaviour changing strategy

Task

Let's do an experiment to find out what happens to your discomfort when you stop trying to fix it. For the next week, try the following:

- on Sunday, Tuesday, Thursday, Saturday – don't carry out any neutralizing or compulsions. Just acknowledge when intrusive thoughts or urges come along. ('There's another one!')
- on Monday, Wednesday, Friday – carry on with 'business as usual', i.e. carry out any neutralizing or compulsions in your usual way.

At the end of each day, rate:
- how anxious or distressed you felt overall (e.g. 50%)
- how often obsessional thoughts or urges occurred (a rough estimate of how many is fine).

What happens next?

Have you noticed that your anxiety doesn't keep getting worse? Or that you seem to get fewer intrusive thoughts or doubts? If we can just allow ourselves to experience the discomfort, the feeling gradually goes away. This is called **habituation.** For example, you get into the swimming pool and the water feels absolutely freezing, but if you stay in the water it seems to warm up. Of course, the temperature of the water hasn't really increased, it's just that you've become used to it. In other words, you've habituated yourself to the feeling.

Anxiety discomfort works slightly differently because when our 'fight or flight' response is triggered, it causes a rush of adrenalin. Adrenalin is the hormone responsible for the physical sensations we get when we're anxious. As well as getting used to feeling the discomfort, habituation also allows adrenalin levels to reduce.

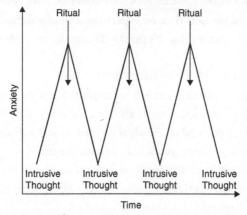

Figure 10.1: How rituals prevent habituation.
Rituals prevent us discovering that anxiety reduces on its own.

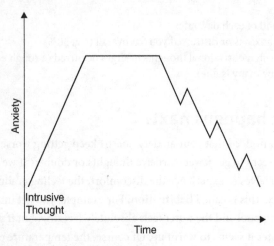

Figure 10.2: How habituation works.
Anxiety may continue to go up for a while. It then levels off and
eventually comes down again. It doesn't always come down smooth-
ly, but it will reduce as long as we don't do anything to fix it.

When we carry out a ritual, it can seem as if our anxiety levels will
keep on increasing. We mistakenly believe that our compulsions were
the reason for the decrease in anxiety when in fact it comes down on
its own. It works the same with OCD doubts too. If we believe this is
what saved us, the next time we experience a similar difficulty we're
likely to do the same thing. It's that OCD con all over again.

Mindfulness and habituation

Instead of doing rituals when you get anxious, allow the urge to be
there and 'urge surf'. OCD urges are like a wave: if you try to fight it
or jump into it, you end up smashed on the rocks. But if you allow
yourself to surf the urge, you'll float towards the shore.

When we feel in a crisis, we often feel as if our emotions are driving
us. Instead of acting on this urge, we can equally choose *not* to act on
it. Don't try to get rid of it – just don't act on it.

Only solve the problem you have right now

When we try to work out how to deal with an imagined problem we have to come up with an endless number of solutions since we can't be certain what we have to deal with. Do you remember what we've previously said about **impossible criteria**? Do you think that trying to find the ideal solution to every problem is an example of that?

We kid ourselves into believing that it's a 'good idea' to plan ahead and be prepared for any disaster that might come our way. The trouble is that very few (if any) of these disasters will happen, so all our planning is a waste of time. Plus it often means that we don't have the time, effort or energy to live our lives in the here and now – 'living in the moment' as it might be described from a mindfulness perspective.

If we only attempt to solve a problem when we actually have a problem, it is much easier to work out the most appropriate and effective strategy to deal with it. Why do you think that is? Well, we know exactly what the problem is and therefore we don't waste time considering solutions that aren't helpful. If it's not an immediate danger, it's a waste of time thinking about it.

Maybe it will … maybe it won't

While you're tackling OCD and attempting to do things differently – the non-OCD way – your active imagination will most likely be in overdrive. OCD never gives up easily and as a consequence your mind will be sending you a stream of ideas, images, doubts and predictions. Don't get caught up in this torrent. Remember, thinking is what brains do. Just acknowledge the thoughts and carry on with what you have chosen to do, rather than what OCD is telling you to do. Embrace the uncertainty that inevitably follows such thoughts, but instead of trying to work it out in your head, carrying out a ritual or a compulsion or avoiding the situation, just deflect these concerns with a dismissive, 'Maybe it will … maybe it won't'.

Reality is never as bad as our imagination

When we worry, our imaginations often run riot and we picture all kinds of disasters in our heads. What we picture in our minds often makes a big-budget disaster movie look as scary as a grainy old silent movie in which the heroine is tied to the railway track while some little steam engine chugs its way towards her at walking pace. It seems such a shame to 'waste' our imagination on creating worries for ourselves.

Most of the things we worry about rarely happen to us. Carol has never lost control and harmed someone, Janet's son hasn't gone blind although he plays football in the park several times a week. And even if something bad happens, it's never as bad as we think it's going to be. Despite his constant checking, Tadeusz once had a burglary. The thieves removed a pane of glass and managed to wriggle through, taking his laptop, the watch he'd been given for his 21st birthday and some money he'd put away towards celebrating a friend's stag do. But he admitted it wasn't a big deal. Yes, it took up time, making statements to the police, getting someone to fix the window and dealing with the insurance company. But everything was sorted out fairly quickly, and he even managed to buy a watch with the insurance money that he liked far more than the one his grandmother had chosen. In fact, the burglary proved to be quite an incentive for Tadeusz to change his ways: OCD hadn't been the friend he thought it was. He decided that the risk was probably not much greater if he stopped all his checking and worrying, and then he could focus his attention on things that were far more important. If he was burgled again, or there was a flood, fire or other problem, he was confident that he could deal with it.

Chapter summary

In this chapter, you have discovered:

- it is possible to live with uncertainty and doubt
- trying too hard keeps OCD going
- learning to 'urge surf' leads to habituation.

The only antidote to uncertainty is to put up with the discomfort. By learning to 'urge surf', you will find out that the discomfort goes away on its own. Seeking reassurance is a common response to doubts, but the effect is short-lived and often leads to further doubts. Reality is never as bad as our imagination. Only solve the problem you have right now. And even if feared consequences become a reality, we have to find a way of coping and carry on. Respond to doubts and worries with 'Maybe it will … maybe it won't.' Embrace uncertainty.

Your new life begins here. Are you ready to create a new outlook? In Chapter 11, find out whether OCD really is the friend it makes itself out to be and learn how to imagine your life without it.

CHAPTER 11

Your new life begins here

Overview

In Chapter 10, we discussed how uncertainty is a fact of life and how trying less hard enables us to discover how anxiety really works. In this chapter we ask:

- is OCD really your friend?
- how can I imagine life without OCD?
- what do I need to do to create a new 'normal'?

Whether OCD has been in your life for a long time or only a short time, it will have shaped what you do and how you do it. Your life may be quite different from how it was before. Maybe there doesn't even seem to be a 'before'. While it's tempting to plan for a future that may be a little way off – 'When I've tackled my OCD, I want to …' – the future starts now. By reclaiming the things that OCD has deprived us of, we begin to reclaim our lives.

If OCD was a person, what would they be like?

When John looks back to the time he started checking his car for signs that he might have clipped another car in the car park, it seemed like a sensible thing to do – a small price to pay to put his mind at rest when he had a doubt about whether he might have been involved in a prang without realizing it. It didn't seem a big deal at the time. After all, it only took a few seconds to have a quick look for any damage. As time went on, though, John began to experience these doubts more frequently. What's more, the doubts weren't confined only to minor prangs. They became more disturbing, with worries that he might have caused more serious accidents or even run somebody over.

A quick look no longer set his mind at rest and he began elaborate, time-consuming routines to check for any possible signs of damage: any scratch or dent would have to be logged in a notebook he kept specifically for the purpose. He would examine anything that had got stuck to the paintwork in case it was blood, hair or fibres from the imagined casualty's clothing, even checking underneath the car with a mirror for indications that he had been involved in an incident. To begin with, OCD seemed like a good friend offering sound advice to eliminate his worry: 'Have a quick check and then you'll feel better'. And so he did ... for a while.

While OCD might feel like a trusted friend, it's more helpful to think about it as a bully, or even a protection racket. The bullying racketeers tell you (in a menacing way) about all the dreadful things that could happen to you, your loved ones and your property. However, through the goodness of their (criminal) hearts, they explain how they can help you safeguard all the things you hold dear ... for a price. The cost of this 'safeguarding' might seem quite reasonable to begin with – after all, isn't it worth it for peace of mind? But each time they come calling, they demand more ... and more. And if you decide to put a stop to it, they're hardly going to simply shrug their shoulders at your refusal and walk away. They'll put on even more pressure with worse threats. They might even rough you up a bit until you pay up. It can feel too terrifying not to give in to their demands. The thing is, that is exactly what you need to do: dig your heels in and refuse, no matter what they threaten. In time, they will give up and leave you alone. They might beat you up a bit, but they're not into heavy violence because they know there are other easier targets to intimidate. And, in fact, even without their 'protection', these kinds of things aren't any more likely to happen.

So is OCD really your friend?

It can be hard to stand up to the OCD bully, but wouldn't it be worth it in the long term? This next exercise helps you to identify the ways in which OCD seems helpful to you and to compare this with the ways in which it is *not* helpful to you. Don't get tied up in trying to make both lists equal – they won't necessarily balance out. To get you started, let's have a look at what John wrote.

OCD is my friend because:	OCD is *not* my friend because:
It stops me worrying about accidents.	It takes such a long time to check my car properly.
It keeps me safe.	I seem to worry about everything now.
It tells me what to do to reduce my anxiety.	I've had to do more and more checks to make me feel OK.... and I still don't feel OK.
It helps me spot potential dangers.	
I can be sure I haven't caused an accident.	It gives me even more ideas to worry about.
I pay really close attention when I'm driving.	I'm always late because of the time I take checking.
	I end up taking the bus because it's too much trouble to use my car.
	I can't even listen to the radio when I'm driving because I'm worried I'm not paying enough attention to the road.

What do you notice about John's list? Maybe the most striking difference between the two lists is that he was able to come up with far more reasons why OCD is *not* his friend. That's maybe not that surprising. You might also have noticed that although John feels OCD keeps him safe and reduces his anxiety and worries, he also recognizes that OCD causes him to feel less safe and creates even more worries. And if OCD really was his friend, what kind of friend makes you catch the bus when you have a car? I don't suppose that's the kind of friend you would want.

Cost–benefit analysis

A cost–benefit analysis is a straightforward technique used in business to help make decisions about whether it's worth going ahead with a project. As the name suggests, it involves adding up the benefits and comparing these to the costs. In other words, it's about weighing up all the pros and cons associated with taking a course of action. Psychologists have been known to borrow this approach to use in therapy, with a few tweaks here and there – after all, the costs from a psychological point of view are less likely to be in terms of money (although some of them might be). Generating our own cost–benefit analysis spurs us on to make the most helpful choices in line with the new (non-OCD) outlook we want to take. John's list is a simple example of a cost–benefit analysis.

Instead of setting about the analysis on the basis of whether OCD is or isn't a friend, let's look at the advantages and disadvantages of OCD in terms of a project we're thinking about embarking on. Seeing it from this viewpoint can protect us from the kind of pitfalls we could stumble into if OCD really was a friend, even if they weren't a very good friend and caused us all kinds of problems. Thinking about the costs and benefits of changing can help us stay more neutral and unbiased.

Actually, why don't we first consider the advantages and disadvantages of *not* changing. After all, when we feel stuck and are struggling to do things differently, the question we're really asking is, 'Is it worth the bother?' To put this into OCD terms, we need to look at:

- the benefits or advantages of continuing to do things in the way we have been doing them (doing things the OCD way)
- the costs or disadvantages of continuing to do things in the way we have been doing them (doing things the OCD way).

Behaviour changing strategy

Task

So is OCD really your friend? In the cost–benefit analysis table below, or a copy of it, write any reasons why it seems as if it is, and any reasons why it isn't. It doesn't matter if some of the reasons seem similar – John also found there was a lot of overlap. Here are some tips to get you started.

- Brain storm – include anything that comes into your head. It doesn't matter if it seems silly, odd in some way, or a crazy notion that isn't likely to happen. If you've thought it, write it down. Otherwise it could be lurking in the background and whispering things that hold you back.
- What are the costs to you in the short and long term?
- How about the costs to others in the short and long term?
- Are there any financial costs, e.g. soap, replacing taps, etc?

Cost–benefit analysis I	
OCD is my friend because these are the benefits of doing things the OCD way:	**OCD is *not* my friend because these are the costs of doing things the OCD way:**

Now that you've considered the evidence, what do you think? Is OCD the kind of friend you really want in your life?

Let's not stop here. It's one thing to weigh up whether we're content to live with things the way they are. But it's a different question altogether whether or not it's worth doing things differently, changing what have probably become long-term, entrenched habits. So what we have now is a slightly different chart, considering:

- the benefits of changing (not doing things the OCD way)
- the costs of changing (not doing things the OCD way).

Cost–benefit analysis II	
Benefits of changing *(i.e. not doing things the OCD way)*	**Costs of changing *(i.e. not doing things the OCD way)***

Let's see what Janet's cost–benefit analysis looked like:

OCD is my friend because these are the benefits of doing things the OCD way:	OCD is *not* my friend because these are the costs of doing things the OCD way:
I am keeping my family safe.	It's so hard trying to avoid anything to do with dogs.
I don't feel so worried.	I spend so much time washing and cleaning.
I know that no dog poo has come into the house.	My hands are always raw from washing.
We're less likely to get dog poo on us.	Detergents and soap cost a fortune.
I know that everything in the house is clean.	I don't have time for much else.
	My husband gets angry with me.
	It's not normal to take your clothes off in the garage.
	No one can come to the house; I've lost a lot of friends.
	My son can't have his friends round.
	I can't enjoy watching him play football.
	There are so many things I'm scared to let my son do.
	We don't have a normal life.
	People probably think I'm weird.
	I worry that my husband will leave me and take our son with him.

Benefits of changing *(i.e. not doing things the OCD way)*	Costs of changing *(i.e. not doing things the OCD way)*
We could be like a normal family.	It will be difficult to change what I do.
It would be nice not to have to wash so much.	I worry that I'll be anxious all the time.
My husband and son would be happier.	My son could get dog poo on him and get ill (or worse).
We'd have fewer arguments.	
Friends could come to the house.	
I wouldn't be so lonely.	
I could be more relaxed about what my son does.	
I wouldn't always be asking if their shoes were clean.	
My hands would be nicer.	
We could treat ourselves with money saved on soap powder.	
I'd have time to do things I want to do.	

Not only does a cost–benefit analysis enable us to see that OCD isn't the friend it makes itself out to be, it also gets us to rethink our goals. By taking stock of what we truly value, we can get a new perspective on our problems.

Case study: Janet

'I like everything to be clean and want my family to have a lovely safe home. I have my cost–benefit list, and I can see that the cost of keeping on trying to do all I can to protect them is too great. I've already lost so much as a result of OCD and so have my family. I need to live with the doubt. I live with uncertainty all the time and cope with it – it's a fact of life – like when I was trying to get pregnant. It was upsetting at times, but I survived it. Even if I hadn't conceived my lovely son I'd have survived.

Dropping all my cleaning and avoidances sounds really awful, but at the moment my life is just as awful.'

Imagining life without OCD

Even if it still feels as if you have a long way to go before you've made a dramatic impact on your OCD, it's never too soon to begin creating a new outlook on life and taking steps towards living your life free from OCD. The rest of our lives start here, at this very moment. Therefore it makes sense to begin doing the kinds of things you would want to do if OCD wasn't a problem. Some of these things might spring easily to mind (e.g. Miriam longed for her grandchildren to be able to visit her, but hadn't been able to have any visitors to her house because she was afraid they would become contaminated by her 'dirty' home), but there are probably many things that you might not think of so readily. Some of the ways in which OCD has taken over your life can be so subtle that they're not obvious. Dread of bringing in traces of spit or vomit that she might have picked up outside meant that Daria had never been able to come straight in from work, put the kettle on and relax for a few minutes. Instead, she had to go through a lengthy sequence of undressing in the kitchen, putting all her clothes in the machine to wash and then making her way to the bathroom to shower and wash her hair without touching anything on the way. Only when she felt perfectly clean and dressed in her 'indoor' clothes could she settle down with a cuppa. This often took the best part of two hours, and longer if she got distracted while going through her exacting procedure and had to repeat some of the steps. There were so many 'rules' OCD made her believe she had to obey that she had lost sight of what most people did.

It may be that struggling with OCD has meant that you have set your sights quite low. David never applied for promotion at work, remaining a junior clerk for almost 20 years even though he had a wealth of knowledge and experience on which his younger (and often more senior) colleagues relied. Maxine put up with living in bare, unfurnished rooms after getting rid of her furniture and carpets because she was worried that they smelled, even though living this way was at odds with her values. Her arty and creative nature meant she appreciated beautiful things and had surrounded herself with lovely belongings before OCD forced her to get rid of them. She had come to believe that functional and unlovely was the best she could hope for.

When we allow OCD to rule our lives, the way we live can seem normal to us, even if it isn't how most people live. We need to create a new 'normal' for ourselves.

Creating a new 'normal'

OCD can fill our lives with what seems like meaningful and important activity even though it is not. What are we going to do with the spare time that freeing ourselves from OCD will inevitably leave? We all need to fill our time but it's important to fill it wisely, in ways that that make us feel fulfilled and happy, give us a sense of purpose and fit with our values and the things that are important to us.

There are many ways in which OCD takes its toll on us.

- It takes up a lot of time.
- It lowers our mood, making us feel less inclined to do things.
- It dictates how we do things.
- It prevents us doing things we want to do.
- It distances us from the outside world.
- It lowers our expectations.

Creating a new outlook helps tackle OCD from different angles: it helps us create a new way of being that leaves less room for OCD as well as providing us with opportunities to boost our mood, increase our self-confidence and dip our toes into the world that is waiting for us to take full advantage of the wonderful things it has to offer.

What is 'normal' anyway?

Because of OCD, you might have forgotten how life used to be. It can be hard to imagine what you might want to do if there were no restrictions. Perhaps you've been so caught up with OCD that you've lost sight of how other people do things. This may be just one of the lies that OCD has told you to keep you in its grasp.

There is no such thing as 'normal'. How can we really know exactly what other people do? The new rule is that there are no 'rules'. Take the risk and try things out – that applies to new (non-OCD) ways of behaving as well as developing new interests and hobbies. It's important to move away from the idea that there's a 'right' way or a 'wrong' way. Without OCD, you are free to live the way that you want to.

Behaviour changing strategy

Task: My valued direction

Imagine that you wake up tomorrow morning and OCD is no longer a problem. What would you be doing? How would different aspects of your life have changed? This exercise can help you define what is important to you. It will help you decide what you need to do to move in the direction of your personal values.

	My valued direction
Personal relationships What do you want to be like as a partner? What kinds of things are important to you in close relationships? If you're not in a relationship at the moment, what sort of relationship would you like to have? How would you like to be with a partner?	
Family relationships What is important to you in how you want to be with family members? How do you want to treat your parents? What kind of sister or brother would you like to be? If you have children, what kind of parent would you like to be? If you're not in contact with some of your family, would you like to be? How would you want to act in such a relationship?	
Friends and social life What kinds of things do you value in your friendships? What are the important aspects of being a good friend? How would you like your friends to think of you? What kind of social life would you enjoy? Would you like to expand your social network – make more friends or increase your social activity?	

	My valued direction
Home How would you like to live? What is important to you? Is there anything that you would like to change in your home to reflect your interests, values or the kind of person you are? What would you like to be able to do at home, e.g. have visitors, spend time in the garden?	
Work or education What is important to you in your work (if you're not in paid work, think about your role as a parent or carer)? Is there anything you would like to do to further your career? What would make it more meaningful? What skills or knowledge would you like to develop? Why is learning important to you?	
Leisure What do you do to relax? What kinds of hobbies, interests or sports do you enjoy (or would you like to follow)? What is important to you about them? What would make your leisure time more satisfying? How could you have more fun? What would you enjoy doing on your own? Or with other people?	

Our personal values are the measures we use to determine whether our lives are turning out the way we want them to. Use them to make decisions and to identify your real priorities in life. Choose to take up opportunities that fit with what you truly want, rather than what OCD says you can have.

Practical advice ⇒

Helpful habits III: Becoming more active

Don't forget that looking after yourself is an important feature in maintaining your new life. Here is the next instalment of helpful habits. This time the topic is becoming more active.

It's a fact that few of us get enough exercise in a day. We're a nation of couch potatoes, spending far too much time sitting down – at our desks at work, in front of the television or playing computer games. Many of us turn up our noses at the prospect of exercise. Maybe we have bad memories of PE at school. Or perhaps you like the idea of doing something more physical but consider yourself to be too busy to fit it in to your day. It can seem hard to find a few minutes for yourself along with working or looking after your family. But it is an essential part of a healthy lifestyle. It's essential for:

- maintaining a healthy heart
- keeping muscles and bones strong
- reducing the likelihood of developing a serious illness
- reducing stress and lifting our mood.

As adults, we should be aiming for 150 minutes of exercise each week. This might seem a lot, but if we break it down, it's not much more than 20–25 minutes each day. And it doesn't have to be done in one chunk of activity either, although it is recommended that we have at least 10 minutes of aerobic activity each day – activity that raises our heart rate and makes us mildly out of breath – in order to have positive benefits on our cardiac health.

If we can build exercise into our daily routine, rather than it being 'something I mean to do when I have the time' or an activity that needs special arrangements in some way (like having to go to the gym, wear special clothing or have a big block of time available for it), so much the better. Stefan found that he could do 20 'star jumps' and touch his toes a dozen times in the time it took for the kettle to boil before he made tea in the morning. Making just small changes to what we already do is a great way to increase our activity levels. Maybe make it a rule to always use the stairs and never take the lift. Every little bit helps us build our activity levels.

Although experts don't seem to be able to agree whether vigorous housework counts as exercise, the way a thorough session with the vacuum cleaner makes us break into a sweat certainly suggests that something is happening in our bodies, even if it doesn't match a workout at the gym. Plus you get the added bonus of a clean house – what's not to like?

And how about including a few fun things in the mix? Dancing along to your favourite tunes on the radio while you dust or peel the potatoes brings cheer to even the dullest chores. And there are many short videos available free on the internet about everything from jiving lessons to boxing workouts. Of course, if you want to incorporate such fun activities into your leisure time you could join a local class, some of which are either free or don't cost much.

How about some of these ideas?

- Run on the spot while the kettle is boiling.
- Walk to the shops or the station instead of driving.
- Dance along to a song on the radio.
- Go for a walk whenever you use your mobile phone.
- Clean the windows.
- Walk to the next bus stop instead of catching the bus at the nearest one.
- Vacuum the house.
- Park your car in the furthest part of the car park.
- Sweep the patio or front path.
- Take the dog for a brisk walk.
- Play tickling games with your children (or partner!)
- Use a bike instead of the car.
- Carry heavy grocery shopping home from the shops.
- Garden.
- Learn to rock and roll.
- Make love.

- Move the furniture so you can clean in the corners of the room.
- Mow the lawn with a push-along mower.
- Paint your bedroom.
- Use the stairs instead of the lift at work or when shopping.
- Use a skipping rope (real or imaginary!)
- Play 'tag' with the kids.
- Go for a swim.
- Clean the car.
- Do 20 sit-ups.
- Meet a friend for a walk.
- Use an exercise bike while watching your favourite soap opera.
- Run for the bus!
- Join a football or netball team.
- Get an exercise DVD (or find a video on the internet).

Chapter summary

Now that you've finished this chapter, you have seen:

- OCD is not the friend it claimed to be
- OCD prevents us from living our lives according to our true values
- the importance of reclaiming your life while you tackle OCD.

Remember who you used to be before OCD sapped your confidence. Start living your life as if OCD was no longer an issue. Allow yourself to take up opportunities that OCD has denied you. Be patient: it takes time for our confidence to drain away, so it will take time to build it up again. Don't let the fact that you've suffered from OCD define you forever – it's just an episode in your life.

With your life in better shape, it's easy to settle for this. Why is it important to keep going? In Chapter 12, we'll be asking whether it's best to reduce or eliminate compulsions. Challenging thoughts and changing behaviour also steps up a gear.

PART 4

Practice

*Keep catching your behaviour
and letting your thoughts go
each time*

CHAPTER 12

Challenging thoughts and changing behaviour steps up a gear

Overview

Chapter 11 helped you to imagine your life without the OCD bully. This chapter explains:

● why it's best to eliminate OCD completely
● whether extreme exposure is necessary for success
● how to avoid slipping back into old habits.

By now you will have made some changes to loosen the hold that OCD has had on you. It won't have been easy; in fact, it may still seem a real struggle not to get swept away in the tide of obsessional worries, or drawn in to doing things that you now understand are unhelpful and prolong the agony in the longer term.

What is your ultimate goal in tackling OCD? To do things the non-OCD way, the way most people do things? To enable you to achieve this, it can be helpful to go that extra mile. Maxine wanted to enjoy a takeaway without having to wash her clothes afterwards. By smearing dabs of curry on her hair and clothes and not washing, she became more comfortable with the idea that food smells might linger. If we can do the more extreme things, then you know you can cope with all eventualities in real life.

OCD – reduce or eliminate?

Janet found it hard work but eventually managed to make a lot of changes. Life was so much more relaxed at home: she no longer insisted her husband and son strip off in the garage when they come in from football, and she enjoys hearing about the match while they sit in the kitchen with a hard-earned drink and snack. She's so proud that her son has actually gained a place in his school's first team, although her husband reckons it's the result of *his* coaching. As long as they leave their muddy football boots outside or in the garage, she's quite happy. 'Of course, they go and shower straight away,' she explained, 'and then I pop their kit in to wash … no point leaving it, is there?' she added. Janet described how much better things were now.

As the team's top goal-scorer that season, her son was extremely popular among his team-mates and often invited them round. Janet no longer minded them coming to their house either. Well, as long as it was only a couple of them – and not the lad who had a couple of those dogs with the long hair. 'It's not the dogs,' she insisted, 'he just seems a bit …you know …'. She reminds them to leave their shoes by the door; 'Well, we all do. It's only sensible with beige carpet.'

Janet went on to say how nice it was to be able to go out without a coat now that the weather was so warm, and she certainly didn't miss the odd looks she used to get when she always wore gloves. 'And look how much softer my hands are now,' she exclaimed, 'I'm not washing them all the time.' (Although she confessed she hadn't got around to chucking out the hand gel that was in the bottom of her handbag.)

Tadeusz had cut down the time it took to leave the house in the morning. He was content to have a quick look in each room and just try the window catch once. 'Naturally I make sure all the lights have been turned off, and I unplug the TV before I go to bed', he said, 'So

I know that I don't need to check them again in the morning.' But he had stopped watching the news while eating his breakfast some time ago, so he had no need to go into the lounge before work as he ate his cereal standing in the kitchen. 'I can leave the flat in 20 minutes', he pronounced delightedly.

Why cutting down is not enough

The idea of 'OCD Lite' might be appealing, but just as with cakes, biscuits and crisps marketed in a similar way, we haven't learned to change our unhelpful habits. On a weight-loss diet, we need to acquire the habit of snacking on wholesome and healthy foods, or just breaking the habit of having biscuits with our cup of tea. Developing helpful habits in relation to OCD works in a similar way: it's important to make a complete change from your old OCD way of doing things.

The changes Janet has made are brilliant. They've made such a difference not only to her life but also that of her family. It's wonderful to see how she can now do the kinds of things she really wants to do. If we asked Janet to put herself on a scale ranging from obsessively clean to filthy dirty, she'd probably rate herself as being on the clean side of average. While that shows fantastic progress, should she be content with that? It's understandable that Janet wouldn't want to 'rock the boat' by pushing herself too hard now that she isn't overwhelmed by anxiety every time she sets foot out of the door, and that she can be relaxed in her home and enjoy having visitors. Yet it would concern me that OCD might still be just around the corner, waiting for an opportunity to creep back into Janet's life. In Chapter 7 we examined two different ways of looking at OCD: Theory A and Theory B. Both Janet and Tadeusz are still dealing with OCD as a danger problem.

> ## Don't get re infected!
>
> The doctor examines your wound after you've completed a course of treatment. 'That's looks much better ... there's only a bit of infection left. Nothing too serious. Let's leave it at that.'
>
> Would you be happy with this? Why not?
>
> That's right. Unless the infection has cleared up completely, it can still come back and cause more problems.

So it's important not to just cut down on rituals and compulsions, or take the 'OCD express' approach by doing them more quickly. Having fewer worries may seem great, but to really free ourselves from OCD we need to create more!

Do I need to do extreme things?

Television programmes in recent years have depicted OCD sufferers doing some extreme things to overcome their OCD. It's not surprising that many people are put off seeking help when we see someone who, only moments after admitting that they are petrified of germs, is plunging their hand down the toilet in a fairly spectacular fashion. Programme makers are looking for something 'sexy' with visual impact to draw in viewing audiences. Nevertheless, exposing ourselves to situations that are outside our comfort zone is essential to ensure long-term freedom from OCD.

So is it necessary to do extreme things in order to tackle OCD? It isn't the case that doing the most extreme things you can think of in connection with your OCD problem will make it better, as if by magic. What is important is to do things that take us outside our comfort zone. For example, the ultimate goal of someone who has an extreme fear of heights may be to visit their friend on the sixth floor of a block of flats. Would it be enough just to work up to that? Or is it more helpful to do something more? Doing more extreme things, such as going to the 50th floor of a building, would mean that they wouldn't be concerned at the thought of the lift bypassing the sixth floor, or their friend moving to a higher floor.

Anxiety is what you need to expose yourself to, not necessarily the feared substance or situation (no therapist would be keen on putting their fingers in dog mess!). If we're having fewer worries, we get fewer opportunities to expose ourselves to the anxiety that goes with those worries.

The key thing to remember about OCD is that it is an **anxiety problem**. And in order to free ourselves from an anxiety problem, we have to do things that make us feel anxious. Anxiety isn't something we can go over, under or around; we *have* to go through it. In fact, trying to avoid anxiety is one of the key reasons why it persists. Although you probably struggle to believe it, facing up to situations that make us feel anxious is often not as bad as we think it will be. It's like being told that you have to go into a lion's cage and stick your head into its mouth. What a terrifying idea – it's roaring like crazy, it's not surprising you're shaking in your shoes. But when you dare to enter the cage and (gasp!) put your face close to its gaping jaws, you see that the lion has no teeth.

But for exposure to be successful we have to make sure that we really are exposing ourselves fully to the anxiety – closing our eyes, holding our nose and jumping into the deep end is not exposure (even metaphorically). Being 'present', i.e. in the moment and willingly accepting uncomfortable experiences without avoidance or other efforts to control them, is vital.

Doing things the anti-OCD way

So far, the focus has been on dropping OCD habits and doing things in the way most people would. We've called it the 'non-OCD' way. It's one thing to refuse to listen to OCD and wait for it to go away, but to rid yourself of it for good you need to CHASE it away.

The anti-OCD way means going that extra mile to bring on some of your worst worries. What we're aiming for is to be able to accept and tolerate the worst OCD worries without trying to soothe our discomfort. Have a look at some anti-OCD examples to give you an idea.

	OCD way	Non-OCD way	Anti-OCD way
Maxine	Avoid cooking smelly foods, e.g. fish, garlic.	Cook whatever I fancy.	Chop an onion and leave it in the lounge.
Carol	Hide sharp knives, scissors and other potential weapons.	Use sharp knives or other tools when I need to.	Put the bread knife on my bedside table at night.
Janet	Avoid walking near dog mess or even looking at it.	Walk in areas where dog-walkers go.	Put a joke dog poo on my bed. Make some chocolate cakes that look like dog poo for my son.
Tadeusz	Unplug all appliances before leaving the house.	Leave the kettle, TV, alarm clock and table lamps plugged in all the time.	Switch the lights, TV, radio, oven, kettle and toaster on and go out for the afternoon.
Stefan	Avoid 'unlucky' numbers.	Ignore thoughts about unlucky numbers, buy four-packs of cans or chocolate bars.	Have a T-shirt printed with 666 on the back. Stick the number 13 where I'll see it.
David	Ask my mother to check my mail before shredding it.	Decide for myself what to throw out. Only shred bank statements.	Put some bank or credit card statements in the recycling bin without tearing them up.

	OCD way	Non-OCD way	Anti-OCD way
Richard	Check if I get aroused by images of men or women.	Be friendly and chatty with both sexes without wondering if I fancy them.	Play 'Glad to be gay' on my MP3 player … on repeat.

Perhaps you're thinking, 'But no one does that kind of thing!' Certainly, most people don't do the kinds of things listed in the anti-OCD column. Unless they're tackling OCD. Think of it like this: who raises and lowers their leg 100 times a day? Not many people … unless their leg is recently out of plaster following a fracture. The muscle would need building up again, so a physiotherapist might recommend an exercise like this. Doing these more unusual things will help you build up your anti-OCD muscles.

'I'll do anything to get rid of OCD' … but not this? If you've been reluctant to write down some more unusual ideas for anti-OCD challenges, it's important to reflect on why that might be. It usually suggests that's where the action is, and that some unhelpful beliefs are still holding you back. Have you slipped back into accepting the old OCD view that there is a danger that you need to avoid? If it's because you feel too nervous to have a go, it's fine to start with something less anxiety-provoking. But at some stage maybe you will accept the thoughts and the anxiety and do it anyway.

Case study: Carol

'My therapist helped me see how my way of thinking had been based on the way I felt, rather than on what was real. Sometimes she would suggest ways of dealing with habits or things I had been avoiding and I would think, "I don't want to do that", but I knew that I needed to, to get rid of the problem. And the more times I did something the anti-OCD way, the better it became. Most importantly, by stopping the rituals the feeling that I needed to do them went away. When I stopped trying to feel 'all right', then I just did. Moreover, I experienced a wonderful sense of freedom when I realized I didn't have to follow the rules OCD was persuading me to do.'

Dare to be dangerous

Don't let OCD call the shots. Choosing to do things the anti-OCD way treats the OCD bully with the contempt it deserves. It can feel scary to begin with, but it is possible to have some fun with it too – who says therapy has to be serious all the time? So engage your naughty side and think up some fun challenges. It's saying to OCD, 'Come and get me … if you think you're hard enough!'

Have a look at some of these ideas for inspiration (and yes, these are things that have really been done to tackle OCD).

Dare to be dirty …

… if your concerns are about cleanliness or contamination. For example:

- use a 'contaminated' duster to clean your home – Maxine dirtied hers on the dustbin and dabbed some tuna on it
- put your bag and coat on the floor in a public toilet
- choose cutlery with dried-on food deposits when you eat out
- rub your hands over clean crockery after stroking the cat
- sit at the dirtiest table in a café
- stick a picture of maggots inside your fridge
- skip washing your hands for a whole day
- lick the sole of your shoe!

Come on, be careless …

… especially if your concerns are about checking or doubting, tidiness, order, perfection or you have repeating rituals. For example:

- play Remote Control Lotto when you lock your car so you can't be sure it's locked
- leave the oven on all day while you go out
- write your bank details and your signature on a slip of paper and leave it on the bus

- put a ballpoint mark on a brand-new item of clothing
- deliberately make a mistake when sending emails or letters
- mess up your neatly arranged DVD or book collection
- make the bed and then lie on it without straightening it up afterwards
- put canned goods away upside down.

Happy to be harmful ...

...especially if your concerns are about causing harm to yourself or others. For example:

- deliberately bump into someone in the street
- kick some debris into the middle of the road where a car could run over it
- move an item to the edge of the shelf in a shop where it could get knocked off
- wish something bad on someone
- drive with the radio on full blast and a heavy item rolling around in the boot so you couldn't hear if you hit something
- put sharp cans or broken glass in the dustbin without wrapping them
- watch the film *Psycho* with the bread knife on your lap.

Fun with flights of fancy ...

... especially if your concerns are about sex, blasphemy or morality. This is also helpful if ruminations are the main problem. For example:

- rather than stop your thoughts, embellish them. Sahib didn't just agree with his thoughts, but deliberately imagined everyone in his class naked on their bikes
- Mandy found she could sing, 'I'm a paedophile and a murderer' to the tune of the *William Tell* overture
- saying a swear word when you walk past a place of worship
- ask the devil to come and get you, and picture burning in hell for all eternity

- stick pictures of famous murderers around your house, and have one as a screensaver on your phone too.

Dare to be dangerous …

… especially if your concerns are about checking, doubting, numbers or superstition. For example:

- deliberately break a mirror, walk under ladders, etc.
- stick your 'unlucky' numbers all over the place
- leave your car for 15 minutes after your parking ticket has run out
- get 'D.I.V.O.R.C.E.' as your ring tone
- throw a handful of old correspondence out without looking at it – at all!
- throw nearly empty bottles/packets of bleach or weedkiller into a public bin near a school or children's play area
- Carol danced around the house wielding a knife and singing the Tom Jones song 'Delilah'.

So, as you can see, we have quite a range of unusual things to do! What will you do today to chase OCD away? Make your list in the table in the next box.

But these are real worries …

No, most people *don't* do this kind of thing. The aim of the anti-OCD approach is to build up your resilience to uncertainty and risk.

Is it possible that you're worrying more than you need to? Remember that OCD gets you to appraise things as being more dangerous than they actually are. For example, even if something is dirty, it doesn't mean it will definitely cause disease or that you need to do something about it. Feeling responsible for harm often leads to, say, lengthy washing, which in turn makes it feel like it's important to keep paying attention to dirt or germs.

Behaviour changing strategy

Task

You'll need your Theory A/Theory B sheet from Chapter 7 to help you with this exercise. On the sheet below, or a copy of it, fill in the 'OCD way' column with items from your Theory A answers, and the 'Non-OCD way' column with items from your Theory B answers.

Now, have fun thinking of interesting items to put in the 'Anti-OCD way' column that will really rock the boat and challenge OCD.

OCD way	Non-OCD way	Anti-OCD way

Worrying too much about the dangers and feeling highly responsible for preventing bad things from happening have the effect of making you over-sensitive to potential hazards. You see dangers everywhere. We talked about trying too hard to achieve certainty in Chapter 10.

Compulsions and rituals are often unrealistic or out of proportion to the risk. What you're in fact doing is attempting to get rid of the anxiety that the thoughts cause you. Do others share your concerns or do the kinds of things you do? Is it only through luck that they've managed not to have bad things happen to them?

If you change the things you do, there's no guarantee that you won't leave a window open accidentally, step in dog poo, lose your keys or get food poisoning. But if you keep on doing what you have been doing, you're guaranteed to be troubled by OCD.

Once you have conquered OCD, you will be able to *choose* exactly how you want to live your life. However, it may be that occasionally you will find it helpful to have done some of these bizarre things. Maxine enjoyed her first foreign holiday for years, and laughed as she explained that she hadn't been able to shower for three whole days on a trekking holiday in South America. How could the anti-OCD approach liberate you?

Case study: Niamh

'When I started doing anti-OCD stuff … I felt like I had the power instead of OCD. It meant I was no longer the victim … I was the *doer*. It was so much better having something to actually *do* rather than doing something more passive.'

Chapter summary

In this chapter you have learned:

- why it's necessary to eliminate compulsions and avoidance rather than just reducing them
- how doing more extreme things aids recovery
- what you can do to challenge your OCD concerns further.

As we change our relationship with OCD, unwanted thoughts often reduce and we spend less time carrying out compulsions. While this seems like a good thing, there is still scope for OCD to creep back in. By doing 'just enough' it is likely that we'll still be afraid of events that would take us out of our comfort zone. By this stage, it often takes more to trigger concerns. If you are 'prepared to do anything to get rid of OCD but not *that*', *that* is exactly what you need to do. By going that extra mile and doing some unusual things, we not only refuse to listen to OCD but actively chase it away. Doing the anti-OCD things invites OCD to come and get us. Not only are you encouraged to allow such thoughts into your head, but urged to embellish them beyond your wildest imaginings. The message is that if you want to think about it *less*, think about it more.

By building and strengthening your alternative view of OCD, you are developing a new outlook and a new way of being. In Chapter 13, we will look at how life experiences may influence underlying beliefs and assumptions. Are you ready to find out more?

Why am I like this?

Overview

Chapter 12 enabled you to understand how doing more extreme things helps eliminate OCD. This chapter takes a look at the broader context of your experience of OCD and explores:

- the role of life experiences
- underlying beliefs and assumptions
- how to generate a more helpful outlook.

Experiences shape and influence how we are – they're not causes as such, but they create filters through which we see the world. We refer to these filters as beliefs and assumptions. Although we are advised against trying to work out why we are the way we are with regard to 'causes' (see Chapter 5) it is helpful to examine the underlying beliefs and assumptions we hold that may benefit from being modified to a more balanced view.

Beliefs and assumptions can outgrow their usefulness. For example, most parents instruct their children not to talk to strangers. While that can be a useful rule when we're five years old, or even 10, if we still operate under that rule when we're 25 our lives will have suffered greatly as a consequence. What beliefs and assumptions might contribute to OCD?

Why am I like this?

According to cognitive behavioural theory, life experiences shape our beliefs and assumptions about ourselves, the world and other people. Experiences from our childhood often play a significant role in the development of these. The beliefs and assumptions provide meaning and understanding, guiding our thinking and our actions and helping us to navigate our way through life. However, not all our beliefs and assumptions are beneficial.

Some of us are more sensitive to interpreting situations as dangerous or harmful. This is because we have underlying beliefs (sometimes called **core beliefs** or **schema**) and **assumptions** about danger. Once these beliefs and assumptions have been triggered, we are more likely to keep having more thoughts about danger and keep viewing things in this way. Because we tend to accept these beliefs and assumptions as being true, it is understandable that we'd want to reduce the likelihood of danger or harm.

Core beliefs are central rules or guides through which we see ourselves, the world and other people. They are shaped by experiences from childhood as well as things that happen later in life. Beliefs take the form of fixed statements:

● I am ...
● Other people are ...
● The world is ...

An assumption is something that is accepted as true or certain to happen, without proof. Assumptions take the form of conditional statements:

● If ... then ...
● If I don't .... then ....
● I should ...

Safety-behaviours and avoidance cause their own problems. They intensify anxiety symptoms and prevent us finding out that our beliefs about danger might not be true. They often lead to further unhelpful thoughts that produce unhelpful behaviours, creating vicious circles. We have seen how a series of vicious circles keeps OCD going in our Vicious Flower formulation in Chapter 6.

While core beliefs about danger and harm lie beneath anxiety disorders as a whole, there are certain beliefs and assumptions that are mainly linked to OCD. These include:

- over-estimation of risk
- increased sense of responsibility
- unacceptability of certain types of thoughts.

What makes us vulnerable to OCD?

It is likely that vulnerability to developing OCD occurs as a combination of factors including the biological, genetic, behavioural, cognitive, social and environmental.

Biological factors

A popular idea about OCD is that it is caused by a fault or chemical imbalance in the brain. Although there has been a lot of research into biological causes of OCD, so far there have been no definite findings. Biological explanations do not currently enhance our understanding of how OCD can be treated.

Although some types of antidepressant medication can reduce OCD symptoms, this should not be taken as evidence for a chemical imbalance. After all, paracetamol reduces pain but it doesn't mean that pain is caused by a shortage of paracetamol in the brain!

Sometimes a number of people in a family may have OCD. While this could seem to confirm a genetic component, a different explanation is just as likely.

Psychological and social factors

Could you have 'caught' OCD from a parent? We learn a great deal from our families in all kinds of ways. Ways of doing things, little habits and traditions, even certain mannerisms run in families. Most of these we have simply learned from being around others who do things in a certain way. Do you think there could be a gene for preferring to drink tea from a mug rather than a cup and saucer?

In this way, we might pick up particular ways of doing things. If adults around us when we are children tend to worry about harm or cleanliness, we might develop similar attitudes. When others are engaged in routines and rituals arising from obsessional concerns, it's easy for things we do to slip by unnoticed and unchallenged.

If we are victims of criticism or blame, our core beliefs are shaped to reflect our interpretation of these experiences. Constantly being blamed for things we hadn't done ('Who did that? I bet it was you!) may make us over-cautious, not wanting to risk mistakes. We form our own rules for protection and survival. We may also develop rules about responsibility based on those experiences. Strict codes of conduct can also make us prone to rigid beliefs about right and wrong, or having to do things in a perfect or exacting manner.

If we've never been allowed to take responsibility for anything, we may develop beliefs about incompetence or vulnerability and that danger is just around the corner. Some of us may have been burdened with responsibility from a young age – perhaps having to care for a parent with a disability – and may then believe that the onus is always on us to be in control or to ensure things don't go wrong. In other instances, we may mistake events outside our control as something we had influenced. For example, we might attribute an accident to something we did or didn't do. Magical thinking or superstitious behaviour can be an example of this, perhaps believing that the reason for the accident was because we didn't say goodbye in the 'right' way or had removed a good luck charm.

Pathways to responsibility sensitivity include:

- taking on too much responsibility in childhood (either through choice or circumstances)
- strict religious, moral or behavioural codes
- being sheltered from responsibility

- an incident in which our actions (or inaction) actually contributed to misfortune
- an incident in which our thoughts, actions or inactions appeared to contribute to misfortune.

Not everyone in a family turns out to be the same. There's a complex interaction of many factors. An important factor appears to be our own interpretation of experiences. These are filtered through our core beliefs and acted on in accordance with our assumptions. Factors such as personality play a part. We might have a generally anxious temperament, be dependent on others or have low self-esteem. Equally, someone with unrelenting high standards (especially for themselves) and a tendency to perfectionism may also be vulnerable to developing OCD.

External factors

Certain experiences in our lives can trigger core beliefs and assumptions which increase the likelihood of us developing OCD. If we already have a certain vulnerability, even events such as leaving home, getting a promotion at work or having a baby may lead to the onset of OCD. These incidents alone are unlikely to trigger OCD. However, they can combine with beliefs and assumptions that we already have.

At times, more dramatic events provide the spark, such as a fire or a flood, being falsely accused of a crime or a death in the family. Critical incidents such as these don't necessarily set off OCD at the time. It might be years before some other event finally starts it off.

Case study

As a young boy, Tadeusz and his friend enjoyed roaming freely in the lakeland area of his native Poland. His friend's dog, Spifka, always trotted along after them. The boys enjoyed throwing a stick for the dog, tossing it into the lake for him to fetch. They did this several times over, laughing as the dog jumped into the chilly water to retrieve it and doggy-paddled back to the shore. Again, they flung the stick and the dog duly plunged in to get it. Only this time, Spifka didn't return.

Interestingly, this vivid and catastrophic incident didn't have any obvious impact on Tadeuz for almost 15 years. It was only after moving to the UK and getting his own flat that he began to worry about safety and being responsible for things going wrong if he wasn't careful enough. The unfortunate incident with the dog may have added to his store of beliefs and assumptions, beliefs and assumptions that had already developed while he was growing up. Never having to do anything for himself, he had been shielded from all responsibility until now.

Underlying beliefs and early experiences

While all our experiences are unique to us and we make sense of them in different ways, certain core beliefs occur regularly in OCD:

- I am a bad person.
- I am dangerous.
- I am weak and vulnerable.
- My judgment can't be trusted.

Of course, our belief-system is far more complicated than that. However, these themes often arise in some form. Here you can see how past events and underlying beliefs and assumptions fit in with each person's experience of OCD.

	Underlying beliefs and assumptions	Life experiences	Critical incident
Janet	I am a clean person. Unless I protect my child from all harm, I am a bad mother.	Several miscarriages – struggled to conceive. Mother house-proud and critical.	Reading about toxoplasmosis during pregnancy.

	Children are vulnerable.	Parents not cuddly; showed care in practical ways.	
Maxine	I am unacceptable. I am not good enough.	Only child of single mother. Not much money. Importance of 'being nice'. Never had a long-term relationship.	
David	I am stupid. Better safe than sorry. We live in a dangerous world. People will take advantage of me.	Bullied at school. Always 'away with the fairies'. Found school work a struggle although he passed his exams. Parents were both worriers. Low self-esteem.	
Mandy	I am a bad person. Sin by thought. I must always be in control (of my thoughts).	Experienced OCD during teens. Playing 'doctors & nurses' as child; feeling guilty and dirty. Religious school (even though parents weren't); always talking about sin.	Birth of her first baby.

(Continued)

Tadeusz	Bad things happen out of the blue. It's irresponsible not to be careful about things that could cause harm.	Playing with my friend's dog.	Accident with his friend's dog. Moving to UK.

Sahib and Mandy both assumed that someone who experienced the kinds of sexual thoughts they had were deviant. Leila and David assumed that unless they were 100 per cent certain, they would make terrible mistakes or errors of judgment.

Core beliefs and assumptions	Appraisals of intrusive thoughts
I am a bad person.	I am bad for thinking this way.
I am stupid.	I will get it wrong.
Other people will judge me.	I will be blamed if I make a mistake.
Bad things happen out of the blue.	I have to be sure nothing will happen.
Better safe than sorry.	I can't take the risk of things going wrong.
I must always be in control of my thoughts.	I shouldn't be thinking like this.
Children are vulnerable and need protecting.	I need to do all I can to protect my child.
I am vulnerable.	Getting too anxious is dangerous.

Figure 13.1 shows how core beliefs and assumptions contribute to intrusive thoughts.

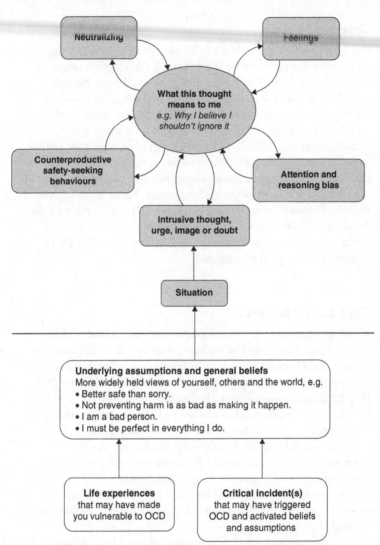

Figure 13.1: Our vicious flower revisited ... complete with roots. Like other flowers, our vicious flower has not just appeared from nowhere. These underlying beliefs and assumptions that we develop as a result of our experiences form the roots that may contribute to our sensitivity to developing OCD.

Case study: Arun

When Arun was only a child his father died of a heart attack brought on by stress. His mother used to say, 'Don't let that happen to you'. As a consequence, Arun worried that anxiety would damage his heart. Once he understood how OCD had developed and taken a hold, he was determined to test out these unhelpful (and inaccurate) thoughts. Rather than try to soothe himself when he became stressed and anxious, Arun determinedly pictured himself in his mind's eye getting so worked up, with a purple face and steam coming out of his ears, that he eventually popped like a balloon. Not only was he able to test out his belief that he would have a heart attack, but he began to build up a more balanced view of himself. He could see that he was no more vulnerable than most people. In fact, he noticed that since allowing thoughts to come and go (a strategy he didn't reserve just for OCD thoughts) he was generally calmer.

Case study: Mandy

Mandy struggled with unwanted, and very graphic, thoughts about her baby girl. They pushed all the buttons for her: she swung between trying to hold back certain memories from her own childhood and not becoming overwhelmed. 'What kind of mother thinks like this?' Her long-held assumptions provided her with an immediate answer: only a terrible one. A terrible mother who is a bad person. Mandy's conclusion fitted with a belief about herself that she had tried to hide.

Mandy dated her belief that she was a bad person back to experiences when she was a child. When she was seven, she and a schoolfriend played 'doctors and nurses', taking it in turns to have a look at each other's genitals. She felt guilty and ashamed at the time in case her parents or teachers got to know. She reflected on why she believed she was bad.

At Mandy's school, religious instruction played a large part in the timetable. Having pure thoughts was something the children were instructed to strive for. The notion that thinking bad things was as bad as doing them – sin by thought – was drummed into them. Mandy believed she should always be 'good' in thought, word and deed if she was to be a good person.

However, now she could use her 'wise mind' to challenge her seven-year-old way of thinking. 'It's natural to be curious about our bodies at that age,' she agreed, 'but I convinced myself I was bad because of what we were always being told at school.' She then came to a new conclusion. 'I wasn't being bad … I was just being a kid.'

How much do we need to challenge core beliefs?

While some of our underlying beliefs do not provide a helpful filter through which to see ourselves and the world, it isn't necessary to directly challenge them in order to free ourselves from OCD. We can just do things differently, despite the ideas our mind may be sending us. By continuing to act differently, we develop different viewpoints which back up other (more helpful) beliefs.

An awareness of *how* we're thinking can assist us in letting thoughts and ideas go. **All-or-nothing thinking** is a common tendency in OCD. Unless Maxine could be certain she was completely clean and fragrant, she reckoned she was smelly and dirty. When Tadeusz had doubts about whether it was safe to leave the toaster plugged in, he decided it must be dangerous. Although you now know that accepting uncertainty is vital to living life free from OCD, it's useful to recognize this thinking style. In Mandy's case, she supposed that if she wasn't a good person, she must be a bad one.

We all have a tendency to accept the beliefs we have about ourselves and the world without questioning them. Sometimes simple rules we may have been given (or devised for ourselves) outgrow their usefulness, as with the 'Don't talk to strangers' example given at the start of this chapter. In a moment there will be an opportunity to examine some of your beliefs and assumptions, but let's look at how else responsibility beliefs can be altered.

All-or-nothing thinking

Mandy's belief that she was a bad person had only surfaced after Betsy was born and she began to experience intrusive thoughts. The responsibility for preventing others discovering what she had always suspected felt immense: 'I must control these thoughts at all costs'. The assumption that went with that was 'Unless I control unwanted thoughts, I'm a bad mother'. Notice that it's one of those 'If ... then ...' statements again. We make rules for ourselves in this way based on beliefs we hold.

Using a **responsibility pie chart**, Mandy was encouraged to consider whether other factors might also be relevant to being a good mother. She came up with several ideas, which were allocated pieces of pie, leaving her original belief about controlling unwanted thoughts until last (Figure 13.2).

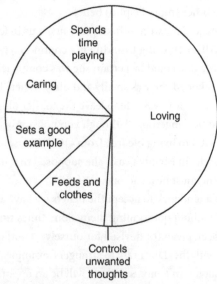

Figure 13.2: What makes a good mother?

What do you think she made of this? Well, she could see that even if controlling thoughts seemed important to her, it was only a very small part of what she really thought being a good mother was. So it wasn't a case of being either a good mother or a bad one; there were lots of points in between. No one is all one thing or another, nor are we fixed at a certain point. Mandy also recognized that the other factors were in fact even more important to her and part of her personal value system.

Think about these questions for a moment.

- What kind of person would be most upset by the kind of thoughts Mandy had?
- If Mandy was a bad person, what would she think, feel and do if she had these thoughts?
- Was that what her response was?

Mandy admitted that someone who was gentle, kind and loved children would be most upset by the thoughts she had. She went on to say that a bad person wouldn't be upset by them; in fact, she reckoned a paedophile would probably be happy to have them. Such people certainly wouldn't avoid children or babies in the way she did. 'So perhaps I'm not really a bad person after all … I only find them upsetting because they just don't reflect the kind of person I really am.'

Reviewing behaviour

Task: Loosening unhelpful beliefs

Consider the following.

- What kind of person would be most upset by the kind of thoughts you have?
- What do you think, feel and do when you get these thoughts?
- What does that say about you as a person?
- How well does that fit with your core beliefs about yourself?

Perfectionism

While healthy striving can be a good thing from time to time, continually setting yourself high standards and make yourself unhappy trying to reach them may be a sign of perfectionism. While this isn't exclusive to OCD, trying to do things perfectly (including things like washing) or attempting to 'feel right' and be free from doubts may be a sign that perfectionism is a problem for you. Beliefs about perfection can be modified using the same methods described above. You may also find it helpful to revisit the 'Trying too hard' section in Chapter 10.

Generating a more helpful outlook

We used Mandy's experience to work through some examples of how certain beliefs may have developed as a result of experiences we have had. She was encouraged to consider whether these beliefs really reflected her nature, and whether there were more helpful ways of looking at it. Use the chart below to guide you through identifying unhelpful beliefs. How could you view it differently?

Behaviour changing strategy

Task: That was then … But this is now

Use this chart to guide you through identifying unhelpful beliefs and how you could view these differently.

That was then …
Some of the significant experiences in my life that may have made me more vulnerable to developing OCD have been: *(e.g. childhood, family, school, life events, things you were told)*

_____

_____

_____

_____

It's understandable that I developed the following rules and beliefs which shaped the way I saw myself and how I looked at the world:
I am …

_____

_____

Thoughts are …

_____

_____

Other people are …

_____

_____

The world is …

_____

_____

What did these rules make me think, feel and do when I experienced intrusive thoughts, doubts or urges?
They made me think …

_____

_____

They made me feel …

_____

_____

They make me believe I had to do the following things …

_____

_____

They seemed helpful because …

_____

_____

_____

235

But this is now
I know now that these were unhelpful habits because: *(e.g. effect on thoughts, feelings and behaviour, what I'm really like as a person)*

_____

_____

_____

_____

A more helpful way to see myself and how I look at the world is:
I am …

_____

_____

Thoughts are …

_____

_____

Other people are …

_____

_____

The world is …

_____

_____

I have a better understanding of OCD in the following ways.
What I now understand about thoughts:

_____

_____

What I now understand about my feelings:

_____

_____

What I now understand about the things I do:

_____

_____

What I now know I should do when I experience these thoughts and feelings:

_____

_____

I can already see that this is helpful because of the following.
Effects on my thoughts:

_____

_____

Effects on how I feel:

_____

_____

Effect on what I do:

_____

_____

If I continue to live my life according to this new way of looking at OCD: *(e.g. What is likely to happen? What will be the effect on your thoughts or feelings? What will be different?)*

_____

_____

_____

_____

Cultivate a new relationship with experiences

Just as we're developing a different relationship with our thoughts, we need to cultivate a new relationship with our experiences too, whether they are things that happened in the past, or something that is happening at the moment. Realize that experience is just that.

'Autopilot' is the force that drives us most of the day. Even when we sit 'doing nothing', we're planning, remembering, worrying, daydreaming. By creating a moment-by-moment friendliness to our experiences, we can notice signs of OCD, respond wisely and with compassion: 'This is OCD and this is what I can do'.

Underlying beliefs and assumptions can create a sense that there's something missing. Maybe we feel that we're lacking in some way. These messages, along with memories of unhappy experiences, are not 'now' or the present. Coming back to the present and recognizing them as echoes from the past enables us to shift out of autopilot into something else.

Recognize when particular appraisals have been activated:

- I can't do this.
- I won't be able to cope with this feeling.
- This is dangerous.
- I can't risk this becoming true.

Behaviour changing strategy

Task

Consider the following:

- When do you believe your thoughts more? Are there particular situations that make them more convincing? How about when you're in a particular mood?
- When do you believe them less? What is different about these occasions? What does this tell you?

When we're in a moment of high pressure, these kinds of thoughts and ideas feel very convincing. Away from this moment, we believe them less.

So what can you do next time you notice yourself feeling troubled in your mind and becoming drawn into your thoughts? The first step is always to take a breathing space. Then remind yourself to step back from the thoughts your mind is sending you. If you are uncertain whether or not there is a problem that needs your attention, treat it as OCD – it's your old war wound being activated. Now you know what you *really* need to do.

The wise choice is to do things that are consistent with your values. Carol had been avoiding visiting her brother and his young family because of her obsessions about losing control and harming them.

Being a close-knit family was part of her personal value system and very important to her. OCD prevented her from seeing them as much as she would like. 'I could go to visit them this afternoon and take my OCD with me ... mindfully.'

Chapter summary

In this chapter you have seen how:

- beliefs and assumptions are filters through which we see the world
- certain beliefs increase our vulnerability to developing OCD
- unhelpful beliefs can be altered.

Our experiences are unique to us, and we make sense of them in our own way. There is no single reason why you have developed OCD. A complicated mixture of life experiences, biological, psychological, social and environmental factors lead us to develop a framework of beliefs and assumptions. Although it isn't helpful to look for causes, it is helpful to amend those beliefs which fuel safety behaviours and avoidance. There's no need to let all-or-nothing thinking hold you back. Good enough is good enough.

Keeping up momentum with your new approach to OCD is rarely easy. Are you ready to discover what to do when the going gets tough? Chapter 14 discusses how to cope with setbacks and get things moving again.

When the going gets tough

Overview

In Chapter 13 we examined how our experiences can shape and influence our beliefs, which may increase our vulnerability to developing OCD. In this chapter, we will concentrate on:

- coping with setbacks
- how to keep up progress
- when life gets in the way.

Overcoming any kind of difficulty is rarely straightforward. Change doesn't always continue at a steady rate. Irregular progress can be very frustrating too, and you may begin to feel that you are getting nowhere. At times like these it's important to remind yourself of your overall improvement. Furthermore, that some progress (no matter how modest) is better than no progress at all. If you think in terms of success or failure, you are more likely to give up attempts at working through OCD. You are only allowing yourself to be one of two things: either a success or a failure; there is no middle ground. Be kinder to yourself. Why not erase the word 'failure' from your vocabulary and replace it with the word 'setback'?

It's no coincidence that the theme of this book is about living your life free from OCD. The overall aim is not to stamp out certain kinds of thoughts, urges, images or impulses but to learn how to live life the way that *you* want despite them. See Chapter 9 for a recap on what we said about this.

Coping with setbacks

Wouldn't it be brilliant if we just sailed through any project we started without a hitch or a hiccup? But it's never like that, is it? It's not unusual to feel a bit stuck or even find ourselves slipping back. It's helpful to recognize this.

Changing our relationship with OCD is a process. Even not making progress can be part of that process. It's like stopping off on a journey; it isn't our destination, yet we might stay there for a while. We might even plan to take a slightly different route. That's fine, as long as we eventually set off on our journey again.

What's keeping you stuck?

- This approach isn't working.
- I've stopped making progress.
- I've had a bad day … I'll never do it.
- I should have cracked it by now … I'm useless!
- I keep forgetting to do it.
- What if this isn't OCD?
- I'm struggling to get started.
- The most awful thing has happened!

This approach isn't working

Leila found that while she was far less bothered by doubts about whether her boyfriend was 'the one' and urges to confess all, other kinds of thoughts started to pop into her mind. She found it particularly upsetting when they were in bed together and the thought, 'Is he really attractive?' flashed into her head. Even though she knew it was a doubt, she still found herself slipping into her old way of having a mental debate in which she tried to weigh up whether or not she still found him attractive. However, the more she tried to make herself feel certain, the worse she felt.

'I ended up thinking that this treatment really can't be working after all if I'm still getting these kinds of thoughts.' Although Leila was so upset she felt like giving up, she made herself carry on using the same techniques that she'd used to free herself from her initial thoughts. 'I'm so glad that I did', she declared, 'Because, although it was so tough at times, all that hard work has really paid off and I have more of an understanding of the condition, which will definitely help me in the future.'

Don't judge success by 'feeling better'. Success is about resisting compulsions and anything else we're tempted to do to make ourselves better in the short term. It's sticking with what will take us towards our long-term values. That's not about feeling better right now. Are you sure you've not been slipping in a few neutralizing strategies here and there? Perhaps telling yourself it will be all right?

It takes time and a lot of patience to stick with the programme. Many people have benefited from this approach, as research shows. They also found it a struggle at times but by carrying on they eventually improved. It's important to remember, too, that if you are seeing a therapist for treatment of your OCD, you would be working on the problem for a long time – usually around three months or more.

I've stopped making progress

When we begin to tackle OCD, a lot of changes often take place within a short period of time. You may have faced some pretty big challenges. Janet hadn't been out without a coat for years. It had been a long time since Maxine had cooked anything. There were so many things Shiralee couldn't do for fear of the name 'Steve' or seeing coffee shops. Those first steps were giant steps for each of them. As they progressed, subsequent steps didn't seem so big.

Sometimes we simply reach a plateau. Nothing much seems to be changing; we haven't slipped back, but we don't seem to have got much better either. Maybe you've become too comfortable with your progress? If so, you may be allowing yourself to coast along without pushing yourself. Staying put for a while is like taking a break on a journey. How about adding a bit more anti-OCD to the mix to give you a kick-start?

It's a good idea to consider *how* you're monitoring your progress. If you are on a diet, how helpful would it be to weigh yourself every day? You might remind yourself not to have biscuits with your coffee (or if you had, to get back to your eating plan straight away). For encouragement, it's better to look at how far we've come rather than at how far we still need to travel.

In the 'This approach isn't working' section, we spoke about allowing enough time to pass before judging how much progress you've made. If you were also asked whether you had spent adequate amount of time challenging your OCD every day, what would your honest answer be? If your answer is, 'Oh, not much. I've been a bit slack recently', you know what you need to do. Keeping a diary (like the Progress Tracker chart, see below) lets you see at a glance where there's scope for improvement.

I've had a bad day ... I'll never do it

Are you thinking yourself into the future? If so, are you thinking that you won't manage to make changes? Just because you didn't manage to stick to the 'diet' today doesn't make you a failure. It's just something that you didn't do ... on this occasion. Even when you're free of OCD it doesn't mean it won't put in an appearance from time to time. After all, intrusive thoughts are entirely normal.

I should have cracked it by now ... I'm useless!

What effect does our mood have on OCD? What happens to it when you're happy, sad, angry, feeling stressed, or anxious for other reasons? What can you learn from this? As well as OCD affecting how we feel, how we feel affects OCD.

Low mood can make us over-critical of ourselves. It can trigger unhelpful beliefs. It also makes us more prone to all-or-nothing

243

thinking – our mind may send us thoughts such as 'I always …' or 'I never …'. Don't be hard on yourself if you have a setback. Don't focus on what's wrong in your life but on what's right.

I keep forgetting to do it

Old habits die hard. While you could just wait for the next opportunity to occur for you to challenge your OCD, why not just 'undo' whatever the compulsion was. If you've accidentally washed your hands, how about doing something to make them 'dirty' again. If you've cancelled out a bad thought with a prayer or some other mental neutralizing action, deliberately think the bad thought again.

It can help to leave yourself a few reminders to prompt you to do things the non- or anti-OCD way. Stick a reminder in the places where you usually get caught out.

What if this isn't OCD?

OCD is a wily old devil. Have you already done quite a lot to tackle your OCD? Perhaps you've been braving it out against the OCD bully. The fear that maybe it isn't OCD after all is extremely common. It's yet another example of a doubt. And you know what you need to do about them. Have another look at Chapter 10 to refresh your memory.

I'm struggling to get started

If you've been reading this thinking 'It's all very well for some', are you stuck at the starting blocks? Sometimes trying to psych ourselves up can get us stuck. Maybe you're spending too much time planning and thinking about what you're going to do and how (or whether) you can do it.

The most awful thing has happened!

Janet panicked when her son came in the kitchen with his school shoes caked in dog poo. She went into a cleaning frenzy, using a whole packet of disinfectant wipes after throwing his shoes in the bin and the whole of his uniform into the washing machine. Even when she had calmed down, Janet wondered whether it really was worth the risk.

She took another look at her cost–benefit chart. Maybe it was worth the risk. After all, she couldn't guarantee there wouldn't be another dog mess incident, no matter what she did. She decided to accept the uncertainty. After all, life had been so much better without OCD.

Get back on the horse

No matter what led to a setback, we need to carry on. If we fall off a horse, even metaphorically, we need to get back on. Allow yourself to feel fearful: 'Thank you, mind, for sending me these thoughts'. Go back to what you were doing despite these thoughts or unpleasant feelings. This fits with the values of riding: in other words, after a fall it's a good thing to get straight back on your horse. It also fits with the values of trying to overcome OCD. After a while, the fear subsides. But if you judged whether or not you should get back on the horse by how you felt, you'd never get back in the saddle. Whatever led to our setback, this is what we have to do.

Here's what to do to 'unstick' yourself.

- Stay in the present moment.
- Choose a couple of things you can do right now.
- Surf those urges – allow any anxiety to stay for as long as it wants.
- Don't create further pain or problems for yourself in the present.
- Plan ahead for what you will do to tackle your OCD.
- Draw up some new goals.
- Create some fresh anti-OCD ideas.
- Keep a record of your progress.

Monitoring progress

Task: How am I doing?

Keep a record of all the things you do each day to actively challenge your OCD in the Progress Tracker chart below. (To make it easier, you only need to write once what you did. Then on other days just tick next to the number each time you do it.) Copy the chart if you need more space or another copy.

Set yourself targets each day. And how about rewarding yourself with a star (you could even buy some stickers) for meeting your daily target?

Also make a note of:

- how often you have put yourself in situations or done activities you used to avoid for OCD reasons. Rate it on a scale from 0 –4. Write it in next to 'Exposure'.
- how often you have avoided situations or activities for OCD reasons, e.g. to prevent triggering intrusive thoughts. Rate it on a scale from 0 –4. Write it in next to 'Avoidance'.

Progress Tracker chart			
	Monday	**Tuesday**	**Wednesday**
What have I done to challenge my OCD today? *Ratings:* 0 = Not at all 1 = Rarely 2 = Sometimes 3 = Often 4 = Always	1 2 3 4 5 6 7 8 9 10 Exposure = Avoidance =	1 2 3 4 5 6 7 8 9 10 Exposure = Avoidance =	1. 2 3 4 5 6 7 8 9 10 Exposure = Avoidance =

Thursday	Friday	Saturday	Sunday
1	1	1	1
2	2	2	2
3	3	3	3
4	4	4	4
5	5	5	5
6	6	6	6
7	7	7	7
8	8	8	8
9	9	9	9
10	10	10	10
Exposure =	Exposure =	Exposure =	Exposure =
Avoidance =	Avoidance =	Avoidance =	Avoidance =

Your Progress Tracker chart shows at a glance how hard you've been working on tackling your OCD. How did you do?

- How active have you been in challenging OCD this week?
- What could you do to improve on this?
- What new challenges could you add to build on your success?

Stuff happens

Stress is something that we all experience in our lives. It can really get in the way of many of our good intentions and make it hard for us to stick to any plans we have. This is especially true of tackling OCD and can often account for the re-emergence of symptoms, even long after you've won the fight against it. The things that cause us to feel stressed (sometimes known as **stressors**) can be of two kinds:

- major life-events, like bereavement, redundancy or an accident
- daily hassles, like traffic jams, domestic arguments, financial problems.

Both can increase the possibility that you'll find it harder to stick with your 'new' ways of responding to OCD concerns and experience setbacks. If we think of stress as demands on us, then it makes more sense. Demands can be physical, mental and emotional – and they are made on us all the time. The way we perceive these demands is the key to whether we take them in our stride or feel unable to cope with them. While we generally attribute stress to negative or unpleasant occurrences, even the nice things that happen to us can create stress. Consider events such as:

- getting engaged
- a promotion at work
- having a baby
- winning the lottery
- retiring from work (or your partner retiring).

You might be thinking how lovely it would be if some or all of these things happened to you, and maybe you'd happily put up with the stress of winning millions. But desirable as such events might be, they still make physical, mental and emotional demands on us.

Certain major life-events are outside our control. As we all know, 'stuff' happens. We can all expect a few major upheavals during the course of our lifetime, and there's never a 'good time' for them to happen. Yet even though things happen that are outside our control – like accidents, illnesses or bereavements – it can make sense not to plan too many life-changing events in a short period of time. If you can help it, don't get married, move house and start a new job all within a month or two.

'I was carrying on minding my own business when Life happened.' Perhaps you recognize this sentiment. Although there's nothing we can do to eliminate stress, it is possible to reduce its impact. This applies to both major stresses which (hopefully) don't happen too regularly as well as the smaller daily hassles that pepper our waking day.

Although it is best to avoid excessive stress, there's nothing wrong with a bit of stress. To expect a totally stress-free life is unrealistic. The challenge of a stressful situation, and the satisfaction gained from coping with it, can be very rewarding.

Helpful habits IV: Stress-busting strategies

Work off stress

Physical activity can work wonders in helping us to burn off the adrenaline which courses around our body when we're stressed. If you're not a gym-goer, then a brisk walk, some energetic dancing to your favourite music or even a vigorous session with the vacuum cleaner can do the trick.

Talk to somebody

As they say, a problem shared is a problem halved. Tell someone – your partner or a friend – how you feel. It doesn't have to be a 'moan-fest' but it can help to get it off your chest and put it into perspective. Of course, it's important not to let this become a way of getting reassurance about an OCD worry (see Chapter 10 for the reasons why this isn't a good move). But just feeling connected to family and friends can help us feel more grounded and less stressed.

Avoid self-medication

Cigarettes, alcohol and tranquillizers (whether prescribed or over-the-counter) are not the answer. They might give you a 'quick fix' but won't help in the longer term; they might even lead to further problems in their own right. Too much caffeine isn't helpful either, whether in the form of coffee, tea, cola, certain types of stimulant energy drinks, some headache or flu remedies, or even chocolate. Very often, too much of any of these can make us feel even twitchier and more stressed.

Get enough sleep and rest

It's important to recharge your batteries. Stress can affect the quality of your sleep. Have another look at Helpful habits ll in Chapter 5 for a reminder of what you can do to improve sleep problems.

Take time out for you

Too often we put all our energy into looking after everyone else – family, friends, colleagues – and it seems we simply don't have time to look after ourselves. Even if it's only five minutes to have a sit-down and a cuppa, or 15 minutes to stroll around the park in our lunch break, it's important not to overlook our own well-being. Build some time into your weekly schedule that is simply for you to do the things you enjoy – maybe join an evening class to learn a new skill, meet up with a friend or go for a jog.

Become more assertive
Learning to say 'no' or asking for help now may prevent too much pressure building up in the future.

Agree with somebody
Life shouldn't be a constant battle ground and some things just aren't worth arguing about.

Manage your time better
Find a system that works for you, not against you. If you find using the internet takes up far more time than intended, set yourself a time (maybe use a timer or free parental control software) and stick to it. Don't let OCD take over either.

Plan ahead
Keep a diary so you know in advance what commitments you have. Don't leave things to the last minute. If you know there's a stressful event coming up, what can you do to prepare for it?

Be kind to yourself
Don't set yourself impossibly high targets. If you don't manage to do something, don't fret about it – there's always another time … or maybe it doesn't matter that much if you don't do it at all. If you're ill, don't try to carry on as if you're not.

Develop a hobby
Work can become an addiction, whether it's a paid job or household chores. It's important to strike a balance with something that can help you to unwind. Remember what they say about 'All work and no play …?'

Eat sensibly
Don't forget your 'five a day'. Are you providing your body with the quality 'fuel' it needs (discussed in Chapter 4)? Even if you just cut down on sweets and chocolate, it will help to avoid the peaks and troughs of yo-yoing blood-sugar levels.

Exercise

Evidence suggests that even just a brisk walk every day has many positive health benefits, from reducing blood pressure to preventing colds. What further changes could you make to become even more active? See Chapter 11 for ideas.

Learn how to relax
Techniques such as yoga, mindfulness or progressive muscular relaxation can be helpful.

Learn to accept what you cannot change
Make your motto 'If you can't fight it or flee it, flow with it'.

Keeping up progress

It's very easy to overlook the positive changes you have made so far. At this point, we're not necessarily talking about the changes you've made unhooking yourself from OCD (although it's fine to include those as well), but about the changes slotted into the way you live your life regardless of whether OCD features in it. How are you doing with those? It doesn't matter how big or small the changes are, you should still give yourself credit for having done them. For example:

- Instead of catching the bus from the nearest stop, I'll walk to the next one five minutes away.
- I'll reduce my caffeine habit by drinking herbal tea on weekdays, while still enjoying a coffee on Saturday morning.
- I'll leave my phone downstairs when I go to bed.
- I'll check emails only three times a day.
- I'll snack on fruit between meals instead of chocolate.

Monitoring progress

Task

What changes have you made in the way you live your life? What other changes could you make soon? Write them in below.

Positive changes that I have made:

_____

_____

_____

Three more things I will do this week:

1 _____

2 _____

3 _____

Identifying future 'danger zones'

'Forewarned is forearmed', or so the saying goes. It can be helpful to plan ahead so that we are prepared for things that we know might be stressful for us or lead to setbacks. By doing some forward planning we can give consideration to how we might tackle such situations. Some of these are the kinds of things most people find a bit stressful even if they don't have OCD, such as work deadlines or getting ready to go on holiday. These events may cause particular concerns if they activate some of our OCD worries. A bit of planning can help keep stress at a more manageable level. There are ways of coping which do not involve compulsions, rituals or other kinds of safety behaviours. It's not a bad idea to use these ways of making life more manageable. These are labelled as 'non-OCD' in the examples below. It's also possible to use these stressful events as an opportunity to work on tackling OCD. For instance, there may be things you can practise to make it easier to deal with an event that is coming up or it may give you a chance to tackle it in a way you've previously avoided. These are in italics and labelled as 'OCD' in our examples below:

	Stressor	How I could deal with it
Maxine	**In the next week:** My period is due. It always makes me stressed (and more worried about smelling).	Take it easy. Remind myself I'll feel OK after a couple of days (non-OCD). *Use a pad instead of a tampon but ditch the wipes and feminine deodorant I usually use (OCD).*
Janet	**In the next month:** Mother-in-law coming to stay.	Prepare the guest room well in advance (non-OCD). Book a table for the whole family to eat out to cut down on cooking (non-OCD). *Get plenty of practice of other people using the upstairs toilet, e.g. friends (OCD). Work on putting 'dirty' things in the bedroom and all over the bed so I get used to having doubts about whether things are clean enough (OCD).*

(Continued)

| David | **In the next three months:** The end of the financial year means all the filing needs to be up to date at work. | Ask for help to clear the backlog (non-OCD). *File all new correspondence as it comes in (OCD/non-OCD).* *File at least 20 items every day (OCD).* |
| Tadeusz | **In the next year:** Going abroad on holiday. | Pack my bag a few days before I go (non-OCD). Book the taxi to the airport at least a month before (non-OCD). *Practise staying away from home overnight and leaving things plugged in, etc. (I could stay with a friend) (OCD).* |

Behaviour changing strategy

Task: Planning ahead

In the chart, note the kind of stressors that might arise and some possible ways in which you could deal with them (taking into account what you have learned so far). It's helpful to include OCD-related stressors as well as non-OCD stressors.

Timescale	How I could deal with it
In the next week	
In the next month	

In the next three months	
In the next year	

Chapter summary

In this chapter you have learned:

- why we sometimes get 'stuck'
- what to do to get moving again
- how to plan for future stressors.

Don't think of setbacks as failures – they're just 'hiccups'. They can be dealt with in the same way that you tackled the problem initially. Just get back to your plan and you'll be fine. Remember that changing your relationship with OCD is a process. Even not making progress is part of the process – it's like stopping off on a journey. It helps to revisit our goals, make sure that we're not just coasting in our comfort zone, and put more time into challenging OCD every day. By trying a little harder today, we can make living a little easier tomorrow. While we can't avoid stress, we can build up our resilience to it with stress-management strategies. Remember, if you can't fight it or flee it, flow with it!

The process of change brings about many things. Are you ready to find out more? Chapter 15 explores what change means for us and those around us and encourages us to take a kinder and more compassionate view of ourselves.

PART 5

Progress

Test your new ways of thinking and behaving in fresh contexts to progress towards change

A change for the better

Overview

In Chapter 14, you found out how to cope with setbacks and continue to make progress. Here we will look at:

- the implications of change
- family, friends and OCD
- building the new you.

All the changes you have made still need nurturing and support. It's part of the process of discovering how to live your life free of OCD. OCD can also take its toll by knocking self-confidence, especially if you've had the problem for a long while. Maybe it has been the way that you have defined yourself as a person. It's important to remember that you are not the OCD. It's just a problem you have had. Building up a more positive self-image can strengthen your defence against relapse.

Although you can see that it is a change for the better, the effects of change can send out ripples of many kinds. When we are troubled by OCD, its effects can be felt by family and friends. But although we have changed our relationship with OCD, family and friends may not have made the same journey.

What are the effects of changing?

Developing the freedom to live your life how you want without the burden of OCD is wonderful. Yet oddly it *is* possible to miss it. How could that be? Maybe it's like an old friend who's no good for you, gets you into all kinds of scrapes and leads you astray. Although you can see that, you've known them for a long time. They're familiar and you're comfortable in their company. Possibly you miss the strict rules it set. When OCD called the shots, you knew exactly what you could and couldn't do and how it needed to be done. Now the world is your oyster but it may seem as if there are too many options. Don't be scared by this. As we've seen, living your life free from OCD is about having choice. You will gradually begin to establish your preferences for what you do and how you want to do them, but this time with greater flexibility.

Those close to you have also been passengers on your journey. They may have been drawn into your difficulties with OCD, either knowingly or unsuspectingly. You may have relied on them to provide reassurance or to relieve you of the responsibility of certain tasks. Have they perhaps changed how *they* do things because of your OCD rules? They may have gradually absorbed OCD 'rules', or it could be that you insisted. It's not because you're a bully but someone who was worried. Not only did fear make you follow OCD's orders, but it caused you to believe everyone else should too. For instance, while Olivia rejoiced in her new-found freedom, her partner just couldn't come to terms with it. 'Oh, don't bother doing that,' she'd declare. But after years of doing so many things according to her wishes, he'd lost sight of how else he could do them.

Although OCD isn't 'catching', Chapters 13 and 14 have explained how we can develop ways of being simply by following conventions. It's not always easy to accept a more casual approach. If your partner has actually developed OCD, could you help them overcome it using the method in this book?

Once you're open to going to new places and enjoying different activities, it can also uncover aspects of relationships that you were unaware of. Family and friends will need time to adjust to your new role as a person who doesn't have OCD. It's a good idea to talk about the changes you've made and your fresh outlook on life. Or haven't you spoken about OCD to them yet? Even the act of telling someone is an important step to reduce the significance or importance of intrusive thoughts. You could say this is the ultimate exposure task!

Behaviour changing strategy

Task

If you've yet to tell your partner or a close friend about your difficulties, take another look at the advice in Chapter 4.

Before

- Why have you kept these thoughts secret?
- What do you imagine their reaction would be if you told them?
- What do you predict they would think, do or say?
- Are there people you would never tell?
- Why wouldn't you want to tell them?

After

- Who did you tell?
- What was their reaction?
- Were they sympathetic or not?
- Did anyone react badly when you told them?
- Did anyone change their attitudes or behaviour towards you? In what way?
- How did you feel as you started to tell them?
- How do you feel now?

Case study

Carol's mouth dried up completely. It was hard to get the words out … 'I need to tell you something.' All her worries came tumbling out as she spoke. 'Blimey', exclaimed her husband, 'Is that all?' Convinced that she was about to tell him she was leaving him, he was relieved. He also laughingly admitted that he gets weird thoughts like that all the time.

Grief, sadness and even anger aren't uncommon reactions after beating OCD. David regretted the missed opportunities at work and socially. Janet mourned not being a fun and carefree mum when her son was small. While we cannot change the past, we can use the knowledge we have now to pave the way for a better future. OCD is not our fault.

Who am I now?

It may sound peculiar, but OCD can make us feel special. If we've had it for as long as we can remember, it can seem as much a part of us as our feet and hands. Others may even have acknowledged our specialness by complying with our quirky ways or shielding us from the many things we struggled with or avoided. Who wants to be normal anyway? It sounds so bland and dull. Is it time for you to stop being so harsh on yourself?

Practical advice ⇨

Helpful habits V: Self-prejudice

You now know that having OCD doesn't mean that you're mad and you can now see that it is more like being stuck in a loop. By now you've almost certainly made quite a few changes in how you approach the problem and are gradually managing to live your life free from OCD. However, up to this point you probably spent a lot of time worrying about being different from other people. You perhaps felt that you had something missing that everyone else has (though maybe you now realize that is more like having something extra). Because you might have been very reluctant to discuss it with anyone else, you might not have had the chance to find out how many other people get stuck in similar loops and how normal it is to have odd intrusive thoughts. Believing things like that about yourself makes you feel pretty bad about yourself. Often it undermines your confidence and makes you feel that you are not as good as other people in some way. In short, it results in **low self-esteem**. As if having a poor opinion of yourself isn't bad enough, low self-esteem makes us more vulnerable to feeling that we have to get things right. And if that's what we believe, we're more likely to feel devastated by our mistakes and to feel that we have to try even harder (and we've already established that OCD often fools us into trying too hard). So low self-esteem feeds into a vicious circle which either keeps the problem going or could be a potential cause of relapse.

Why is low self-esteem a problem?

If we look at the more general effects of low self-esteem we can see how it causes us to overestimate our faults and weaknesses and to underestimate our qualities and strengths. It leads us to make predictions in a negative way about how we'll cope in certain situations, so it's not surprising that we feel anxious at the prospect. If we feel anxious enough, we might even avoid the situation completely, as a result denying ourselves the chance to discover that we would in fact cope just fine. And the more we avoid, the more our self-esteem shrivels.

Carol always found it difficult to accept compliments from anyone. She would brush them aside, thinking, 'Oh, she's only saying that to cheer me up' or 'I wonder what he's after … he probably wants a favour from me'. She found it hard to believe that anyone could ever think anything nice about her. Low self-esteem makes us very critical of ourselves. It's like having a parrot on your shoulder that is always ready with some remark to put you down: 'You made a right mess of that, didn't you?', 'Anyone else would have known that the door was locked with just one check', or 'No one else gets the kinds of ridiculous thoughts you do'. It's not surprising that our mood and self-confidence suffer under such a torrent of criticism. It would seem sensible to try to do something about changing it. But what can we do to change something that has probably been around for a very long time?

Combating low self-esteem

Let's start by having a look at ways of changing other types of beliefs that people hold strongly and may have held for a long time. Do you know of anyone who has a prejudice that you disagree with? If not, we could use as an example a person who is prejudiced against all people with red hair. Imagine we were going to try to change this person's prejudice. If he or she were to see a red-haired person behaving in a selfless, brave or generous manner, do you think that this one event would alter their prejudice? Probably not. They would find ways of making this piece of information fit in with their beliefs about red-haired people. For example, they might think that this person is an exception to the rule and that they weren't acting like red-haired people usually do. Or they might think that the red-haired person had some ulterior motive for what they'd just done, some sly way of getting something for themselves.

Or it might be that they don't even notice what the red-haired person has done because it wasn't the kind of thing that fitted with their long-standing deeply held beliefs about red-haired people.

Discounting, distorting or just plain ignoring are common features of prejudice and serve to keep prejudices in place. How could we do something to change these prejudiced ideas? Perhaps if we could put this person in a position where they had lots of opportunities to see many examples of behaviour that didn't fit with their distorted beliefs there might be a bit of movement. On the other hand, of course, it's possible that they might still discount what they see. How about getting the person to write down what they have seen and keep a log of it? When there is written evidence it is so much harder to overlook it or brush it aside. Gradually, by accumulating evidence which doesn't fit with their prejudice about redheads, those beliefs will be weakened as the person begins to build up more positive and appropriate ideas about them.

Low self-esteem as prejudice against yourself

You've probably already guessed the moral of this story and how it might fit with our discussion about low self-esteem. It's like having a prejudice against *yourself*. Like Carol, when we feel unhappy about ourselves, anything we achieve or do well or any compliments we're paid fail to make us feel good. This is because we're doing precisely what the person in the redheads example was doing: discounting, distorting or not noticing. By gathering evidence that doesn't fit with our poor self-image we can begin to build up a more balanced view of ourselves.

The following exercises will help you put together examples from your own personal experiences. Hold on a minute – don't just skip to the next chapter! Although it's tempting to ignore the exercise, don't forget what we said about the power of having something in writing.

Although Maxine had made enormous progress tackling her worries about smells, her underlying belief that she wasn't a likeable person had a tendency to come to the surface especially in social situations. Not surprisingly, intrusive thoughts about whether or not she was smelly tended to pop into her head at such times. It's not difficult to see how the combination of intrusive thoughts and underlying beliefs made it hard for Maxine to keep up a healthy level of self-esteem. To counteract this, Maxine began to keep a diary of good things about herself. Each evening, she looked back over the day and jotted down anything that made her feel good about herself. She made a particular effort to collect instances that fitted with a more positive belief that she was likeable. In other words, she was looking for evidence to support what was *right* with her!

Daily diary of good things	
Monday	Jo at work stayed in the kitchen chatting after she'd made her coffee.
Tuesday	The guy in the newsagent winked at me as he handed me my change.
	My manager praised me for completing an urgent letter before lunch.
Wednesday	I got a surprise text from a friend I haven't seen for ages (Ella). She sounded pleased to hear from me when I phoned. She asked if I wanted to meet up.
Thursday	An old lady at the bus stop smiled at me and commented on the weather.
	My manager asked my opinion in a meeting.
Friday	Saw the bus-stop lady again. She told me about her dog.
	Went to cinema with Ella. She asked if I'd go shopping with her at the weekend.

To add to this, Maxine also drew up a list of 25 positive qualities she had or things she liked about herself. She found this a real struggle to begin with, not just because she wasn't used to thinking nice things about herself but also because it seemed rather big-headed. It's a commonly held view that to voice things we're proud of is somehow boastful, and that 'nice' people don't blow their own trumpet. Yet valuing our qualities and achievements should never be viewed as boastful. If we don't value ourselves, others probably won't either. In fact, telling yourself this is to put yourself down. It's saying that you don't deserve to hear nice things about yourself, or that your opinions don't count. Although Maxine managed to list lots of examples that flew in the face of her old belief that she was unlikeable, the little voice in her head kept trying to discount her experiences.

List your good points

One way of building up a catalogue of evidence to help create your new (healthier) self-image is to give some thought to your good points. Try to write down 25 things you like about yourself. At this point, you're probably thinking, 'Twenty-five? I'll be lucky to find five, never mind twenty-five!' Remember what we've just been talking about. Recognizing our positive qualities isn't always bragging – and on this occasion, you have permission to blow your own trumpet for the sake of helping yourself achieve the quality of life you want.

Your good points don't have to be Nobel Prize-winning things. Because low self-esteem often causes us to disregard little achievements or less mind-blowing features, it's really helpful to give these small things their moment in the limelight. And don't get hung up on things you do *really* well. Leila enjoys playing the piano. She hits a lot of wrong notes and wouldn't want to play in front of an audience, but she delights in picking out a few tunes for her own pleasure. On her list she wrote: 'I can play the piano … badly'. Even without high levels of accomplishment or expertise, playing the piano is still a skill, and one that not everyone has. While you're considering what to include, mull over the following:

- What kinds of abstract qualities do you have?
- Are you kind, considerate, thoughtful, honest?
- What physical features do you like? For example, do you have a nice smile, long legs, your own hair and teeth(!)
- What skills are you proud of? For example, can you bake a cake, drive a car or use a power drill?
- How about some unusual skills? For example, can you do the splits, do impressions or whistle with your fingers?

Don't forget that it doesn't matter how good you are at something; it's more important that it's something that you value, gives you pleasure or something not everyone can do (even if it's blowing raspberries on your baby's tummy to the tune of 'Baa-baa black sheep'). Even if your mind is sending you thoughts like: 'But you're not as good at it as your sister' or 'The last cake you baked was burnt', don't either be put off from writing it down or get drawn into debating these ideas. If you're still struggling to come up with things for your list, perhaps you could ask your partner or a close friend to suggest some to you, but only after you've *really* tried for yourself.

Monitoring progress

Task

Write your list on the chart here, or make a copy of it.

25 things to blow my own trumpet about	
1	14
2	15
3	16
4	17
5	18
6	19
7	20
8	21
9	22
10	23
11	24
12	25
13	

Diary/journal write-in

Now start your own daily diary of good things.

My daily diary of good things	
Monday	
Tuesday	
Wednesday	
Thursday	
Friday	
Saturday	
Sunday	

What's *right* with me?

Once you have your list of 25 things you like about yourself and have begun the diary in which you note pleasant events, don't put the list away in a drawer and forget about it. Self-esteem is like a muscle: it needs to be flexed both repeatedly and often to build it up. Although it had been really hard to begin with, both Carol and Maxine noticed that, by adding to their diary every day, noticing pleasurable things that happened during the day became easier. They had tuned themselves into all kinds of things that gladdened their hearts or made them smile for a moment, and felt they had become kinder and less critical of themselves. This daily 'flexing' of their newly found self-esteem 'muscle' allowed this new information to continue to chip away at their self-prejudice.

You too can change your focus by actively trying to notice the good things about yourself instead of being so self-critical. Do you remember how we talked about 'Looking for trouble' in connection with OCD worries in Chapter 6? In the same way that we might have homed in on puddles on the floor of public toilets, newspaper reports about child abuse or references to burglaries, we can retrain our attention to pick up on positive things. By refocusing our attention on positive events and personal traits, we develop new pathways in the brain with practice. In time these replace the well-worn tendency of only looking on the negative side and help us to take a 'glass half-full' instead of the more depressing 'glass half empty' view of the world.

One of the many benefits of building up our self-esteem is that we're often better able to survive times when our confidence gets a knock. If we have a more robust sense of being an 'OK' person, we're less likely to perceive mistakes as a disaster, and as a result don't feel the need to work so hard to prevent them. Another benefit is that we're less likely to have so many negative, critical thoughts about our ability to cope in different situations, so we feel less anxious. Be kind, not critical. You wouldn't be so hard on your best friend, so why be so much harder on yourself? Remind yourself that we are all the same – a mixture of strengths and weaknesses, good points and bad points. That's what being human is all about. Give yourself credit for the things you do, especially the progress you are making in understanding and overcoming your OCD.

A change for the better

Recognize the changes you have made. Arun and Benita wrote letters to themselves to acknowledge the effect OCD used to have on their lives and how much better it was now. As you can see, they both took a slightly different approach. Arun wrote from the perspective of his 'wise' self describing his experience of OCD and learning how to overcome it. Benita preferred to write a letter to a dear friend, showing wisdom and compassion, forgiveness and understanding.

Case study: Arun

Before I learned to tackle it, my previous years were blighted by anxiety and OCD behaviours. These significantly affected my working life and my social life – I was at risk of losing my job and had become socially avoidant.

Life felt unbearable. If I hadn't tackled my OCD I believe I might have come to breaking point. For me, taking this approach meant immediate improvement in the quality of my life. It wasn't always easy, but I could see the results each time I stood up to OCD and just let the thoughts and urges come in. And each time I did that, the easier it became, until my anxiety levels fell to a negligible level – where they have stayed to this day. Sure, there are times when OCD comes 'knocking at my door', but I know how to recognize it and what to do about it to prevent it taking hold again.

Not only has life become 'bearable' again, but I have become highly successful in my work and very happy in my social life. This approach has given me an invaluable 'toolkit' for life. It allows me to manage and defeat anxieties and OCD whenever they re-occur. Consequently, my personal confidence has expanded and I've been drawing up plans for a career change next year.

Case study: Benita

For as long as you can remember, you have done things you felt you had to do because they seemed to make you feel all right again. You just thought that these rituals were something you had to do to make you feel better – like drinking when you were thirsty, sleeping when you were tired. You thought you needed to do them, even though they were time-consuming and inconvenient, and that if you didn't the bad feeling wouldn't go away and would affect your life in other ways. Deep down you knew this behaviour was illogical and therefore hid it from other people. It came and went at various times, but never disappeared completely. You didn't realize then that this was OCD and that the rituals you had been doing, rather than solving anything, were actually making your problem worse.

There were times when it seemed that the things you needed to do or avoid doing suddenly multiplied and got really out of hand, resulting in you feeling so overwhelmed you felt physically ill with it all. You wanted to understand what had been happening to you and prevent the problem escalating as it had before.

You learned that the things you had been doing had been the cause of your problems and that even though OCD was telling you that you had to do something, you didn't have to go along with it. You had moments of deep insight into what had been driving the OCD. Taking this step-by-step approach encouraged you to make your own decisions about what you needed to do to get rid of the OCD. You were interested to discover how your way of thinking had been based on the way you felt rather than on what was real.

Behaviour changing strategy

Task: Compassionate letter writing

You can write your letter as if you were writing to a dear friend (i.e. 'You …') or in the first person (i.e. 'I …'). Either way, begin it with 'Dear …… (*your name*)'.

There's no right or wrong way to write your letter. If you wish, you can include some or all of these ideas to get you started:

- the difficulties you used to have
- the ways of thinking, feeling and doing you used to have
- what has changed
- how you see the problem now
- show compassion for how you felt
- remind yourself that you are not alone in having experienced OCD.

Here are some things that wouldn't be helpful:

- don't criticize, condemn or blame yourself
- don't dwell on the past
- avoid the use of 'should', 'ought', 'must'.

If thoughts come to your mind that make you feel worse, let them go and refocus. Engage with your warm and sensitive side to encourage yourself in the future.

Chapter summary

Now that you've finished this chapter you understand.

● why positive changes can have a downside
● how family and friends need time to adjust to the 'new you'
● what you can do to boost your self-esteem.

Adjusting to life unencumbered by OCD takes time. While we're practising our new role as a person without OCD, our nearest and dearest are also trying to find their place in the new order of things. Change can uncover difficulties that were previously masked or disguised. Although freedom from our worries and anxieties is something we longed for, unexpected feelings of sadness, anger and regret are not uncommon. Learning to recognize our many strengths and positive qualities is essential to our long-term well-being.

Although you may still have some way to go before you are able to say that OCD was something you *used* to have, are you ready to review your journey so far? In Chapter 16, our final chapter, you will find out how to summarize what you have learned and what to do if you would like further support.

Living your life free from OCD

Overview

In Chapter 15, we talked about change, adapting to change and how to boost your self-confidence by recognizing your personal qualities and talents. This final chapter will help you:

- summarize what you have learned
- prevent setbacks turning into a major relapse
- live your life free from OCD.

In the time that it has taken you to read this book, it is unlikely that your life has become completely free of OCD. It's important to remember that change is a journey, not just a destination. Even if you have only travelled a short way on your journey, you will still be some way along the road from where you started out. Perhaps you discovered something you didn't know about OCD, or thought about your difficulties from a different perspective. This is still a step in the right direction. If you have other difficulties as well as OCD, it can slow you down.

Now that you've reached the final chapter of this book, let's take the time to recap what you've learned about OCD and reflect on the things you've changed in your life.

Keeping OCD at bay

You've learned a lot about your problem in the course of the book, and have worked hard to change the things that you now know kept

OCD going. You have your worksheets from the exercises to refer to, as well as this book. It's still helpful to write things down in a clear, brief way. You then have a handy crib-sheet whenever you need a quick reminder. It's surprisingly easy to forget some of the strategies that you've found useful. A blueprint (see below) is a way of summing up all the things you have learned about OCD and how to tackle it.

Having a plan for the future is another way in which we will use our blueprint. By identifying the situations that could lead to a setback we can decide on some suitable tactics. This way, we can prevent a small setback turning into a major relapse. What signs would you notice that might signal you were at risk of slipping back? How about including these ideas as part of your relapse prevention plan:

- I will do at least one thing each day to confront OCD.
- I will remind myself that if I do something I find hard today, it will be easier tomorrow.
- If I slip up and do a compulsion, I will 'undo' whatever I have done so that I re-expose myself.
- I will do at least one anti-OCD thing each day until I no longer have the problem.

Your personal experience will give you a good indication of your progress. To back this up, you might find it interesting to fill in a new version of the Obsessive–Compulsive Inventory (OCI) that you first completed in Chapter 2.

- How do your initial scores compare to your scores today?
- Where have you made the most changes?
- Which areas could do with a bit more attention?

Use what you know to set yourself a few new goals.

Even when OCD is no longer a problem for you, it's important not to get too smug and cocky about it. It still helps to flex your anti-OCD muscles and keep them toned. Setting a date for a monthly anti-OCD review is a great way to make sure you're still in charge.

And once you've agreed a date, don't put it off with some excuse or another – that's leaving the door open for your unwelcome 'friend' to creep back in.

Monitoring progress

Task: My OCD blueprint

Use this worksheet to fill in your own personal summary, or make a copy of it.

My OCD blueprint

What have I learned?

_____

_____

What were the main thoughts/images/urges/doubts that bothered me?

_____

_____

Why did I think I was having them? What did I think they meant about me?

_____

_____

What do I now know they mean?

_____

_____

What kinds of things was I doing that kept the problem going?

_____

_____

Why did I believe it was helpful?

_____

_____

What do I now know about these behaviours?

_____

_____

What have I done that has been most helpful?

_____

_____

Why was it helpful? What did I learn from doing it?

_____

_____

What can I do now that I struggled to do before?

_____

_____

What could lead to a setback?

_____

_____

How will I deal with this?

_____

_____

What kinds of things would I notice if I was starting to slip back?

_____

_____

What can I do about it?

_____

_____

Life doesn't have to be perfect

Case study: Benita

When I had different kinds of OCD worries in the past, I'd managed to stop some of the OCD habits by myself. I was really surprised when my therapist praised me, saying that it was good that I had broken lots of rules. I had never thought of the things I did as 'rules' before and it seemed to change the way I felt about the things I did. In my non-OCD life I would query rules and the reasons for them, but I now realized I had been making up literally hundreds of crazy rules that had no basis in logic. But I had kept acting on these rules because when I did I seemed to feel better. Since using this approach I have discovered that when I don't do things or follow the OCD 'rules', I feel better than when I did them.

If you haven't reached the stage on your journey where you feel that you have made sufficient progress to enable you to make choices about how you live your life unburdened by OCD rules, what can you do now? To begin with, ask yourself the following questions.

- Have I read this book all the way through?
- Have I completed all the exercises and written down my answers to questions?
- Did I set myself clear goals for therapy?
- Did I include anti-OCD tasks as part of my daily/weekly goals?
- Did I spend adequate time on challenging my OCD every day?
- Have I applied these strategies every day for at least three months?

In your heart of hearts, you know the real answers to these questions. If you've answered 'No' to any of them, you know what you need to do next. As the late American opera singer Beverley Sills famously said: 'There are no shortcuts to any place worth going.' That is as true for overcoming our anxiety problems as it is for developing a skill or talent. We simply have to put in the time and the effort. By tackling OCD one step at a time it *is* possible to live your life free of it. The key, however, is to progress *through* each step, as these are the building blocks to success.

Case study: Niamh

I'm not free of OCD altogether yet – I might have to do anti-OCD things every so often just to keep me on track. But now I have 'real things' in my head … like living my life. It felt weird not having all those old thoughts and urges but now I just do what I want to do. It's about having a choice. And although it sounds really weird, I feel so much more in control by *not trying* to be in control.

Take the risk and put it down to OCD, because it probably is. And not to take the risk isn't worth the cost. 'Life does not have to be perfect to be wonderful' (Annette Funicello, 1942–2013). Living our lives free of OCD gives us back the choice to live however we choose.

Resources

What to do if you still need help

It's hard, of course, to always be as disciplined as we might want to be. After all, would there be a need for slimming clubs if we could turn on self-control like a light switch? You may have followed the advice in this book but still struggle with OCD. Taking the journey alone can seem daunting. And there's no denying that trying to change longstanding habits – especially when we fear that *not* doing some of those things is somehow risky or dangerous to ourselves or other people – is *very* hard and scary.

To have someone who understands our feelings and can guide and coach us through the process might be what we're looking for. Sometimes a wise friend or family member can help in this way, although often it's hard for us to open up to them completely because their lives are intertwined with ours. Furthermore, they may not fully understand how OCD works and the ways in which it can affect us.

Maybe it's time to look for that support outside your personal contacts. We can often feel alone with our problems, especially with difficulties like OCD as it can seem as if no one else has the same kind of concerns. It may be that OCD isn't your only problem. That can make using self-help methods harder too.

Further support

So what options are there if you feel that a bit of 'hand-holding' can help you on the way?

Medication

It is possible to overcome OCD without taking medication; many people do. However, sometimes we can benefit from a bit of a 'leg-up' to boost our mood and make it easier to get started. While your GP can prescribe appropriate medication for OCD, you may be referred to a psychiatrist for a specialist opinion.

There is no medication specifically for OCD, although certain types of antidepressants can be effective. Tranquillizers and sleeping tablets are not recommended drug treatments. They can offer short-term relief for sleep or anxiety problems but should not be taken for more than two weeks under the guidance of your doctor. They do not help OCD and can be addictive.

Over-the-counter remedies like vitamin supplements, herbal remedies or other so-called 'natural' products are also not specifically useful for OCD, and in some cases taking too many can be bad for you. If you are concerned about vitamin deficiency, it is better to make sure you have a balanced diet and to get checked out by your GP. With vitamins, it isn't a case that more is better – having too much of a particular vitamin can create more of a problem than having too little.

Choosing a therapist and a therapy

Seeking professional help can provide you with specialist support and expert knowledge to help you move on. Many therapists promise expertise in many things; avoid those who claim success with everything.

The treatment of choice for OCD is cognitive behavioural therapy (CBT). It is recommended by the National Institute for Health and Clinical Excellence (NICE). You can view their guidelines at www.nice.org.uk/CG31

Your GP can refer you to your local mental health service. Some services, such as IAPT (Improving Access to Psychological Therapy programme), are happy for you to refer yourself. All IAPT services offer CBT. There are a number of specialist services for OCD around the country. Your GP should know what they are and how to refer you.

If you wish to seek private treatment, make sure that the therapist is registered with at least one of the professional bodies. These are:

- The Health Care Professions Council (www.hpc-uk.org)
- The British Psychological Society (www.bps.org.uk)
- The British Association for Behavioural and Cognitive Psychotherapy (www.babcp.com).

Don't be afraid to ask your therapist whether they are qualified and experienced in CBT for OCD. Further advice on choosing therapists can be found on the websites listed at the end of this section.

Charitable organizations

There are a number of charities that provide information, advice and support on OCD and other anxiety-related conditions. The main ones are: OCD-UK, OCD Action, Maternal OCD and Anxiety UK (see 'OCD resources' below for contact details).

As well as useful information on their websites, these charities can offer support in other ways. Some of them co-ordinate support groups for people like yourself. Occasionally these are run by a mental health professional who has a special interest in OCD, or they may be organized by individuals who have personal experience of the difficulties, either themselves or as a carer.

Internet forums

It can be useful to hear about the experiences of others who have similar difficulties, either sufferers themselves or family and friends. Many people find internet chat rooms and forums a useful resource. They can provide a fairly anonymous way to find out more about OCD or to make contact with other sufferers. One of the benefits is that, because they draw followers from all over the world, it is more likely that you will come across others whose difficulties are very similar to your own. This can be a really positive experience if it means we don't feel like we're battling alone or it shows that the way in which OCD affects us is not unique, odd or unusual (the concerns that can lie behind doubts about whether our problem really is OCD, as we explored in the book). However, the internet forums etc. can have their drawbacks too. Because chat rooms often aren't monitored, they can become a source of unhelpful ideas or be used in ways that this book would not recommend, e.g. as a source of reassurance or unhelpful (or just plain useless) suggestions for tackling the difficulty.

OCD and employment

OCD is a registered disability. You are not legally obliged to disclose to your employer that you have OCD. However, there can be some benefits. Employers have to make reasonable adjustments for an employee with a disability. Detailed information can be found on the OCD Action website and on the government website at: www.gov.uk/equality-act-2010-guidance

OCD resources

NICE guidelines
www.nice.org.uk/guidance/CG31

OCD UK
www.ocduk.org
PO Box 8955, Nottingham NG10 9AU
Tel: 0845 120 3778

Maternal OCD
www.maternalocd.org
Tel: 0845 057 9345

OCD Action
www.ocdaction.org.uk
Suite 506–507, Davina House, 137–149 Goswell Road, London EC1V 7ET
Tel: 0845 390 6232

Anxiety UK
www.anxietyuk.org.uk
Tel: 0844 477 5774

References

Foa, E. B., Kozak, M. J., Salkovskis, P. M., Coles, M. E. and Amir, N., 'The validation of a new obsessive compulsive disorder scale: The Obsessive Compulsive Inventory (OCI)', *Psychological Assessment, 10 (3)* (1998), 206–214.

Rachman, S. and De Silva, P., 'Normal and abnormal obsessions', *Behaviour Research and Therapy, 16* (1978), 233–248.

Salkovskis, P. M., Richards, H. C. and Forrester, E., 'The Relationship Between Obsessional Problems and Intrusive Thoughts', *Behavioural and Cognitive Psychotherapy, 23* (1995), 281–300.

Salkovskis, P. M., Wroe, A., Gledhill, A., Morrison, N., Forrester, E., Richards, H. C., Reynolds, M. and Thorpe, S. J., 'Responsibility attitudes and interpretations are characteristic of obsessive compulsive disorder', *Behavioural and Cognitive Psychotherapy, 38* (2000), 347–372.

Index